Catherine O'Brien

The Celluloid Madonna
FROM SCRIPTURE TO SCREEN

WALLFLOWER PRESS
LONDON & NEW YORK

A Wallflower Book
Published by
Columbia University Press
Publishers Since 1893
New York • Chichester, West Sussex
cup.columbia.edu

A complete CIP record is available from the Library of Congress

ISBN 978-1-906660-28-4 (cloth : alk. paper)
ISBN 978-1-906660-27-7 (pbk. : alk. paper)
ISBN 978-0-231-50181-1 (e-book)

Book design by Elsa Mathern

Columbia University Press books are printed on permanent and durable acid-free paper.
This book is printed on paper with recycled content.
Printed in the United States of America

c 10 9 8 7 6 5 4 3 2 1
p 10 9 8 7 6 5 4 3 2 1

The Celluloid Madonna

contents

acknowledgements

I am obviously very indebted to Yoram Allon, who showed an interest in this project and has been extremely patient and supportive throughout its gestation, and to all the staff at Wallflower Press: Del Cullen, Tom Cabot, and particularly Jodie Taylor. Ian Cooper provided his excellent copy-editing skills, which are very much appreciated.

Many thanks to my stimulating colleagues in the departments of Film Studies and French at Kingston University, especially to Frank Whately, Carol Gartrell, Carrie Tarr, Noëlle Brick, Will Brooker and Simon Brown for sustaining my research efforts. Stephen Barber offered valuable guidance, and Lieve Spaas and Keith Reader have also kept me focused.

Some of the research that informed this monograph was undertaken during a sabbatical funded by the Arts and Humanities Research Board (now the Arts and Humanities Research Council), for which I am very grateful.

My desire to learn more about the Virgin Mary in film has taken me to the British Film Institute National Library and the British Library in London; the Bibliothèque Nationale and the Bibliothèque de Film in Paris; the National Library of Congress in Washington; the Margaret Herrick Library and the University of Southern California in Los Angeles; and the International Marian Research Institute at the University of Dayton in Ohio. During all my travels, I have received advice and untiring help from librarians and archivists. Mike Witt also kindly lent me material on Jean-Luc Godard.

Matt Page's Bible Films Blog at http://www.biblefilms.blogspot.com/ has been discovered as a superb source of news and film criticism.

I have discussed my work with Sarah Boss, the director of the UK Centre for Marian Studies, and members of the Mariological Society of America. The work of Fr Johann Roten is always a major source of inspiration. Although I have benefited personally from the vast knowledge of these experts in Marian Studies, they bear no responsibility for any mistakes that I have subsequently generated and may not necessarily agree with my approach.

Most sincere appreciation to Michael Duricy, who is a pioneer in the field and whose database of Marian films at the University of Dayton is an invaluable resource. Michael very generously gave his time to make many worthwhile suggestions for corrections to portions of the manuscript. He should be credited for any improvements to the original text but he is not accountable for any errors of fact or judgement that remain.

Finally, the more emotional thanks go to Andrea Rinke (my 'cell mate' and constant source of good cheer in difficult times); to Jan Hurst, loyal friend and fellow sufferer of deadlines; to my wonderful mother-in-law, who has always taken an interest in my work; to my beloved parents, who have never failed to support me in all my endeavours; and, it goes without saying (but should always be emphasised), to Tom Ennis. I would certainly exceed my word limit if I were to try to record his contribution on paper.

abbreviations

The following abbreviations are used for books of the Bible:

Dt	Deuteronomy
Gal	Galatians
Gn	Genesis
Is	Isaiah
Jn	John
Lk	Luke
Lv	Leviticus
Mi	Micah
Mk	Mark
Mt	Matthew

Introduction

Over two millennia, the life of Mary of Nazareth has inspired magnificent works of art that reveal the complexities of the Marian tradition. She is the principal woman in Christian Salvation History; a symbol of beauty, purity and sanctity; a figure implicated in gender, ecclesiastical and ecumenical politics; and a link between the three Abrahamic faiths as a Jewish mother whose son Jesus is worshipped by Christians and revered by Muslims. Since the late nineteenth century, the film industry has added to Mary's vast pictorial legacy by capturing her image on celluloid. Writers have transformed the Scriptures into a script. Casting directors have sought an appropriate actress to incarnate the Virgin Mother. And filmmakers have encountered the tensions between religion, originality and profit for the film studios.

As a consequence, the films selected for analysis in this book embrace a notably wide range of angles. The majority have been designed as entertainment for cinema release, with box-office returns remaining inevitable concerns for the producers. Only a few of the productions have been deliberately developed as teaching tools: *The Jesus Film* (Peter Sykes and John Krisch, 1979) is a work of Protestant evangelism that has reportedly been dubbed into more than a thousand languages and seen by several billion viewers; and Dayspring International, an organisation set up to bring the message of Christianity to India, maintains that its mobile film units have shown the Life of Christ film *Dayasagar* (A. Bhimsingh, 1978) to at least 140 million people across the country.[1]

Unlike theologians, who must defend their theories before Church and academic authorities, filmmakers are at liberty to follow their creative notions within the boundaries of censorship. Consequently, the biography of Mary has fuelled the imagination of a rather odd assortment of film directors. Pope Paul VI, writing in his apostolic exhortation on Marian devotion entitled *Marialis Cultus*, stated: 'It should be considered quite normal for succeeding generations of Christians in differing sociocultural contexts to have expressed their sentiments about the Mother of Jesus in a way and a manner which reflected their own age' (1974). However, not only committed Christians have taken up that proposition. Amongst the people who have accepted the challenge are the Catholic Mel Gibson, the Protestant Jean Delannoy, the atheist Pier Paolo Pasolini, and the maverick Jean-Luc Godard, who has earned fame as a Marxist fellow traveller.

Nevertheless, whatever the primary intentions of the filmmakers, close readings of their on-screen presentations of Mary reveal that narrative and artistic choices (such as dialogue, framing, *mise-en-scène*, editing and special effects) have a theological dimension that allows the audience to encounter the life of the mother of Jesus (and therefore of Jesus himself) from a fresh perspective. While this 'fresh perspective' may not meet with the approval of all spectators, there is no doubt that the film industry has a continuing impact on the public's perception of Scripture. Cecil B. DeMille suggested that more people had been told the story of Jesus through his film *The King of Kings* (1927) 'than through any other single work, except the Bible itself' (in Telford 1997: 122). And the spectacular, although undoubtedly unexpected, profit for Mel Gibson's *The Passion of the Christ* (2004) underlined the ongoing capacity of the cinema to disseminate versions of the Gospel story to huge audience numbers in the twenty-first century.

Although reviews of 'the celluloid Jesus' have led to a substantial body of academic criticism (see, for example, Kinnard and Davis 1992; Telford 1997; Baugh 1997; Stern *et al.* 1999; and Reinhartz 2007), the screen image of Mary has received less sustained analytical commentary, despite the fact that the role offers one of the most intriguing opportunities for spiritual reflection. There are several articles and book chapters on the subject (Malone 1992; Zwick 1997; Roten 2001; Duricy 2003; Langkau 2007; O'Brien 2007a; Reinhartz 2007; Roubach 2007), but the most extensive investigation into Marian films has been carried out at the International Marian Research Institute at the University of Dayton, Ohio. Michael Duricy has set up a magnificent database of films with Marian references including traditional biblical epics, documentaries, academic lectures, traces of Marian symbolic figures, and glimpses of statues and rosary beads in Hollywood movies.[2]

Given the wealth of material available and the necessity to draw boundaries, this particular study focuses on feature films that relate incidents from Mary's earthly biography as the mother of Jesus. The central corpus is drawn predominantly from Hollywood and Europe. Some of the films under discussion are well-known New Testament epics that fall into the Life of Christ category in which Mary plays a secondary role. But there are also a number of narratives in which Mary figures as a chief protagonist.[3]

Film can function as a myth, which explains the status quo, or as an allegory that subverts it and attempts to rethink the religious tradition. A few of the selected films are re-workings, in which biblical episodes have been updated, parodied or reconfigured.[4] Some, not surprisingly, have received famously polarised reactions. Jean-Luc Godard's effort to relocate the story of Mary and Joseph to contemporary Switzerland in *Hail Mary* (1984) generated an uproar that has been widely documented, with Pope John Paul II himself joining in the condemnation (see Locke 1993; and Sterritt 1999). Martin Scorsese's attempt to make *The Last Temptation of Christ* (1988) was initially thwarted when the French government refused to finance his film in the wake of the Godardian controversy.[5] However, even Philippe Garrel's drug-fuelled *The Virgin's Bed* (1969), which purports to use elements of the story of Jesus to comment on the events of May 68, reveals that the sacred figures of the Bible have a significance that survives perceived acts of sacrilege.

The majority of the scriptwriters examined here present the biblical events within their specific historical and political framework, emphasising that Mary's child was born under the Roman occupation of Palestine. Consequently, the plot potentially encompasses a rather impressive range of themes: love, faith, hope, courage, morality, poverty, genocide, exile, politics, messianic prophecies, miracles, capital punishment, salvation, resurrection and eternal life. The location is chiefly first-century Galilee and Judea (often replicated by the landscapes of North America, Tunisia, Morocco, Spain or Southern Italy) and concentration is on a Jewish woman from Nazareth (frequently played by a gentile actress).

THE FACE OF MARY

There are legends that St Luke painted a picture of Mary that formed the template for future Marian images (Ebertshäuser *et al.* 1998: 222); and both St Bernard of Clairvaux and the poet Dante spoke of Mary's face 'as the one through which to view the face of Jesus Christ, through which in turn the face of God was visible' (Pelikan 1996: 30). In the light of this assessment, casting the role of Mary for film creates a notable dilemma. 'Who may fairly pass on camera in this secular age as the Mother of God?' asked a *Variety* critic in the review of George Stevens' *The Greatest Story Ever Told* on 17 February 1965 (Land 1965).

Pope Paul VI introduced the idea of Mary as 'the way of beauty' in 1975 (Académie Mariale Pontificale Internationale 2005: 58); and Pope John Paul II wrote in his 'Letter to Artists': 'Beauty is a key to the mystery and a call to transcendence' (1999). As feminist theologian Elizabeth Johnson points out in her study *Truly Our Sister: A Theology of Mary in the Communion of Saints*, Renaissance painters worked according to the principle 'that great beauty implies lofty virtue and, conversely, that spiritual beauty shows itself in physical ways' (2003: 205), so they used their Eurocentric ideal of female grace as the template for their images of the Virgin without regard for historical or ethnographic accuracy. In Franco Zeffirelli's *Jesus of Nazareth* (1977), Mary is 'the perfectly-featured, definitely-Caucasian Olivia Hussey who, first half-hidden behind the threads of her weaving loom but then, accompanied by a cresting wave of music, rises dramatically to reveal the breathtaking splendour of her refined beauty' (Baugh 1997: 77).

Ethnicity is a particularly contentious issue when a blue-eyed, fair-haired Virgin Mary has often been found in popular representations in western culture, so that the Jewishness of Jesus's family has frequently been overlooked. In Nicolas Ray's *King of Kings* (1961), Siobhan McKenna retains her original Irish accent in the role of Mary, causing a critic to remark humorously on the 'Irish touch for the Jewish mother' (in Baugh 1997: 19). But serious reflections on Judeo-Christian relations have pointed to 'a de-Judaizing process' in the early Christian Church that subsequently obscured awareness of Jesus's Jewish origins.

Conversely, the story of Jesus has a universal meaning beyond its historical and geographical framework, and transracial devotion demonstrates that Marian iconography 'has transcended every culture and ethnic group' (Ball 2004: 9). The faces of Mary and Jesus mirror the appearance of the believers who have created iconography in their honour across the world. The Black Madonnas of Czestochowa (Poland) and Guadalupe (Mexico) have made Mary 'a special ambassador to that vast majority of the human race who [are] not white' (Pelikan 1996: 26). Jean Claude La Marre's *Color of the Cross* (2006) and Mark Dornford-May's *Son of Man* (2006), which both feature a black Jesus (and, therefore, a black Madonna), are obvious filmic examples of such inculturation.

There are descriptions of Mary's physical appearance in the thousands of recorded Marian apparitions, although the desire to recreate the image of the Virgin sometimes met with the dissatisfaction of the seers. When St Catherine Labouré, a French nun who had visions of the Virgin Mary in a Parisian convent in 1830, saw the Marian statue that was sculptured to commemorate the event, she reportedly grimaced and said: 'Actually, it is not bad; but the Holy Virgin is much lovelier than that' (in Franciscan Friars 1998: 22). St Bernadette Soubirous, who had repeated visions of the Virgin in a grotto in the little village of Lourdes in the Pyrenees in 1858, was also critical of the statue placed at the apparition site, describing the Marian figure as too big and too old (see Harris 1999: 72).

Zeffirelli relates in detail in his *Spiritual Diary* of the making of *Jesus of Nazareth* that he searched in many countries for the right actress to play the part of Mary. As she had only a few lines of dialogue in his 382-minute mini-series, he circumnavigated the language barrier but needed 'a convincing *presence*' (Zeffirelli 1984: 71 [emphasis in original]). Indeed, an iconic presence appears to have been the major concern for George Stevens in *The Greatest Story Ever Told*, as he presented Dorothy McGuire as a virtually silent, figurative Madonna. The *Variety* critic was happy to suggest that her 'large, soft, womanly eyes and pensive expression' made her a plausible choice: 'A reviewer may only guess that the Marianists, always a potent bloc in the Catholic Church, should be satisfied with Miss McGuire' (Land 1965).

There are also extratextual and intertextual dimensions that some directors take into consideration in selecting an appropriate actress, for she evidently has a life beyond the confines of the set. When Olivia Hussey appeared in public wearing tight jeans and a T-shirt while filming *Jesus of Nazareth* in Morocco, a village elder asked Zeffirelli to persuade the actress to dress more modestly so as not to upset the sensitivities of the local people, who revered the mother of Jesus (see Zeffirelli 1986: 281). Reinhold Zwick comments critically on the western European features of Myriam Muller in the titular role in Jean Delannoy's *Mary of Nazareth* (1994) (1997: 273) but it becomes clear in the director's autobiographical writings that he was mainly concerned to select a relatively unknown actress whose previous filmography would not taint her performance (see Delannoy 1998: 252). The fact that Pernilla August played Mary in Kevin Connor's *Mary, mother of Jesus* (1999) in the same year that she appeared as Shmi Skywalker, the virgin mother of Anakin in George Lucas's *The Phantom Menace*, did not pass unnoticed by critics.

In making DeMille's *The King of Kings* the actors were expected to sign a clause that demanded their exemplary behaviour. Dorothy Cumming, who portrayed Mary, reportedly agreed to let the director approve her choice of roles for the next five years. When Cumming divorced her husband during the early distribution of *The King of Kings*, she 'was effectively blacklisted in Hollywood as a result' (Birchard 2004: 393). These issues were brought to the fore in the publicity for Catherine Hardwicke's *The Nativity Story* (2006), where the pregnancy of Keisha Castle-Hughes, the sixteen-year old unmarried actress who played Mary, became news before the film's release. When Pope Benedict XVI did not attend the film's première at the Vatican in November 2006 (an unusual location in itself for the launch of a secular film), there were 'Pregnant Mary embarrasses Vatican' headlines and suggestions of a Papal boycott. However, Father Melchor Sánchez de Toca y Alameda, a member of the Papal Council for Culture, strove to downplay the rumours by pointing out that Castle-Hughes was 'not expected to be a saint herself, only to do her work as an actress properly' (in Owen 2006).

In fact, Hardwicke's film was more notable for the choice of a suitably aged actress to represent Mary at the time of the Annunciation. The fact that biblical historians indicate that Mary would have been aged about twelve or thirteen when she was considered ready for marriage is consistently, if not consciously, overlooked in the casting process, in keeping with western sensibilities. The same actress generally follows Mary's narrative trajectory from the Annunciation to the Crucifixion. In the films discussed here, only Pier Paolo Pasolini (*The Gospel According to St Matthew*) and Kevin Connor (*Mary, mother of Jesus*) employ a younger actress to embody the role of Mary at the time of the Annunciation.

In his diary reflections, Zeffirelli points out a key distinction between religious art and cinema:

> When you have that face [of Mary] in front of you in the silence of the chapel in St Peter's [Basilica in Rome], a ray of light falling upon it from above, you remove it entirely from any human context, from all reality. But when you see it in the world of Nazareth, with the chickens, the little donkey, at the loom, during the engagement ceremony, or on the journey to Bethlehem, you need human qualities approaching the sublime as convincing as possible, and beauty, too, not artificial or disturbing, but a true inner beauty. (1984: 71–2)

Art critic Xavier Bray claims that the glory of painting lies in an 'ability to grasp and transmit a sense of beauty and grace – rather than literally to copy nature' (2004: 38). However, filmmakers are relying on human nature and human flesh to convey such beauty and grace. Responding to the outcry surrounding the film *Hail Mary*, Charles Warren remarked on the physical beauty of the actress who plays Mary, and asked audiences to compare Godard's work with Renaissance art and 'to think how like or unlike painting of the Madonna is the filming of Myriem Roussel, alive and moving, playing this role?' (1993: 17–18).

The following investigation strives to address some of these issues within cinematic visualisations of Mary's story in the hope that 'where exposition (film) and explanation (religious meaning) complement each other, the religious film will lead to a better understanding of the nature of faith and disclose at least some of the beauty of mystery' (Roten 2007). The films under consideration are obviously not theological texts. However, in choosing to engage with the New Testament narrative, the filmmakers are treading on theological ground, whether or not they (and I myself) are fully aware of the size of the minefield ahead.

'Contexts' provides information on developments in Mariology (the study of Mary in theology and cult) that are relevant to an analysis of the filmic corpus. The subsequent discussion takes a thematic approach, highlighting key scenes in the life of Mary taken from the New Testament. 'Announcement and Commission' explores the consequences of the Annunciation to Mary in Luke's Gospel and the difficulties of transmitting a spiritual dimension via the industrialised process of cinema. 'Mary and Joseph' captures the filmic reactions of the betrothed Jewish couple, who find themselves in an extraordinary situation when Mary becomes miraculously pregnant. 'Virgin and Mother' examines the cinematic staging of the Nativity against a background of liberation theology and Incarnation theology (in which God took on human form). And 'Mother and Disciple' traces Mary's journey to the place of Calvary, at which her son is executed.

Adele Reinhartz's highly informative *Jesus of Hollywood* is rather reductive in its summary that most films 'treat Mary with kid gloves. They reverentially highlight her serene beauty, her chastity, and her special relationship with both God and Jesus' (2007: 69). The next chapters argue that the reality is more complex and nuanced. The filmed tableaux of early silent cinema contrast with the twenty-first century renderings that bear the legacy of feminist and post-colonial theory. Vast multi-million dollar extravaganzas are distinguished from the TV movies, the latter being the source of the more daring (and occasionally ill-advised) experiments with narrative. And the focus on Mary brings together the ideas of devout Catholics and renowned atheists who would be strange bedfellows in other circumstances. Yet, the diversity of perspectives and religious beliefs illuminate crucial aspects of the life of Mary, re-visioning on film the world's most significant female cultural icon. It is hoped that the approach will offer suggestions for an analysis of extant films not discussed in detail, as well as for those productions to be made in the future.

contexts

Religion has always provided thematic material for the cinema, beginning with the filming of Passion Plays in the late nineteenth century. In focusing on Mary of Nazareth, the following study will consider how her screen role has evolved over the twentieth century and beyond, examining the intersections between the sacred and the secular.

Within the cinema industry, a number of specific events have impacted on the presentation and reception of films with Marian content. The coming of sound allowed Mary's key lines of New Testament dialogue to be audibly delivered. Biblical epics of the 1950s and 1960s provided a magnificent vista in 70mm Technicolor that tried to woo viewers away from their new-fangled television sets. Italian Neo-realism and the French New Wave inspired new methods of filmmaking that affected the work of Pasolini and Godard, who both created memorable (and controversial) Marian figures, and paved the way for low-budget projects. The end of the Production Code saw the demise of the Catholic Church's once powerful influence in Hollywood, and a liberalisation with regard to moral and religious content. And the application of psychoanalytic, poststructuralist and gender theory to film studies opened up new avenues for analysis of the Marian image. While theologians have engaged with the religious dimension, film scholars have 'framed the discussion of the female presence in the filmic text' (Deacy and Williams Ortiz 2008: 98).

In analysing the cinematic representation of Mary of Nazareth, there are a number of visible dangers (not to mention the pitfalls that escape one's notice). One difficulty is an attempt to categorise reviews of films using terms such as 'feminist', 'Protestant' or 'Catholic'. For example, feminist theology may be further divided into a range of different subgroupings, including liberal feminism and radical feminism, whose approaches may substantially differ. While Protestants traditionally *'do not talk about Mary'* (Gaventa 2005: 121 [emphasis in original]), Protestant and evangelical scholars have begun to focus attention on the mother of Jesus (see Gaventa 1999; Perry 2006; McKnight 2007). And, on the release of Godard's *Hail Mary*, there were Catholics who took to the streets and held candle-lit vigils in protest against a film that had won an award from the Catholic Film Office at the Berlin Film Festival. These paradoxical reactions demonstrate the power of the cinema to awaken theological disputes, regardless of whether the filmmakers and audiences are particularly schooled in theology. Thomas Merton wrote in *New Seeds of Contemplation* that people's views about Mary often reveal more about themselves than about the mother of Jesus (1972: 167), and that analysis holds true for directors, screenwriters and critics (and, no doubt, the author of this book).

In transferring Mary's story onto the screen, there are a variety of sources on which to draw. There is the Bible; the apocryphal writings; the Koran; the historical evidence of daily existence in first-century Palestine; existing poetic and fictional meditations on Mary's life; and two thousand years of developments in Mariology. In order to tackle this complex subject, an understanding of elements of Mariology is relevant to an examination of Mary's on-screen role. But, given the vastness of the field, this chapter will merely attempt to highlight themes that are germane to the specific filmic analysis undertaken here.[1]

THE BIBLE

The writer attempting to transform Mary's life into a screenplay would presumably turn first to the verses in the Bible that contain Marian references. In the opening scenes of Emilio Cordero's Italian film *Mater Dei* (1950), which is a visual hymn of praise to the Virgin Mary, a woman's hand reaches out and plucks an apple. The inclusion of this episode from the Garden of Eden is one example of how prophetic allusions to the mother of Jesus have been identified by Catholic theologians in the Old Testament. According to the Book of Genesis, Eve, the first woman, fell into temptation, disobeyed God and ate the forbidden fruit, leading to exile from Paradise. In contrast, Mary accepted the will of God, and became the mother of the Messiah who brought salvation to the world. St Justin Martyr (d. 165) introduced the idea of Mary as the 'New Eve'; and the Eve-Mary typology was taken up by St Irenaeus (d. 202) when he claimed that 'Eve's disobedience was untied by Mary's obedience; what the virgin Eve bound through her unbelief, the Virgin Mary loosened by her faith' (in Anon. 1997: 132). However, some feminist theologians have rejected the 'New Eve' presentation because it is seen to honour Mary while identifying ordinary women with Eve 'as fickle, unreliable, morally inferior beings' (in Carroll 1994: 54).

Additionally, the Book of Genesis introduces humankind's ongoing combat with the Devil, when God said, 'I will put enmity between you and the woman, and between your offspring and hers' (Gn 3:15). This verse has long had Mariological resonance, particularly because a mistranslation in the Latin Vulgate Bible meant that Catholics across the centuries read the line: 'She will crush your head, and you will lie in wait for her heel' (a prophesy in which the pronoun 'she' was interpreted as a reference to the Virgin Mary crushing the serpent). In fact, the verse should read: 'He will strike at your head, while you strike at his heel' (Gn 3:15), taking the woman out of the equation and presenting Christ as the Devil's chief enemy. However, in the Counter-Reformation period, Catholic exegetes argued that the Marian reference had justification because the mother of Jesus was an active participant in the destruction of evil (see Boss 2000: 142). Paintings and statues of Mary crushing the snake beneath her foot have become part of traditional Marian iconography.[2]

The prophecies of the coming of the Messiah are obviously relevant to the Marian narrative. The Book of Micah signals the birthplace:

> But you, Bethlehem-Ephrathah,
>   too small to be among the clans of Judah,
> From you shall come forth for me
>   one who is to be ruler in Israel. (Mi 5:1)

And the prophet Isaiah foretells the birth of Jesus: 'Therefore the Lord himself will give you this sign: the virgin shall be with child, and bear a son, and shall name him Immanuel' (Is 7:14). In fact, Isaiah 7:14 is one of the most contested verses in biblical exegesis, leading to disputes over the use of the Greek word *parthenos* as a translation of the Hebrew *almâ*. There have been arguments as to whether the prophecy in Isaiah referred to a 'virgin' or a 'young girl' and the potential consequences for belief in the virginal conception of Jesus. As biblical scholar Raymond Brown pointed out in his in-depth analysis of the Infancy Narratives, the translation has led to heated reactions, ranging from Justin's *Dialogue with Trypho* in the mid-second century to the burning of the *Revised Standard Version of the Bible* (which used the translation 'young girl') in 1952 (Brown 1993: 145–6).

However, it is the New Testament that provides the details about the earthly existence of Mary. Chronologically, the first reference to Jesus's mother (albeit not by name) appears in the Letter to the Galatians, when St Paul writes that 'God sent his Son, born of a woman, born under the Law' (Gal 4:4), which indicates both the humanity and Jewishness of Jesus (see Perry 2006: 29). But the most extensive material on Mary is found in the Gospels of Matthew and Luke in the Infancy Narratives – a title that is itself something of a misnomer, given that the *infancy* of Jesus is not the main focus. The opening chapters in each Gospel recount events surrounding the Nativity; and Luke relates an incident when Jesus was lost in Jerusalem at the age of twelve.

In most overarching attempts to rework the story of Jesus's conception and birth within a secular medium, the Gospels of Matthew and Luke are merged to form a coherent chronicle and the discrepancies are removed. The angel Gabriel's appearance to Mary (in Luke) usually figures in the narrative before Joseph is informed in a dream that Mary has conceived her child by the Holy Spirit (as recorded in Matthew's Gospel); and the Lukan shepherds come to pay homage to the child Jesus before the arrival of Matthew's Magi – a mixture of images that are now familiar in Christmas crib scenes.

Luke records the Annunciation of the angel Gabriel to Mary (Lk 1:26–38); the Visitation of Mary to her kinswoman Elizabeth (Lk 1:39–56); the birth of Jesus in Bethlehem (Lk 2:1–20); the circumcision of Jesus and the prophecy of Simeon that 'a sword will pierce' the heart of Mary (Lk 2:21–38); and the finding of Jesus in the Temple (Lk 2:41–52). Matthew offers Joseph's perspective on the conception of Jesus (Mt 1:18–25) and relates the visit of the Magi (Mt 2:1–12); the flight of the Holy Family into Egypt to escape the slaughter of the innocents (Mt 2:13–18); and the return from exile after Herod's death (Mt 2:19–23).

During the chapters that record Jesus's ministry, there are direct references to Mary as the mother of Jesus in the Gospels of Mark (Mk 6:1–4) and Matthew (Mt 13:54–58); and the 'mother and brothers' pericope is of particular interest because its treatment in a screenplay affects the on-screen relationship between the adult Jesus and his mother, as well as having theological repercussions. The pericope, which is found in the three synoptic Gospels (Mt 12:46–50; Mk 3:31–35; and Lk 8:19–21), is an incident when the relatives of Jesus came to see him when he was preaching. Matthew records: 'While he was still speaking to the crowds, his mother and his brothers [*adelphoi*] appeared outside, wishing to speak with him' (Mt 12:46). The first issue is the interpretation of the 'brothers' of Jesus, who are named in the New Testament as James, Joses, Judas and Simon (Mk 6:3), as well as a number of 'sisters'. Protestants have no difficulty in acknowledging these protagonists as the children of Mary and Joseph (and they appear in this guise in La Marre's film *Color of the Cross*). However, for Catholics who believe that Mary remained a virgin after the birth of Jesus, the word *adelphoi* has been taken to have a wider translation that would include cousins, half-brothers, half-sisters, nephews and nieces.

The second concern is Jesus's reaction to the appearance of his family. '"Who is my mother? Who are my brothers?" And stretching out his hand toward his disciples, he said, "Here are my mother and my brothers. For whoever does the will of my heavenly Father is my brother, and sister, and mother"' (Mt 12:48–50). Some theologians regard the fact that the family of Jesus did not appear to understand him as evidence 'that Mary's awareness of Jesus's mission was not fully formed until the crucifixion' (see Maunder 2007: 18), and that 'Mark declares that despite their blood ties, Jesus's family is distant from him both physically and spiritually' (Perry 2006: 35). However, the verses have also been read as an indication that Mary (who did the will of the Father by becoming the mother of the Messiah) is the foremost amongst the followers of Jesus. When Luke relates how a woman in the crowd praised Mary with the words: 'Blessed is the womb that carried you and the breasts at which you nursed,' and notes that Jesus replied: 'Rather, blessed are those who hear the word of God and observe it' (Lk 11:27–28), the response has been used as evidence to honour Mary as the 'first disciple'.

In addition, John's Gospel incorporates two key Marian events that are not found in the synoptic Gospels: the miracle at Cana when the water is changed into wine (Jn 2:1–11); and the presence of Mary at the foot of the cross (Jn 19:25–27). The Lukan Acts of the Apostles also confirm that Mary was present in the upper room with the disciples in Jerusalem at the time of Pentecost (Acts 1:14). The woman who is 'clothed with the sun, with the moon under her feet, and on her head a crown of twelve stars' in the twelfth chapter of the Book of Revelation has also received a disputed Marian interpretation (see Buby 2000: 77–96).

Theologians have asserted that any inconsistency or omission found in the Gospels does not undermine the veracity of Scripture, but rather it affirms that the word of God has been recorded by human beings who could offer only a partial insight into the mystery of the revelation in Jesus Christ (see Brown *et al.* 1978: 23). The incompleteness of the narrative of Mary of Nazareth may be explained by the fact that the evangelists' focus was the ministry of Jesus rather than the biography of his mother. While attempts to fill the gaps in the canonical texts may cause conflict for the ecumenical movement, given the Protestant insistence on the authority of Scripture, they have proved to be a boon to the fertile imagination of screenwriters and directors.

THE KORAN

The Koran, which Muhammad began to preach in the seventh century, contains the story of Mary and her son Jesus. Sūrah 19, which is called 'Mary' (Maryam), is one of the longest in the Islamic Holy Book, and the only one that has the name of a woman as its title. Mary's father is named 'Imran, and when Mary's mother becomes pregnant, she vows that her child will be dedicated to God: 'And when she was delivered of the child, she said: "Lord, I have given birth to a daughter" – God well knew of what she was delivered: the male is not like the female – "and have called her Mary. Protect her and all her descendants from Satan, the Accursed One"' (3:36). Mary will grow up to be the virgin mother of the prophet Jesus, and both mother and son 'are spoken of as being of exceptional purity' (Jomier 2002: 65).

The Bible and the Koran both recount the angelic annunciation to Mary and the birth of Jesus. Parallels have been drawn 'between Muhammad and Mary as both bearers of the word of God' (Pelikan 1996: 69). However, the Koran concentrates on the oneness of God and excludes the idea of God having a son. Whereas Christians regard Jesus as the Second Person of the Trinity, Muslims honour him as a holy prophet. Timothy Winter indicates that 'the Muslim Mary is not primarily celebrated as mother of Christ, but as a distinctive archetype of female prayerfulness and patience in adversity' (2007: 479). Mary of the Koran was 'enjoined to worship constantly, to submit, to prostrate and to bow, that she might be deserving of this miracle, and might be thankful for this grace' (in Winter 2007: 486).

Of particular interest to Christians seeking to build bridges of understanding with the Islamic community is *The Saint Mary* (Shahriar Bohrani, 2001), an Iranian film that relates the birth and childhood of Mary, the Annunciation and the birth of Jesus as found in the Koran. Mohammed Saeed Bahmanpour, who wrote the script, said that the film came about 'because of an inspiration that I always had about the Virgin Mary' and because of 'how great a lady she is'.[3]

In the Koran, there is no role for Joseph, and Mary is alone as she goes to a remote place and gives birth to Jesus by a palm tree. Timothy Winter argues that, from an Islamic perspective, the virginal birth of Jesus is 'one of Mary's miracles, no more dogmatically significant as such than the miraculous appearance of fruit and water in her cell, or the visitation of Gabriel' (1999). Mary lived 'in isolation from men as a pious worshiper and, hence, a virgin only by implication' (*Ibid.*). In *The Saint Mary*, this sense of isolation is captured in magnificent high-angle shots in which Mary (Shabnam Gholikhani) walks alone across the Temple courtyard.

Islam has 'no cult of a holy female intimately tied to divinity' (Carmody 1992: 112). But Winter points out that there are convergences in the symbolic language of Christianity and Islam 'in their exploration of a gendered dynamic by which heaven and earth are reconciled. Thus, symbolism, rather than founding historical figures, must be considered the basis for any dialogue that hopes to avoid both the dangers of reductionism and the sterility of a simple acknowledgement of difference' (1999). As a consequence, Bohrani's film may serve as 'a starting point for the religion's lively modern debates over the nature and the role of womanhood' (Winter 2007: 479).

LITERARY TEXTS

Additional details about Mary's existence on earth – especially the years before the Annunciation – have come from manuscripts that fall outside the biblical canon. The first Christian text to treat Mary as a person of intrinsic significance in her own right is considered to be the second-century *Protevangelium of James*. It is an apocryphal gospel that records Mary's life prior to the birth of Jesus, as well as additional information not found in the Infancy Narratives. The chapters relate the infertility of Mary's parents Joachim and Anna until angels tell them that the Lord has heard their prayer: 'You shall conceive and bear, and your offspring shall be spoken of in the whole world' (in Elliott 1993: 58); Mary's extraordinary childhood, during which she walked at the age of six months, resided initially in the sanctuary of her bedroom, and then was taken to the Temple at the age of three to serve the Lord (a scene that evokes Mary's dedication to the Temple in the Koran); her betrothal to Joseph, a widower who is chosen by divine intervention; and the attestation of Mary's virginity *ante partum*, *in partu* and *post partum* (referring to the fact that Mary remained a virgin before, during and after the birth of Jesus, with the unbroken hymen as a tangible symbol). A woman named Salome refuses to accept the midwife's account that 'a virgin has brought forth, a thing which her condition does not allow' (in Elliott 1993: 64) without physical proof, a response that echoes the disciple Thomas's doubts about the Resurrection of Jesus (Jn 20: 25). When Salome conducts her test, her hand is consumed by fire and not cured until she touches the baby Jesus in repentance. While *The Protevangelium of James* has been dismissed by some scholars as 'inventive hagiography' it has been influential in the development of the biography of Mary (see Brown *et al.* 1978: 248–9) and in elements of Marian doctrine and devotion.

Many of the films that deal with 'the life of Mary', such as Jean Delannoy's *Mary of Nazareth* (1994) and Kevin Connor's *Mary, mother of Jesus* (1999), begin with the Annunciation in Luke's Gospel. However, Cordero's *Mater Dei* and Fabrizio Costa's film *Maria, Daughter of Her Son* (2000) cover the early childhood of Mary, both drawing on the apocryphal material for Mary's dedication to the Lord. In *Maria, Daughter of Her Son*, Mary is presented as a little girl dressed in white like a tiny bride being carried to the Temple. Her parents are informed that, 'If the child climbs the staircase of the Temple, never once looking back, your offering will be pleasing to the Lord,' and the high Temple steps are shot at a low angle to emphasise the scale of the effort that lies ahead. Her mother calls Mary 'my darling, my little love, my great gift' – which are the words that Mary uses for Jesus in the film's birth and Crucifixion scenes and echo throughout the narrative. Mary accomplishes the task and is greeted by the proclamation: 'The Lord will magnify your name.' In the most ancient account of Mary's presentation in the Temple in *The Protevangelium of James*, Mary is represented 'deliberately as Wisdom' (see Boss 2007: 4).

While Cordero limits the Temple episode (indicating the setting with a curtain and a *menorah*) in *Mater Dei*, he does create some additional incidents for Mary's childhood. A female traveller is invited into Mary's home to rest, and the young girl kneels down to wash the stranger's feet as Jesus did before the Last Supper (Jn 13:5). Mary is taught to read by her mother, whereas many commentators argue that she would presumably have been illiterate (in the sense of 'without writing') given the time frame (see Hazleton 2004: 31).

A few films also widen their scope to incorporate scenes from the childhood of Jesus, sometimes drawing on *The Infancy Gospel of Thomas*, which contains episodes that 'stress in a crudely sensational way the miraculous powers of Jesus' (Elliott 1993: 68). While the films generally play down the *enfant terrible* dimension found in the non-canonical texts, the difficulty of casting a suitable child actor to portray a juvenile Messiah (who is not unintentionally irritating) remains a constant problem. Incidents that are drawn from the apocrypha include the moulding of clay into a sparrow (found in *The Infancy Gospel of Thomas*) that becomes a scene in Franco Rossi's *A Child called Jesus*; and the death of Joseph (recorded in *The History of Joseph the Carpenter*) features in *Maria, Daughter of Her Son*. Other apocryphal works that allude to Mary include the *Odes of Solomon*, the *Acts of Peter*, the *Sibylline Oracles*, the *Ascension of Isaiah*, the *Apocalypse of Paul*, the *Book of the Resurrection of Christ*, the *Assumption of the Virgin* and the *Gospel of Nicodemus*.

The fascination with the Virgin Mary as an independent person began in the Early Christian Church and has continued throughout literary history. The tenth-century *Vitae* told Mary's story anew in poetic form, embellishing and transforming the biblical narrative, and this tradition has been handed down across the centuries in poetry, plays and novels (see Ebertshauser *et al.* 1998; and Boss 2007). A new creative outlet was evidently found in the cinema.

ADDITIONAL SOURCES

Historians have charted the life of Jewish women in Palestine and revealed details of customs and religious practices during the time when Jesus 'acquired celebrity as a faith-healer, exorcist and itinerant preacher' (Goldberg and Rayner 1989: 76). Of particular interest is the Nazareth Village project, which is a 'living museum' in Nazareth that recreates conditions in first-century Galilee.[4] Indeed, a desire for authenticity is now a feature of some biblical films, with Catherine Hardwicke explaining how the actors in *The Nativity Story* went to 'Nativity Camp' to learn how to milk goats and weave cloth (see Lytal 2006). However, not all directors strive for historical accuracy, believing that the New Testament story has a significance beyond its delineated time frame. Mel Gibson's decision to have the crucifixion nails placed through Jesus's hands rather than his wrists in *The Passion of the Christ* is a noted example.

Geographical legitimacy is a further complication, for many of the original locations in the Holy Land have been markedly changed over the centuries. Frequent viewers of religious movies will come to identify a filmic New Testament landscape that has been created in Europe and North Africa. The village of Matera in Italy is identifiable in Pasolini's *The Gospel according to St Matthew*, Gibson's *The Passion of the Christ* and Hardwicke's *The Nativity Story*; and Monastir in Tunisia forms one of the backdrops for Zeffirelli's *Jesus of Nazareth*, Terry Jones's *Monty Python's Life of Brian*, Rossi's *A Child called Jesus*, Giovanni Veronesi's *For Love, Only For Love*, and Fabrizio Costa's *Maria, Daughter of Her Son*. In some films an imposing large-scale model of Jerusalem in the Second Temple period, housed at the Israel Museum in Jerusalem, makes an appearance.

A number of religious films strive to lay out their serious credentials from the beginning. The title card at the start of Cecil B. DeMille's *The Kings of Kings* states: 'The events portrayed by this picture occurred in Palestine nineteen centuries ago, when the Jews were under the complete subjection of Rome – even their own High Priest being appointed by the Roman procurator.' (Then the text is followed by the director's signature as a form of *imprimatur*.) Some fifty years later, a TV movie called *Mary and Joseph, A Story of Faith* (Eric Till, 1979) [henceforth referred to as *Mary and Joseph*] proudly informed the audience: 'This program has been prepared with the advice and support of noted theologians and it is based on scholarly research. The story is true to its time and historical events are faithfully presented.' However, this heartening statement was followed by a significant one-line caveat: 'Yet because biblical accounts of Mary and Joseph are limited, certain events are depicted as they might have happened.' The last sentence makes way for the subsequent (and substantial) flights of fancy.

MARIOLOGY

Theologians approach the biblical material from a variety of angles, and there are two millennia of theological developments within Mariology to provide further stimuli for screenwriters. The historians strive to uncover the historical reality behind the texts; exponents of 'redaction criticism' demonstrate how the evangelists have edited the material to suit their purposes; and literary scholars dissect the texts and search for the construction of meaning. In the twentieth century, 'reader response' approaches began to recognise 'the importance of texts about Mary in feminist and liberationist circles' (Maunder 2007: 15).

The period of 1850–1950 is described as the Golden Age of Mary. It embraces two Marian dogmas (the Immaculate Conception and the Assumption) and the world-famous apparitions of the Virgin Mary in Lourdes (France) and Fatima (Portugal). And cinema itself was born in 1895, halfway through the Golden Age, allowing Marian events to be recorded on film in both documentary and fictional form. Given the extent of the theological material available, the following brief summary will concentrate on five aspects of Mariology that have bearing on this book's filmic analysis: the Marian dogmas; the status of Marian devotion within the Catholic Church; the Second Vatican Council of the 1960s; feminist theology; and liberation Mariology.

THE MARIAN DOGMAS

A dogma is an article of faith that Catholics must accept as defined by the Magisterium (the teaching authority of the Catholic Church). There are four Marian dogmas: the Divine Motherhood (431), the Perpetual Virginity (649), the Immaculate Conception (1854) and the Assumption (1950).

It is in the staging of the filmic Nativity scenes that the first Marian dogma has resonance, for the directors are presenting the birth of a child who is both the Son of God and the son of Mary: the 'human form divine'. Mary was declared to be the *Theotokos* (the God-Bearer) at the Council of Ephesus in 431. This attribution was disputed by the Bishop of Constantinople Nestorius, who claimed that to call Mary the *Theotokos* 'implied that God had a beginning – as if he were a pagan god, or some other created being' (Boss 2007: 54). Consequently, it has been argued that the official title of *Theotokos* 'was not primarily to honour [Mary] but to refute the heresy of Nestorius who had distinguished the human person of Jesus from the divine person of Christ' (Ashley 1985: 535). It was in the high Middle Ages that theology developed the theme of 'Motherhood' within Mariology. The ordinary faithful found solace in the maternal aspect of the Marian cult before it was expressed by theologians, accepting the idea spiritually rather than intellectually (see Buono in Anon. 1997: 336–7).

The Council of the Lateran in 649 proclaimed Mary to be Ever Virgin, insisting that Mary was a virgin before, during and after the birth of Jesus (as detailed in *The Protevangelium of James*). Scriptural support is found in the Song of Songs, where the line 'A garden inclosed is my sister, my spouse; a spring shut up, a fountain sealed' was seen by St Jerome as a reference to Mary (see Pelikan 1996: 29), as was the burning bush that was not consumed by fire (depicted in Cordero's *Mater Dei* in order to make this Marian link). This dogma is significant in relation to a number of artistic choices in the writing of the filmic screenplay: the treatment of the Annunciation, in which Mary is told that she has been chosen to be the virginal mother of Jesus; the effect of this information on her betrothal to Joseph; and, if the Catholic line is followed, the repercussions for subsequent marital relations. Another delicate issue is the filming of the Nativity scene. Does Mary undergo a normal pregnancy and labour, with all its attendant physical consequences? Or is the act of birth itself mysterious and miraculous, as the apocryphal literature testifies?

Latin theologians accepted without question that the Virgin Mary was free of 'personal sin', reflecting St Augustine's view: 'The honor of Christ forbids the least hesitation on the subject of possible sin by His Mother' (in Anon. 1997: 191). At the Council of Trent (1547) it was confirmed that 'through a special privilege Mary once justified was able to avoid all sins, even venial ones, throughout her entire life (Canon 23 on Justification)' (see Anon. 1997: 110). However, it was not until the nineteenth century that the third dogma of the Immaculate Conception was defined by Pope Pius IX in 1854, stating that Mary was 'enriched by God with gifts' appropriate to her role as the mother of the Saviour and 'from the first moment of her conception [was] preserved immune from all stain of original sin' (in *Catechism of the Catholic Church* 1994: 109–10).

It is this dogma that tends to cause the most confusion for secular commentators, who wrongly assume that the term 'immaculate conception' refers to the virginal conception of Jesus rather than Mary's preservation from original sin. The term 'immaculate conception' is used loosely to describe phantom pregnancies, *In Vitro* Fertilization, or the birth of a child where the father is unknown. When George Lucas's *The Phantom Menace* was released in 1999, a number of film critics commented inaccurately that the apparently miraculous birth of Anakin Skywalker (later to become the evil Darth Vader) could be 'the result of an immaculate conception' (see, for example, Clinton 1999).

Jean-Luc Godard recreated El Greco's 'Immaculate Conception' (1608–13) as a *tableau vivant* in his film *Passion* (1982) and the editing of the narrative ensures that it offers a commentary on the loss of virginity of female protagonist, Isabelle. Isabelle and her partner, Jerzy, recite the 'Agnus Dei' in the bedroom as if underlining a sacred dimension to their actions, and then juxtapositions between this scene and the recreation of El Greco's painting of the Immaculate Conception lead to a major distortion.

El Greco's painting has, in itself, raised controversy, for some art critics have believed it to be an Assumption rather than an Immaculate Conception, but Godard sows further confusion. The respected French film critic Alain Bergala then exacerbates the problem, indicating incorrectly that the Immaculate Conception is a virgin's first act of lovemaking (1999: 139). The mistake is then promulgated in Kaja Silverman and Harun Farocki's book *Speaking about Godard*, where Farocki's misunderstanding of the dogma of the Immaculate Conception ensures that the analysis of the scene in *Passion* reproduces the inaccuracy (1998: 192). In his otherwise highly informative study of the films of Godard, Douglas Morrey also describes *Hail Mary* as 'the story of the Annunciation and Immaculate Conception of Christ' (2005: 141).

Even when the theology is fully understood, the difficulty is how to convey the reality of the Immaculate Conception on screen – and it is an issue that affects all films containing a Marian figure. Elizabeth Johnson has complained that the dogma of the Immaculate Conception has sometimes allowed Mary to be presented as if she lived in a vacuum.

> Exempt from human passions, preserved from temptations, especially those of a sexual nature, immune from wrestling with issues, spared ambiguity when it came to decisions, always in full possession of her wits, clearly knowing God's plan for herself and her son and more than willing to carry it out, she moved through life with unearthly ease. (2003: 108)

Consequently, Mary's less than joyful reaction to the arranged marriage with Joseph depicted in Catherine Hardwicke's *The Nativity Story* met with condemnatory comment from some Catholic members of the audience, who found it 'rather disconcerting to see Our Blessed Mother portrayed with "attitude"' (in Geiger 2006). Certainly, the expletives that Godard's female protagonist utters in *Hail Mary* are an unacceptable attribute for any New Testament character, let alone Mary in the light of the Marian dogma.

The fourth Marian dogma relates to questions about the nature of Mary's death, which had been discussed in the East since the second century (for there was no body and no relics) and the feast of the passage of the Virgin has been celebrated on 15 August since around the year 600 (see Warner 1990: 81). The dogma of the Assumption, in which it was declared that the Virgin Mary was assumed body and soul into Heaven, was finally pronounced by Pope Pius XII in 1950.

The dogma moved beyond the Church's teaching that the soul 'separates from the body at death, and [is] reunited with the body at the final Resurrection' (in *Catechism of the Catholic Church* 1994: 83) and stated that the Virgin, 'preserved free from all stain of original sin, when the course of her earthly life was finished, was taken up body and soul into heavenly glory' (in *Catechism of the Catholic Church* 1994: 221).

According to Benedict Ashley, the last two dogmas were used by the Vatican to express resilience in the face of trauma: 'Pius IX saw in the lovely Immaculata the truth that the Church was infallible in its faith in the face of modern unbelief which came to a climax in his time, and Pius XII hoped that the radiant Assumpta would be a rainbow of hope to an age of death and despair' (1985: 539) that had just witnessed World War II and the Holocaust. Only two films analysed in this study directly refer to the Assumption: Cordero's *Mater Dei*, whose release coincides with the proclamation of the dogma; and Costa's *Maria, Daughter of Her Son*, which offers the most complete rendition of Mary's earthly biography and shows the resurrected Jesus returning to carry Mary away in his arms into the light.

MARIAN DEVOTION

The discovery of a third-century Greek papyrus bearing the Marian prayer *Sub Tuum Praesidium* (*Under your Patronage*) in Egypt provided evidence that people had expressed their devotion to Mary in the Early Christian Church. Mary retains a particularly exalted status amongst Catholics, with 'hyperdulia' (superior veneration) officially sanctioned as 'an intrinsic element of Christian worship' (Buono in Anon. 1997: 88). The Catholic Church states that correct Marian devotion, in its subordinate role, 'brings a very human complementary note' to the worship rendered to the Holy Trinity (Billet in Anon. 1997: 257). However, this aspect of Catholic devotion has caused some conflict with Protestants because of the dangers of suspected idolatry.

Christocentric Mariology relates Mary to Christ in a subordinate way, whereas *Christotypical* Mariology 'places Mary's relationship to Christ by way of analogy with the redemptive role of Christ' (Cheah 1995: 72).

Pope John XXIII himself explained, 'The Madonna is not happy when she is placed before her son' (in Cunneen 1996: 9), and this statement can evidently be taken *literally* in cinema (with regard to framing and *mise-en-scène*), but also has repercussions for Mary's significance within the diegesis.

As anthropologist Victor Turner points out, the image of Mary has come to be 'a signifier meant to represent not only the historical woman who once lived in Galilee but the sacred person who resides in heaven, appears at times to living persons, and intercedes with God for the salvation of mankind' (in Cunneen 1996: 18). If the seers are to be believed, the presence of the Virgin Mary on earth does not end with her death. The first recorded Marian apparition was to St Gregory the Wonderworker (d.ca.270) (see Gambero 1999: 94). Since the year 1000 there have been thousands of reported apparitions throughout the world, with notable variations in the physical appearance of the Virgin and the tone and emphasis of her words. The Marian apparitions in Lourdes (1858) and Fatima (1917) led to the creation of pilgrimage sites that drew worldwide attention to the Marian cult. Reports of miraculous sightings have continued into the twenty-first century, despite fresh reservations in the light of psychoanalysis and the relativisation of faith. While Catholics are not obligated to believe in apparitions (it is not an article of faith, unlike a belief in the dogmas), the recorded appearances have had spiritual (and commercial) repercussions. Henry King's *Song of Bernadette* (1943), starring an Oscar-winning Jennifer Jones, is one of the more famous renditions of the happenings at Lourdes; and Jean Delannoy's film *Bernadette* (1988) is regularly screened at a cinema outside the Pyrenean shrine during the pilgrimage season.

Marian apparitions have generated a number of films that reflect the climate in which they were made. The anti-communist message of *The Miracle of Our Lady of Fatima* (John Brahm, 1952) would have struck a chord with an America afraid of 'Reds under the bed'. Jean-Pierre Mocky's *Le Miraculé* (1986), which centres on an insurance fraud that exploits the shrine at Lourdes, appealed to some of France's anti-clerical instincts. When a spokesman for the Catholic Church appeared on the French evening news 48 hours after the film's release and condemned *Le Miraculé*, Mocky achieved his best box-office receipts in years (see Prédal 1988: 114). And the events at Medjugorje in Bosnia-Herzegovina (where the reported apparitions began in 1981) provided the backdrop for a political story of conflict between Communism and the Catholic Church in Jakov Sedlar's *Gospa* (1995).

THE SECOND VATICAN COUNCIL

The 1960s was a period of revolution and transformation from a number of perspectives – and it was a time when the cult of the Virgin Mary found itself assailed from two angles: the Catholic Church and the women's movement. Within the Catholic Church, Marian devotion appeared to be sidelined by the agenda of the Second Vatican Council of 1962–65. The First Vatican Council of 1869 saw the declaration of the dogma of Papal Infallibility. The Second Vatican Council (often referred to as 'Vatican II'), was the inspiration of Pope John XXIII, who wished to modernise the Catholic Church. Pasolini was so encouraged by the efforts of this pope that he dedicated his film *The Gospel according to St Matthew* to him.

The Council left its mark on the lives of the ordinary Catholic faithful. The Latin Mass was replaced by a post-conciliar liturgy in which the priest spoke in the vernacular and faced the congregation (rather than facing east); and the Papal encyclical *Humanae Vitae* (1968), which was the result of the Council's deliberations on sexuality, reiterated the Vatican's ban on artificial contraception at a time when 'free love' was a popular slogan in the secular world. The Church's anti-abortion stance also ran counter to the feminist argument for 'a woman's right to choose' that led to pro-abortion changes to the laws in Western Europe and the United States.

Particularly relevant to a discussion of New Testament films is the Vatican II document *Nostra Aetate* (*Declaration on the Relation of the Church to Non-Christian Religions*) (1965), which sought to repair Jewish-Catholic relations. The stigmatisation of the Jews as 'Christ-killers' was an appellation that had fuelled anti-Semitic literature across the centuries, including the works of prominent Fathers of the Church such as Origen and St John Chrysostom (see Perry and Schweitzer 2004: 4). The sincerity of the continuing desire for reparation was underlined when Pope John Paul II prayed at the Yad Vashem Memorial in March 2002: 'Let us build a new future where there will be no more anti-Jewish feeling among Christians, or anti-Christian feeling among Jews, but rather the mutual respect of those who adore the one Creator and Lord, and look to Abraham as our common father in faith' (in Korn and Pawlikowski 2004: 196).

Directing *Jesus of Nazareth* in 1977, Zeffirelli 'wanted to make most evident that Christ was a Jew, a prophet who grew out of the cultural, social and historical background of Israel at the time' (1986: 274), and he refers specifically to the Vatican II document: 'Both the words of Pope Paul's *Nostra Aetate* and the need to create cinematic reality led to the decision to try to show the historical Jewish Jesus' (1986: 275). From a different perspective, critics of Mel Gibson's *The Passion of the Christ* also referred to the legacy of Vatican II, attacking Gibson himself 'as an ultraconservative Roman Catholic, a traditionalist who does not acknowledge many of the reforms of the Second Vatican Council' (Meacham 2004: 3), which include the *Nostra Aetate* document. Notably, both directors attributed their work to divine inspiration. Referring to heavenly bodies rather than any of the cast of famous faces who populated *Jesus of Nazareth*, Zeffirelli wrote of 'the sign of that Star that surely guided us all' (1984: 25). Commenting on *The Passion of the Christ*, Gibson claimed: '[The] Holy Ghost was working through me on this, and I was just directing traffic' (in Thistlethwaite 2004: 140).

Also of relevance to an analysis of Mary is *Lumen Gentium* (1965), the new Dogmatic Constitution on the Church which resulted from Vatican II. The document included a final chapter entitled 'The Blessed Virgin Mary, Mother of God, in the mystery of Christ and the Church'. The fact that this theological study of the role of the Virgin Mary was positioned at the end of *Lumen Gentium*, rather than having the status of a separate publication, typified the desire to clarify the status of Mary in the economy of salvation in a manner that would not alienate supporters of the ecumenical movement.[5]

At Vatican II, the Council also debated the possibility of declaring a fifth Marian dogma, in which the Virgin Mary would be assigned the title 'Co-redemptrix, Mediatrix of All Graces and Advocate for the People of God'. Some theologians argue that the title Co-Redemptrix 'refers to Mary's cooperation in the Redemption in the sense that she knowingly and willingly gave birth to the Redeemer (indirect, remote cooperation)' (Carol in Anon. 1997: 78). The champions of the cause argue that 'in teaching that [Mary] is the supreme instance of human co-operation in her Son's redeeming work, the Church would be affirming the corresponding, though lesser, vocation of all Christians' (see Yarnold 2002: 242). The argument is then taken further with regard to Mary's contribution to the redemptive action of Christ at the Crucifixion:

> Together with Christ (though in total subordination to Him and in virtue of His power), Mary atoned or satisfied for our sins, merited every grace necessary for salvation, and joined the Saviour's sacrifice on Calvary to appease the wrath of God. It was in view of this joint operation of Son and Mother that God was pleased to cancel our debt and take us back into His friendship broken by sin. (Carol in Anon. 1997: 79)

The Council chose to reject such a dogma although it stated that Mary was invoked by the Church under the titles of *Advocate*, *Auxiliatrix*, *Adjutrix* and *Mediatrix*. However, the merits of a formal definition continue to be debated. The concern 'that any interpretation of the role of Mary must not obscure the unique mediation of Christ' (Miller 2007: 15) is felt in critical reviews of New Testament films as well as in theological deliberations. The status of Mary as 'Co-redemptrix' was particularly discussed in reactions to Mel Gibson's *The Passion of the Christ*.

While *Lumen Gentium* encouraged the practices of Marian piety rec-ommended by the Magisterium, it urged 'theologians and preachers of the divine word to abstain zealously both from all gross exaggerations as well as from petty narrow-mindedness in considering the singular dignity of the Mother of God' and to 'assiduously keep away from whatever, either by word or deed, could lead separated brethren or any other into error regarding the true doctrine of the Church'.[6] However, for many grassroots Catholics, these reforms were to tear the heart out of Marian devotion. Just as the post-conciliar Mass in the vernacular embraced 'a sense of com-munity around the altar' but lost 'the sense of the numinous, of mystery' (Cardinal Hume in Stourton 1998: 5), so the Marian cult gained a vital biblical foundation at the same time as it threatened to lose its lyrical beau-ty. When faced with reports of this downturn in Marian devotion, Karl Rahner responded that Christians are tempted 'to turn the central truths of the faith into abstractions, and abstractions have no need of mothers' (in Jelly 1983: 73–4). Hans Urs von Balthasar warned:

> Without Mariology, Christianity threatens imperceptibly to become inhuman. The Church becomes functionalistic, soulless, a hectic enter-prise without any point of rest, estranged from its true nature by the planners. And because, in this manly – masculine world, all that we have is one ideology replacing another, everything becomes polemical, bitter, humourless, and ultimately boring, and people in their masses run away from such a Church. (In Heft 1980: 56–7)

The language of *Lumen Gentium* was intended to comfort those Prot-estants who were dismayed by suspected idolatry – or, more specifically, Mariolatry – at work within the Catholic Church. One of the aims of the council was to foster ecumenical links. The document *Unitatis Redintegra-tio* 'rejoices in the conspicuous honour paid to the Blessed Virgin by the Orthodox churches,' and 'the Decree on the Eastern Catholic Churches,

Orientalium Ecclesiarum, recommends that her intercession should be sought for the healing of the East-West schism' (Boulding 2002: 143). This desire has continued with ecumenical documents such as Pope John Paul II's *Ut unum sint* (*On Commitment to Ecumenism*) in 1995. The role of Mary within such discussions has been taken forward by the Groupe des Dombes (1998) and the publications of the Anglican-Roman Catholic International Commission (ARCIC). The Ecumenical Society of the Blessed Virgin Mary also strives to further understanding of the role of Mary within the Christian and Orthodox churches. Ecumenical discussions stress that 'even within the Reformation Churches, the question of Mary was related at first more to what was seen as exaggerated devotion to Mary, rather than to dissent about the place she should have in Christian self-understanding' (in McLoughlin and Pinnock 2002: xiii). Protestant theologian Beverly Roberts Gaventa has made the point: 'If we can say that Mary is a disciple, even the first disciple of Jesus, then we have taken an important step together. And if we can say that Mary is a disciple, then is it not a Protestant sort of thing to affirm that Mary is, symbolically speaking, the Mother of Disciples, even the Mother of Believers?' (in Carroll 2002: 34).

fEMINIST THEOLOGY

Although Vatican II had intended to reform Marian devotion, many saw the result as 'the wreckage' of the Marian cult (see Johnson 2003: 131). As the Catholic Church reduced its May processions and Novenas in honour of the Virgin Mary, it might have appeared to outside observers that members of the Catholic clergy and secular feminists were engaged in a common goal: to dismiss the Virgin Mary as an irrelevant symbol for the second half of the twentieth century.

In an article published in 1967 in *Études mariales* (*Marian Studies*), Louis Cognet wrote that the reduction in Marian devotion was notable in the intellectual *milieu* but that the crowds on Marian pilgrimages and the number of candles burning before statues of the Virgin in the churches indicated that the 'crisis' was not yet evident amongst the 'ordinary people' (1967: 37). However, within the intellectual *milieu*, some adherents of the second wave of feminism identified Mary as a symbol of patriarchal oppression and attention was drawn to perceptions of the misogynist connotations of Mariology. There were feminist theologians who perceived the dogmas of 1854 and 1950 as retrograde steps, claiming that, when supplemented by the belief in Mary's perpetual virginity – as symbolised by the unbroken hymen in the apocryphal *Protevangelium of James* – the Marian dogmas identified women with the dangers of sexual conduct: 'Mariology exalts the virginal, obedient, spiritual, feminine and fears all real women in the flesh' (Radford Ruether in Johnson 1985: 117). The apparent downturn in the fortunes of the Marian cult was welcomed by those critics who had highlighted the androcentric nature of the Catholic Church's teaching on the position of women, with Mary regarded as a prominent symbol of female subjugation. First published in 1976, Marina Warner's *Alone of all Her Sex: The Myth and Cult of the Virgin Mary* (the work of a lapsed Catholic) became a key source text for non-theological scholars in search of a Marian reference, and there was wide dissemination of her conclusion that the Virgin Mary would be reduced to a legend that was 'emptied of [...] its present real powers to heal and to harm' (1990: 339).

However, liberation theologian Maria Clara Bingemer takes a different line: 'The female body, which was for so many centuries regarded by large sections of the Church – on the basis of a dubious interpretation of the Genesis story – as the cause of original sin, something which left the whole female sex with a heavy burden of guilt, is rehabilitated by the Catholic Church when it declares blessed this female body animated by the divine Spirit' (1991: 102). And in the years following the Council there was an attempt by the Catholic Church to extricate Mary from the static role that she had come to play as the ideal mother, the guardian of purity and the intercessor in both personal and apostolic prayer (see Roten 1991: 25).

The US Bishops released a document in 1973 called *Behold your Mother* that re-examined the importance of Mary in the light of developments in contemporary society:

> The dignity that Christ's redemption won for all women was fulfilled uniquely in Mary as the model of all real feminine freedom. The Mother of Jesus is portrayed in the Gospel as *intelligent* (the Annunciation, 'How can this be?'); *apostolic* (the visit to Elizabeth); *inquiring and contemplative* (the Child lost in the Temple); *responsive and creative* (at Cana); *compassionate and courageous* (at Calvary); a woman of *great faith*. These implications in the lives of Jesus and Mary need to be elaborated into a sound theology on the role of Christian women in the contemporary Church and Society. (In Anon. 1997: 496 [emphasis in original])

A year later, Pope Paul VI set out four criteria with regard to Marian devotion in *Marialis Cultus*: conformity with contemporary biblical understanding; conformity with liturgical renewal; ecumenical accord; and sensitivity to cultural difference (see Brennan 1995: 49). Johann Roten records the changing tone in the Papacy's attitude to women, which came with a growing awareness of the momentum of the feminist movement (1991: 25). In *Marialis Cultus*, Pope Paul VI acknowledged that some people were becoming disenchanted with Marian devotion because the horizons of the life of Mary of Nazareth 'seem rather restricted in comparison with the vast spheres of activity open to mankind [sic] today' (1974). He continued that Mary should be imitable not precisely in the type of life she led, with its specific socio-cultural background:

> She is held up as an example to the faithful rather for the way in which, in her own particular life, she fully and responsibly accepted the will of God (cf. Lk 1:38), because she heard the word of God and acted on it, and because charity and a spirit of service were the driving force of her actions. She is worthy of imitation because she was the first and the most perfect of Christ's disciples. All of this has a permanent and universal exemplary value.

As feminist film theorist Laura Mulvey was drawing attention to the sexist depiction of women on screen in her seminal article 'Visual Pleasure and Narrative Cinema' (1975), so the Catholic Church was rethinking the representation of Mary.

However, there was far from ecstatic applause amongst all feminists for the efforts of the Catholic Church. Writing in 1985, Elizabeth Johnson accepted that Pope Paul VI had replaced 'timid, submissive images of Mary with the picture of one who gave active and responsible consent, one who proclaimed God's vindication of the humble and oppressed' (1985: 121). However, she argued that this revisioning did not lead women back to the Church to honour and emulate Mary because the Church still suffered from patriarchal values. Indeed, the argument that 'theology as normally understood is a male-defined subject' (in Carroll 1994: 49) led many feminists to point out that traditional Mariology had been supported by 'markedly androcentric anthropologies, conceived on the basis of the human male, whom they make the model of humanity and also, therefore, the model for the image of God' (Bingemer 1991: 100).

Yet, despite these reservations, some feminist theologians began to refocus attention on Mary. Quite understandably, they began to question whether the Church's most famous female figure should be discarded in the name of women's emancipation. Johnson conceded that, 'for all its debilities', the Marian cult remained 'one of the few female-focused symbols which has persisted in the Christian community' (1985: 130).

LIBERATION MARIOLOGY

While some critics found no inspiration in the Marian cult, claiming that Mary's role was irrelevant for women because it was 'either unique to her or universally significant for all Christians' (in Carroll 1994: 60), members of the Ecumenical Association of Third World Theologians pointed out the oppressiveness of a theology that was 'concerned only with sexism, and not with the liberation of the whole human race' (in Cheah 1995: 75). Renewed interest in the Marian cult in the latter part of the twentieth century stemmed partly from the development of liberation theology, which assigns particular importance to the mother of Jesus in the ongoing struggle to aid poor and oppressed people. *The Magnificat*, which is the canticle attributed to Mary during the Visitation scene (Lk 1:46–55), 'has become the Church's song of predilection for praising the ineffable gratuitousness of the Lord's salvific intervention toward the poor and lowly' (Prévost in Anon. 1997: 271). The words of *The Magnificat* fall into the prophetic genre and underline Mary's 'role as intercessor, first at Cana and then repeatedly within the non-Biblical tradition of the Church' (Massingberd Ford 1972: 92). Certain branches of feminist theology have sought to free the Marian symbol from patriarchal doctrine rather than abandoning it altogether, and 'liberation Mariology' (a term coined by Rosemary Radford Ruether) has striven to refocus the Virgin Mary 'in an empowering manner consistent with liberation theology' (Hamington 1995: 106).

Although liberation Mariology has met with some criticisms, it has been complimented for avoiding Marxist dialectics: 'Liberation under Mary becomes, without alienation, reconciliation; Mary as Mother reconciles the members of her family, the brothers of Jesus' (Margerie 1987: 59). Bertrand de Margerie concludes that 'Mary is concerned not only with our eternal happiness, but also with our temporal destiny in view of (*insofar* as it concerns) our eternal salvation' (Margerie 1987: 61 [emphasis in original]).

Liberation Mariology speaks to 'the poor, the oppressed and the powerless, of whom women are in the majority' (Cheah 1995: 76). It seeks to expose patriarchal distortions and unearth evidence of female autonomy at the heart of the Marian cult. Consequently, running alongside the post-Christian stance epitomised by Mary Daly, there has been a 'revisionist' trend which hopes 'that ancient symbols might be reinterpreted without their pejorative patriarchal trappings' (Carroll 1994: 50). The revisionists have sought 'a Christianity and Catholicity purged of the patriarchal prejudices that have progressively encumbered it since Jesus walked on earth' (*Ibid.*).

Seeking support for their theories in biblical exegesis and popular religion, some feminist theologians have begun to re-image the human and transcendent elements of the Marian cult as a source of power rather than oppression: re-focusing the Annunciation as a scene of co-operation rather than servitude, and re-visioning Mary of Nazareth as a brave advocate of social justice. A number of book titles on Marian themes have underlined the need 'to find' Mary in contemporary society, including Els Maeckelberghe's *Desperately Seeking Mary* (1991), Sally Cunneen's *In Search of Mary* (1996) and Charlene Spretnak's *Missing Mary* (2004). This search is continuing through cultural expression, as the following filmic analysis will testify.

CONTINUING SIGNIFICANCE

In the decades following Vatican II, Mary found one of her greatest champions in Pope John Paul II, who was elected in 1978 and dedicated his Papacy to her under the slogan *Totus Tuus* (*Totally Yours*). On Sunday 8 October 2000, Pope John Paul II made an 'Act of Entrustment' to the Immaculate Heart of Mary, placing the third millennium under the protection of the mother of Jesus 'so that with you as our guide, all people may know Christ, the light of the world and its only Saviour, who reigns with the Father and the Holy Spirit for ever and ever'.

Not only has the Catholic Church continued to underline the ongoing importance of Mary, but some feminist theologians have also indicated the need for Mary to 'enter into dialogue with the time, space, culture, problems and actual people who relate to her' (in Cunneen 1996: 23). Rather than simply dismissing the cult of Mary as irrelevant to women, they have begun to 'discover the hidden themes of liberation that have been submerged in the tradition' (Hamington 1995: 47). Even Mary Daly, one of the major opponents of Mariology, has suggested that there are some elements of the Marian cult that 'have broken out of the stranglehold of Christian patriarchalism and managed to convey a message (partial and blurred) of women's becoming' (1986: 83).

However, any presentation of Mary's character beyond the New Testament verses is fraught with particular risks. When Tissa Balasuriya wrote his book *Mary and Human Liberation* and presented Mary as 'a feminist icon and political activist, a woman who played a full part in her Son's revolution against the establishment of the time and the ruling colonial power' (see Stourton 1998: 161–2), he encountered the wrath of the Vatican's Congregation for the Doctrine of the Faith as well as the bemusement of secular commentators, who suspected that he had 'made up his own Mary to suit his political message' (Stourton 1998: 162). The criticisms of Balasuriya tie in with the fears expressed by French Mariologist René Laurentin, who suspected that feminism's goal would be to tear down the patriarchal image of Mary and attempt to 're-mythologise' it – an action that is made possible because the lack of historical information on Mary makes her malleable (1989: 90). This is the danger that faces all biographers of Mary: that she will become the spokeswoman for a personal agenda that is divorced from the reality of her existence. Although it is also an issue that is addressed by all writers of 'biopics', Mary's status as the mother of God ensures that there are repercussions not normally encountered in the screen adaptation of the life of a famous personality.

However, despite these warning signs, filmmakers have continued to realise the scope of the Marian narrative. When Marina Warner's *Alone of all Her Sex* was reprinted in 1990, the author admitted in her 'Afterthoughts' that the cult of Mary 'remains an extraordinary and fertile site of the feminine, constantly available for questioning and reshaping. [...] Mary offers a field of language and a proving ground, where the essential struggle for sexual and personal identity continues to take place' (1990: 344). This identity struggle is visualised in the cinematic responses to the life of Mary that form the foundation of this study. Through textual analysis, the following chapters attempt to demonstrate how film has reflected theological debates over the significance of Mary of Nazareth.

CHAPTER 2

Announcement and commission

In the sixth month, the angel Gabriel was sent from God to a town of Galilee called Nazareth, to a virgin betrothed to a man named Joseph, of the House of David, and the virgin's name was Mary. And coming to her, he said, 'Hail, favored one! The Lord is with you.' But she was greatly troubled at what was said and pondered what sort of greeting this might be. Then the angel said to her, 'Do not be afraid, Mary, for you have found favor with God. Behold, you will conceive in your womb and bear a son, and you shall name him Jesus. He will be great and will be called Son of the Most High, and the Lord God will give him the throne of David his father, and he will rule over the house of Jacob forever, and of his kingdom there will be no end.' But Mary said to the angel, 'How can this be, since I have no relations with a man?' And the angel said to her in reply, 'The holy Spirit will come upon you, and the power of the Most High will overshadow you. Therefore the child to be born will be called holy, the Son of God. And behold, Elizabeth, your relative, has also conceived a son in her old age, and this is the sixth month for her who was called barren; for nothing will be impossible for God.' Mary said, 'Behold, I am the handmaid of the Lord. May it be done to me according to your word.' Then the angel departed from her. (Luke 1: 26–38)

The first chapter of Luke's Gospel has generated one of the most memorable themes in Marian art. Annunciation paintings are rife with symbolism as they represent the intersection of the sacred and the secular. A lily connotes Mary's virginity; a tripartite pattern signifies the Trinity; and a visible dove represents the Holy Spirit (because the spirit of God 'hovers' over the waters of Creation like a bird (see Ben-Chorin 2001: 67)). Sometimes a golden ray penetrates the ear of the Virgin to signal the moment of conception. There is relevance in the manipulation of space (with pillars often separating the earthly and heavenly realms), while the stance of Mary and the angel (standing or kneeling) indicates respective status. In traditional paintings, Mary has the Bible open on a *prie-dieu* in front of her (see LaVerdiere 2004: 4), without regard for historical reality but as a sign that the Word is about to be made flesh. When the figures of Adam and Eve appear towards the edges of the frame, the onlooker is also reminded that Mary is honoured as the New Eve (as, for example, in Fra Angelico's Annunciation altarpiece (ca.1426), now in the Prado Museum in Madrid).

The addition of cinematic images to the wealth of available Annunciation material allows the emotional intensity of the event to be captured together with its theological significance. The painter must privilege a specific moment – such as the angelic salutation or the instance of Mary's acceptance – which relates to a single shot in the sequence that the filmmaker records diachronically (see Paris 1997: 18). The filmmaker has the opportunity to open out the scene, which 'is perhaps the pivotal moment in the history of God's relationship with his people' (Benedict XVI 2008), to address the range of human emotions that lie behind the short Lukan text.

Moreover, the episode offers a specific challenge to the director: the recording on celluloid of divine intervention. While screenwriter Paul Schrader has argued that the function of transcendental art is 'to express the Holy itself (the Transcendent), and not to express or illustrate holy feelings' (1972: 7), the transcendent is beyond normal sense experience and the scientific, industrialised process of cinema struggles to convey the spiritual and the divine: 'Visual in essence and by obligation, [religious movies] are damned if they are not making visible what escapes all visual categories' (Roten 2007).

Although 'God is above and beyond our ways of thinking, our mental processes, intellectual representations, inductions and deductions' (Larrañga 1991: 44–5), there are still filmmakers who make brave attempts to record the sacred through the camera lens. However, in many cases, the effort demonstrates how much further human creativity has to go in order to embrace the miraculous in any convincing fashion. Some of the most transcendent moments in cinema (in the work of Robert Bresson, for example) are not in traditional biblical films. In contrast, the transpositions of Scripture 'usually have a hard time being inspired or believable to filmgoers' (Anker 2004: 6).

Human creativity seems to flounder when faced with divine intervention. After the silent era, the wings and halo (favoured by the school nativity play) are generally avoided. However, disembodied male voices, choral music, light, wind, or an actor dressed in a white robe are frequently the limits to which the imagination stretches. Perhaps rather predictably, the unpredictable Jean-Luc Godard bucked the trend by introducing an unkempt 'Uncle Gabriel' in an overcoat in *Hail Mary*.

Having familiar faces in biblical earthly roles is fraught with problems, as Stevens's *The Greatest Story Ever Told* amply demonstrated. The danger is compounded when the spirit realm is entered, for the moment of transcendence is immediately destroyed if the performer is recognised from a previous incarnation. When Alexander Siddig appeared as the angel Gabriel in Catherine Hardwicke's *The Nativity Story*, some spectators were distracted by the actor's *curriculum vitae* ('Look, it's Dr Bashir from *Star Trek: Deep Space Nine*!'). Unfortunately, the sense of mystery was lost for some viewers despite the 'outer space' allusion that Siddig clearly brought to the role.

Across the centuries, Mary and the angel Gabriel have been depicted by painters with variations in elements of the staging, including Fra Angelico's calm monastic fresco (1440–41) and Titien's dark and stormy setting (ca.1560–66). *The Jerusalem Bible* translation of Luke's Gospel reports that the angel 'went in', indicating that Gabriel entered Mary's home, but leaves the interior furnishing to the fantasy of the reader. Elizabeth Johnson remarks that 'so much Christian art from medieval times on has depicted Mary beautifully dressed and living in a palace, upper-class room, or monastery, that our memory needs to be refreshed about the fact that her historical life was shaped by the limits of her time, place, and class' (2003: 204). Archaeological studies of the Galilee region reveal that the small dwellings in Nazareth would have been constructed from local stone and have had earthen floors: 'Each family occupied a domestic space or "house" of one or two small rooms. Three or four of these dwellings were built around a courtyard open to the sky' (Johnson 2003: 142). The filmic text must concretise the setting that the biblical account left to the imagination. And the historical reality is interpreted with considerable artistic licence by production designers.

Indeed, many directors ignore this potential stage direction altogether and rely on the vaguer New Testament translation of the *New American Bible*: 'he came to her'. Consequently, a range of venues are chosen, frequently in the open air. More controversially, the films that have re-worked the New Testament narrative present more contemporary Annunciation locations that include a petrol station (*Hail Mary*), an amusement park on Coney Island (*The Second Greatest Story Ever Told*), and a schoolroom in Africa that contains the corpses of murdered children (*Son of Man*).

The Annunciation is Mary's key moment of personhood, and its treatment (or, indeed, its omission) indicates how Mary's personality will evolve during the remainder of the screenplay. Without denying the Annunciation as 'a happening', not all directors choose to grant Mary that privileged scene, even when the script incorporates the birth of Jesus. Ray's *King of Kings*, with its tendency to circumnavigate the miraculous, avoids moments of angelic intervention. Rossellini's *The Messiah* introduces Mary at the Nativity. And Pasolini and Philip Saville make exclusive use of the Gospels of Matthew and John respectively, in which the Annunciation to Mary plays no part.

George Stevens's *The Greatest Story Ever Told* rejects a visual recording of the Annunciation (although this event features significantly in Fulton Oursler's novel (1949) from which the film draws its title). Stevens signals the angel's visit through Mary's moment of reflection in the stable as she holds the baby Jesus in her arms. There is a close-up of Mary's face as her thoughts are expressed via Dorothy McGuire's voice-over (in one of the few instances that the voice of the actress is heard): 'He shall be great and called the son of the Most High. The Lord God will give him the throne of his ancestor David and his kingdom shall know no end.' Mary ponders on the angel's words in a manner that will make sense only to viewers who already know the origin of the message in Luke's Gospel, and her iconic pose paves the way for Mary's future appearances in the film, where she is chiefly a silent witness.

However, when given an appropriately central place in the diegesis, the Annunciation opens up questions pertaining to divine power, personal autonomy, courage and receptivity. A young Jewish girl plays a part in God's plan of Salvation (for Christians believe that she gave birth to the Messiah, and Muslims regard her as the mother of a holy prophet), and her fulfilment of this role will change not only her own life but also the destiny of humankind.

THE WORDLESS GREETING

There are many meaningful wordless greetings in different cultural settings: 'a warm smile, a tearful embrace, a sincere handshake, a welcoming nod, or a respectful bow' (LaVerdiere 2004: 63). Back in the earliest days of silent cinema, the Annunciation message was conveyed without words, as in *The Life and Passion of Jesus Christ* (Ferdinand Zecca and Lucien Nonquet, 1905[1]), which is the oldest film to be analysed in this study. Apart from the titles of the episodes, there is no written text to assist the viewer, although the first viewings of the film may have been accompanied by a reading from the Bible.

The camera is generally stationary (with a rare panning shot or sporadic insert shot), giving the impression of filmed theatre. The series of tableaux serve as picture book illustrations of the New Testament story that was presumably well known to the early twentieth-century audience who chose to watch it. The images are evocative of the popular biblical drawings by Gustave Doré and James Tissot (see Staley and Walsh 2007: 6) and scenes were hand coloured using stencils.

The Annunciation, which is the first scene, takes place on a stage set against a painted backdrop of an interior room. Mary (Madame Moreau) wears a veil and is heavily robed like a pre-Vatican II nun. She enters carrying a pitcher as if returning from the well – a traditional location for the Annunciation within the apocrypha. In *The Protevangelium of James*, the angelic message is delivered in two stages. Mary first hears a voice when she 'took the pitcher and went out to draw water' and 'she looked around to the right and to the left to see where this voice came from' (in Elliott: 1993: 61). Wells – the source of living water – are important places of meeting in the Old Testament for Isaac and Rebecca, Jacob and Rachel, and Moses and Sephora (see Ben-Chorin 2001: 45).[2] The apocryphal narrative continues: 'And, trembling, she went to her house and put down the pitcher and took the purple [thread] and sat down on her seat and drew out the thread. And behold, an angel of the Lord stood before her...' (in Elliott 1993: 61). (Notably, Mary has been given the royal colour purple to weave, indicating her special status.) However, in *The Life and Passion of Jesus Christ*, there is no indication of further domestic duties. Nor is there any sign of fear. Mary kneels to pray just to the left of centre of the screen – the act of spontaneous prayer indicating her piety.[3] Here, cinematic illusion (famously admired in the work of Georges Méliès, a French contem-

FIG. 1 The Annunciation scene in *The Life and Passion of Jesus Christ*

porary of Zecca and Nonquet) is used to introduce the divine. An angel appears through superimposition in a traditional representation, with a halo and wings much in evidence.

The angel is holding a lily in his left hand as a symbol of purity (see Popelard 2002: 37) rather than a gift (which would have been in his right hand), and he hovers in mid-air on a cloud rather than setting foot on the ground, indicating that he is a mediator between heaven and earth (see Popelard 2002: 42). In Western art, the angel is popularly (although not exclusively) painted on the left of the canvas – as Westerners read from left to right – pointing with his finger to indicate the transmission of his message to Mary. However, in *The Life and Passion of Jesus Christ*, Mary is on the left of the screen and Gabriel on the right as if summoned by her act of devotion. Certainly, Mary expresses no surprise at his arrival and bows down before the angel without visible fear.[4] There is only one angelic verbal intervention, which is conveyed with hand gestures and moving lips (presumably informing Mary that she is to be the mother of Jesus). Consequently, there are no mimed questions on the part of Mary. Her response is acceptance (the audience sees her lips move only once) as she bows down again, presumably to indicate her *fiat* ('Let it be done'). When the angel disappears, Mary is on her knees with her hands joined in prayer. She then spreads out her arms in a further sign of agreement, rises to her feet and clasps her hands across her upper body.

This silent scene reduces one of the most momentous moments in the Christian religion to the bare essentials, but also takes a stand on one of the vital questions in Marian theology: was Mary an enthusiastic participant or unwilling servant in the plan of Salvation? When Mary walks to the centre of the frame in *The Life and Passion of Jesus Christ* and stands facing the camera, with eyes gazing upwards and hands outstretched, she is gladly giving herself to God as the 'handmaid of the Lord'. However, the simplification of the action means that Mary accepts the angelic tidings without query (in contrast to the Lukan text). As the second tableau depicts the arrival of Mary and Joseph in Bethlehem, there is no space to consider the repercussions of Mary's pregnancy on the relationship between the betrothed couple.

Tissot illustrations are similarly evoked in *From the Manger to the Cross* (Olcott 1912) in which the Annunciation is also the opening scene. In this case, the viewer is given assistance through the intertitles that contain contextual details (explaining that the initial events take place in Nazareth) and a quotation from the Gospel of Luke recounts that Mary is 'espoused to a man whose name was Joseph, of the house of David'. Although Joseph is not visible before the Annunciation, his role in the narrative is established.

As in *The Life and Passion of Jesus Christ*, Mary is first seen returning from the well carrying a pitcher on her head, which again underlines her domesticity and evokes the apocryphal gospel setting. Mary (played by Gene Gauntier, who also wrote the screenplay) briefly pauses in front of the camera by way of introduction to the audience. Information is then transmitted via an intertitle that the 'angel came unto her' and Mary is shown lying in her bedchamber – a more unusual location as the setting might appear to sexualise the scene of a conception.[5] Theologian Francisco Suárez (1548–1617), for example, was anxious to underline the fact that the Annunciation was not a sexual encounter: 'it did not befit the Holy Spirit [...] to excite any unbecoming movement of passion' (in Warner 1990: 39). In contrast, feminist theologian Tina Beattie argues that the virginal conception 'initiates a new symbolic world of non-phallic fecundity and creativity' but to exclude sexual metaphors 'would impoverish its creative possibilities for both sexes' (2002: 129).

Filmmakers show a hesitation in this domain. (Even Godard's controversial *Hail Mary* created an Annunciation scene in a public space without any overt sexual symbolism.) In *From the Manger to the Cross*, Mary is lying in bed but is heavily robed and veiled so the atmosphere remains chaste. The angel is manifested as a bright light, and Staley and Walsh regard John's Gospel as 'the theological subtext' with the black and white clothes and use of light/dark (2007: 13) but they note that most of the intertitles are quotations from the Gospels of Matthew and Luke. Mary sits up as if aware of a presence in her room and puts her left hand against her heart, as if she has palpitations. Although she is visibly startled, the organ music (on the DVD presentation) does not change in tempo. There is just one musical flourish at the angelic message conveyed by the intertitle (serving the purpose of the male voice-over that is frequently favoured as a sign of angelic intervention in sound films): 'Hail, thou that art highly favoured, the Lord is with thee: blessed art thou among women.' The phrase 'Blessed art thou among women' is found in the *King James Bible* but does not appear in all translations of the Lukan Annunciation, although it forms part of Elizabeth's greeting to Mary in the Visitation scene (Lk 1:42).

Facing away from the camera, Mary falls backwards as if in fear, illuminated by light. At this point it is unclear whether she questions the angel, although with her next gesture she reaches out towards the messenger. However, as only the first part of the message is provided in the intertitle, there is no explicit statement about the birth of Jesus, and the audience is expected to have foreknowledge of the biblical text.

In contrast to *The Life and Passion of Jesus Christ*, Mary undergoes a wide series of emotions, from initial anxiety at the angel's message through to joy, the latter expressed by her smiling face and extension of both her arms as if to physically embrace the news as she turns to face the camera, mouthing her words of response that presumably form the 'handmaid of the Lord' speech. Then she joins her hands and bows her head in prayer. While Mary in *The Life and Passion of Jesus Christ* was a figure in a tableau, the Mary of *From the Manger to the Cross* has developed a wider gamut of feelings. It is in capturing this progression of human responses that cinema adds scope to the painted interpretations of the scene that isolate a single instant. As filmic language developed, so Mary's response has become more complex, from a silent icon in the days of early cinema to the troubled young woman of Catherine Hardwicke's twenty-first century *The Nativity Story*, openly questioning her readiness for motherhood.

THE IMPORTANCE OF WORDS

From a Marian angle, the most disturbing line in Michael Offer's BBC production *The Passion* (2008) occurs when Mary (Penelope Wilton) complains to her adult son Jesus: 'You were in my belly before I knew.' These words indicate that Mary had no choice about becoming the mother of the Saviour, and her apparent disgruntlement sets the tone for the development of her character, which remains overtly pessimistic.

This single line of dialogue in *The Passion* strips away the autonomy of Mary in the way that Ralph Howard and Katharina Otto did when they parodied the Annunciation event (relocating the story to Brooklyn in the 1960s) in the short film entitled *The Second Greatest Story Ever Told* (1993). The 24-year-old Mary Weinstein (Mira Sorvino), who is mocked by her friends 'for having a reputation for not having a reputation,' enters a public convenience on Coney Island. She looks up to find that the cubicle is flooded with light, hears the sound of an angelic choir, and sees toilet paper (like white feathers) floating down around her. Mary's head collapses forward, and she emerges into the sunshine dazed and confused, to discover later (and to her complete bemusement) that she is pregnant. The angel Gabriel (in the form of a cigarette-smoking Malcolm McDowell in a suit) will later give his apologies: 'Oh, I'm sorry that I wasn't the first to give you the good news but, modern medicine being what it is, I'm always a little late.'

Howard and Otto's film is playing with broad humour[6] whereas Offer's production is a reverent treatment of the New Testament text within its historical time frame. Yet these markedly different approaches both undermine the significance of the Lukan Gospel scene. When *The Passion* was screened before an ecumenical audience, Tina Beattie rightly pointed out that Mary's line of dialogue in relation to her pregnancy was 'theologically wrong' because Christianity 'hinges on freedom and Mary had the right to choose'. Mark Goodacre, who was an historical consultant for the BBC film, responded: 'That's one of the interesting things about art. A line is capable of that reading' (in Butt 2008).

Words evidently play a significant role in interpretations of the Annunciation scene that date back to the earliest teachings of the Church Fathers. According to St Ephrem, 'Mary became fertile through the word of God pronounced by the angel Gabriel, which penetrated her through her ear' (see Gambero 1999: 114) – a theory that has been criticised by French psychoanalyst Luce Irigaray, who complained, 'Physical embrace will be banned from this religion of love. Its only unions are celebrated between mouth to ear' (in Beattie 2002: 124). But Irigaray also suggests that there might be a rethinking of the scene in which 'the angel opens the way to a more fertile form of exchange that allows the woman to speak her desire' (see Beattie 2002: 125).

Since the widespread use of sound film beginning in 1927, a single line of audible dialogue in the Annunciation scene creates a fascinating body of material for comparison and contrast. The Annunciation is both the announcement of a birth and a commission or election story (see LaVerdiere 2004: 22–3) and follows a typical five-stage biblical schema: a) the appearance of the messenger; b) fear expressed by the visionary; c) the message; d) an objection uttered by the visionary; and e) the giving of a sign to reassure the visionary. The manner in which Mary responds to the angel can markedly change the dynamic.

In the New Testament, Gabriel greets Mary with the word 'Rejoice!' which is often rather reductively translated as 'Hail!' or 'Greetings!'. In the original Lukan text, the angel does not initially address Mary by her name but calls her 'full of grace' ('Chaire, kecharitomene' in the original Greek), as if that were actually her name, and 'she was greatly troubled at what was said and pondered what sort of greeting this might be'. (It is notable that Luke records that Mary pondered, so that her response is not instantaneous or ill considered.)

Analysing these opening words, LaVerdiere notes that in spoken Greek 'the greeting is very rhythmic and melodious' and 'its wording is very subtle, with a play on words just below the surface' (2004: 67). The words have been variously translated into English as 'Greetings, favoured one', 'Hail, favoured one', 'Rejoice, so highly favoured' but the renderings are 'archaic, stilted and somewhat banal, hardly a cause for Mary or anyone to be troubled, let alone greatly troubled' (LaVerdiere 2004: 68). In the films *Jesus of Nazareth* (Zeffirelli), *The Nativity* (Kowalski) and *Joseph of Nazareth* (Mertes), the angel is manifested only by wind and light, and the message is inaudible to the audience, thereby circumventing this specific dilemma. However, where the angel makes a visible appearance (or is heard in voice-over), the line is reinstated. In *The Jesus Film*, the angel says: 'Fear not, Mary, for you have won favour with God'; in Costa's *Maria, Daughter of Her Son*: 'Greetings, Mary, thou that art highly favoured'; and Hardwicke's angel in *The Nativity Story* says, 'Hail, O favoured one!'

In fact, the verb form that is used in the Greek language occurs on only one other occasion in the New Testament (in Paul's Letter to the Ephesians 1:6). 'The word is rare and therefore, in the context of "grace", signals something that is out of the ordinary' (Rossier 2004: 161). Catholic theologians argue that this uncommon greeting indicates that Mary had been prepared by grace to accept Gabriel's announcement, as Elizabeth Johnson explains: 'The opposite of sin is grace, and the Immaculate Conception means that Mary was uniquely blessed at the outset with the gift of grace' (2003: 108). However, this 'theology of grace' is often lost in translation. Notably Cordero's *Mater Dei*, Delannoy's *Mary of Nazareth* and Connor's *Mary, mother of Jesus* include a reference to grace by employing the opening of the Marian prayer: 'Hail Mary, full of grace, the Lord is with you.'

In response, the actress playing Mary traditionally has only two verses of biblical dialogue to deliver in the Annunciation scene: 'How can this be, since I have no relations with a man?' (Lk 1:34);[7] and 'Behold, I am the handmaid of the Lord. May it be done to me according to your word' (Lk 1:38). The translation and pronouncement of these words reveals much about the reaction of the protagonists.[8] Raymond Brown argues that Mary's question ('How can this be, since I have no relations with a man?') should not be interpreted from a psychological perspective but as a traditional interrogatory device used to reveal the content of the message (see Brown 1993: 307–8). However, Mary's final words in the Lukan scene cannot be explained away by a traditional literary analysis, for it is not a step found in the usual annunciation pattern (see Brown 1993: 316). Three main approaches may be identified in filmic Annunciation scenes: Reluctance; Passive Acceptance; and Active Receptivity. These responses reflect the theological debates surrounding the Marian image that were reinvigorated by the feminist movement.

RELUCTANCE

By the second half of the twentieth century, issues of gender equality had led to an ambivalent reaction to the biblical narrative. A number of feminist commentators rejected Mary as a misogynist ruse, condemning her image as the 'personification of submissiveness and pietism but also of unearthly virginity' (see Cheah 1995: 83) and a repressive instrument of the Catholic Church to keep women in their place. At the furthest extreme, the post-Christian commentator Mary Daly described the Annunciation as the violation of a non-resistant victim: 'The male-angel Gabriel brings poor Mary the news that she is to be impregnated by and with God. Like all rape victims in male myth she submits joyously to this unspeakable degradation' (1984: 74). Jane Schaberg caused additional disquiet in her highly controversial book *The Illegitimacy of Jesus* when she referred 'to the seduction or rape of a betrothed virgin' (in Perry 2006: 71).

While none of the filmmakers discussed in this study adopt the arguments of Daly and Schaberg at their most radical, there are two films that present Mary as an initially reluctant participant in God's plan. In Veronesi's *For Love, Only For Love* (1993), the off-screen Annunciation event is transmitted only through Mary's verbal account to Joseph, which returns the encounter back to the oral tradition from which it originally came.[9] Consequently, the audience is cheated of the visual dimension of cinema, which is turned into scenes 'of people talking' as Alfred Hitchcock famously complained (see Sterritt 1993: 33). But Mary (Penélope Cruz) relates the details with tears streaming down her face, her huddled position indicating that she is a fearful victim. The viewers, placed in the same position as Joseph, are left to draw their own conclusions without the benefit of seeing the event for themselves. The second film, which had a more widespread impact, is Jean-Luc Godard's *Hail Mary*, in which the Annunciation scene is notable for its unconventionality.[10]

Hail Mary

LaVerdiere points out the distances travelled by many of the protagonists in Luke's Gospel but stresses that 'Gabriel's journey, from his exalted position before God to the lowly virgin of Nazareth [...] is not measured in miles' (2004: 66). However, in having Gabriel arrive by aeroplane and taxi, Godard counters this traditional view of the angelic mission.[11] The approach of the messengers is signalled by a plane passing overhead. (Notably, it is not clear whether the plane is taking off or coming into land because of the angle at which it is shot through the trees, adding an element of mystery to the workings of a mechanical mode of transport.) Mary (Myriem Roussel), who is brushing her hair as if making herself ready for an event, looks up at the sound of the aircraft, and there is a cut to a magnificent image of a plane flying across the sun that amplifies the intersection between the earthly and heavenly realms.

However, when Godard staged his Annunciation at a petrol station, the wind blowing on the soundtrack was the only conventional 'special effect' to manifest the presence of the divine. The roof over the petrol pumps creates a little *loggia* (see the discussion of the scene in Bergala 1999: 154–63) and the petrol station itself is an interesting location because of its inflammatory nature, for one spark in the wrong place and the scene could explode.[12] Bergala suggests a play on words, in which the petrol station becomes the first *station* in the life of Christ (1999: 159) in which the *essence* is changed (as *l'essence* is the French word for petrol). Classical heavenly utterances are replaced by the bisexual materialisation of the angelic messenger in the form of the dishevelled Uncle Gabriel and his young female accomplice, sometimes making their announcements off-screen, but clearly visible to protagonists and cinema audience alike. Unusually, the acquaintance of the 'angels' is made by the audience and Joseph (who picks them up in his taxi) before Mary herself, so that there is time to form an impression of their (un-angelic) personalities before the news is given. Godard's Uncle Gabriel and young female partner transform one of the most important communications between God and humankind into a moment of slapstick.

Godard's twentieth-century Mary enters into uneven conversation with the messengers (and Bergala notes that the angels are always shot at the same angle, whereas Mary is framed in a number of different ways). However, the original Lukan text provides a more lucid account than Godard's attempt at updating the dialogue,[13] and Mary's repeated questions to the unprepossessing emissaries are an inevitable consequence of their vague pronouncements, in which God plays no overt role:

Mary:	OK, what is it?
Gabriel (off):	It's you, Mary.
Mary (off):	What do you want? [...]
Gabriel (off):	And you, my lady? Your fiancé?
Joseph (off):	What's it to you?
Gabriel (off):	We couldn't care less. But you're going to have a child.
Mary:	By whom?
Gabriel (whispers, off):	You'll have a baby.
Mary:	I sleep with no one. [...] By whom?
Gabriel:	It won't be his [i.e. Joseph's]. Never!
Mary (off):	By whom?
Gabriel:	Don't play innocent!
Mary (off):	By whom?
Girl (off):	Mary, be pure, be rough. Follow Thy way.
Mary:	What? My way! but the voice or the word?

In a revision to the Gospel story, Joseph witnesses the Annunciation. However, his physical presence does little to lessen his subsequent doubts with regard to Mary's virginity, for the messengers not only refuse to introduce themselves ('Who are these people?' asks Joseph understandably) but also fail to rule out a human father and omit to explain the significance of the child to be born. Given the obtuseness of the message, it is perhaps not surprising that Mary herself offers no immediate words of assent. When Mary sinks down by the petrol pump, it well may be the moment of conception – it certainly appears to be a gesture of surrender.

After the Annunciation, the momentum is disrupted by one of several switches in the film from matters of faith to science (through a subplot involving a teacher and his students). The juxtaposition of the scenes between Mary and a student named Eva is an obvious reminder of the Mary/Eve parallel. In Annunciation paintings, the Garden of Eden story is sometimes represented at the side of the frame, whereas here the crosscutting of the scenes with the students creates a similar effect. Godard's Eva (and Eva spelt backwards is 'Ave') is situated in a classroom or studying a Rubik's Cube, searching for knowledge. By name association, Eva is linked to the story of Genesis, and when she eats an apple (with typically Godardian enhanced sound effects) in a scene with her married lover, her representation as the temptress from Eden is accentuated. As in the Eve/Mary parallel presented by St Irenaeus ('And just as it was through a virgin who disobeyed [namely Eve] that mankind was stricken and fell and died, so too it was through the Virgin [Mary], who obeyed the word of God, that mankind, resuscitated by life, received life' (in Pelikan 1996: 42)), Mary continues the battle against evil. In one of her utterances during the 'dark night of the soul' scene, Godard's Mary says, 'Then Lucifer will die and we'll see… who's weariest, him or me.'

When the focus returns to Mary, her verbal response to the Annunciation tidings is: 'There's no escape.' This is not the reaction of a woman gladly co-operating but of a victim trapped. After a considerable interlude Mary, alone in her bedroom, utters the words: 'Thy will be done….', but this apparent consent is not the culmination of the conflict, and subsequent scenes reveal Mary railing against her situation. In particular, Godard treads on hallowed ground by allowing Mary to utter obscenities, therefore making her ordinary and fallible. This Mary would suit the revisionists who complain that Mary has been robbed of her sexuality (see Ostling 1991: 62) but it is clearly at odds with the Catholic Catechism's 'all-holy Virgin Mary' (*Catechism of the Catholic Church* 1994: 440).

Godard's interpretation of the story pre-dates Tissa Balasuriya's book *Mary and Human Liberation*, in which the author expressed the desire to extricate Mary from 'a presentation which has made her a woman who is not female; a woman who does not know what it is to be human, who does not go through the birth pangs of bringing forth Jesus, who does not know sin, who does not feel the trials of human existence' (1997: 209). *Hail Mary* offers an earlier reflection on this standpoint when, in contrast to tradition, Mary's renunciation of her sexuality in the cause of virgin motherhood is depicted in the film as a painful sacrifice: Godard's Mary claims, 'Being a virgin should mean being available or free, not being hurt,' but she clearly suffers.

David Sterritt suggests that 'Godard's conception of the uncontaminated virgin points to low imperatives of the body as well as high potentialities of the soul' (1999: 175). But the focus in Godard's film is on physicality, whereas Mary's virginity 'is above all an inner and spiritual disposition; it signifies wholeness and integrity – in […] an all-embracing sanctity' (Ware 2002: 359). Although the outwardly radical response to the New Testament in *Hail Mary* means that Godard's twentieth-century Virgin is not the a-sexual, docile handmaid beloved of patriarchy, Mary is restricted to the role of unwilling servant. In the process, Godard's 'celebration here of the low and abject' (Sterritt 1999: 207) obviously runs counter to the belief 'that a woman chosen by Divine Providence for this role in cosmic history must have been prepared by God in such a way as to be entirely fitted for her role' (Ashley 1985: 538).

In addressing the issues raised by the film, critics seem to have adopted two approaches: either concentrating upon the religious symbolism and debating its blasphemous or spiritual qualities; or dismissing the religious furore and analysing the themes, techniques and sexual politics in relation to Godard's canon. Kevin Moore claims that: 'Rather than a film for or against Christianity, the mistaken area of so much critical debate, [*Hail Mary*] attends the claims of the virgin body' (1994: 21), but for the Christian (and, more specifically, the Catholic) spectator, the religious and the corporal dimensions are inextricably linked. The virginal body of Mary has a symbolism that reaches beyond questions of human chastity to the role of a woman in the mystery of the Incarnation.

Mary's biblical response to the angel Gabriel ('Behold, I am the handmaid of the Lord. May it be done to me according to your word') has been read by some feminist critics, notably including Simone de Beauvoir, as a submissive acceptance of women's secondary status within a patriarchal church. In *The Second Sex*, de Beauvoir claims that the religious veneration of women means that they are treated in this world as servants (1949: 366). Godard's film is an illustration of this view of the Annunciation at its most reductive, in which Mary is a grudging participant in God's plan of Salvation. The film concludes: 'I am of the Virgin and I didn't want this being.'

PASSIVE ACCEPTANCE

The interpretation of the Greek word *doulē* (variously translated as handmaid, servant or slave) in Mary's response to the angel in the New Testament opens up major questions regarding patriarchy and co-redemption. Beverly Roberts Gaventa insists that the correct translation of *doulē* should be 'slave', claiming that use of the 'handmaid' appellation 'is to misconstrue Mary's role as that of one who has *chosen* to serve rather than one who has *been chosen* (1999: 54 [emphasis in original]).

47

Nevertheless, Gaventa points out that the problem of using 'slave of the Lord' is that 'generations of Christians have seen Mary as a model or example for all women and have distorted her slavery to the Lord to mean the subjection of women in general to men in general' (1999: 54). Therefore, on the film screen, Mary's physical stance as she speaks (or omits) the words, is an important revelation of the degree or absence of personal autonomy. Four cinematic examples of a form of passive acceptance are the films *Mater Dei*, *The Jesus Film*, *Dayasagar* and *The Nativity Story*.

Mater Dei

Italy's first film in colour, *Mater Dei*, was made prior to Vatican II. Released in 1950, the film honours Mary (Ileana Simova) within a patriarchal framework in which she is depicted carrying out domestic work, fetching water from the well, baking, folding washing, and decorating the house with flowers. Although the narrator informs the audience that, unconsciously, Mary was preparing for a great event – and this event is heralded on the soundtrack by a vibrant fanfare – Mary remains sitting quietly on the right of the screen, with her hands folded in her lap and a green veil covering her hair.

She looks up with a slight start as she hears an off-screen male voice utter the greeting, and as the focus is initially on Mary, the audience sees a light before the angelic visitor. The camera tracks back and pans to the left to reveal Gabriel (an actor dressed in red with curly blond hair – a type familiar from Renaissance painting) and create a link between Mary and the messenger, who is standing on the ground. However, the protagonists are initially separated by spatial distance, then by a series of shot/reverse shots that serve the purpose of the pillar in traditional Annunciation paintings. At first the concentration is on Mary's troubled expression as the angel continues with the message, and she bows her head as she learns that she will bear a son. Then the camera reframes the image to bring the angel back into the equation as he speaks of Jesus ruling over the House of Jacob.

Mary's face is centrally framed (indicating her importance) when she asks how the events foretold will come about as she does not know a man (the objection), and it is notable that she looks the angel directly in the eyes at this point, so that her physical posture does not indicate a servile status. However, as the messenger explains that 'the Holy Spirit will overshadow you,' a low camera angle is chosen so that the angel looks down on Mary, visually replicating the overshadowing motif. Both protagonists are sub-sequently located in the same frame, linking divinity and humanity – al-though separated by space – as the angel says that the child will be the Son of God. Mary's response is to cross her hands across her chest and bow her head as the handmaid of the Lord. Then she looks up: 'May it be done to me according to thy word.' (There is no reference to Elizabeth during the angelic encounter, although the older kinswoman's unexpected pregnancy is introduced in the next scene.) Mary maintains the same seated posture throughout the whole episode, remaining essentially static, so that there is little indication that a transformative act has taken place. As the film is a paean of praise to the life of Mary and her ongoing intercessory role, her quiet calmness is presumably intended as a positive affirmation of her faith in God. However, there is a disappointing lack of wonderment. In considering the role of Mary at the Annunciation, Pope Benedict XVI asks: 'Imagine how she must have felt. She was filled with apprehension, utterly overwhelmed at the prospect that lay before her' (2008). There is certainly no sense that Mary is 'overwhelmed' in *Mater Dei*.

The Jesus Film

Less unexpected is the perfunctory treatment of the Annunciation almost thirty years later in the missionary project *The Jesus Film*, for the film's real interest is the adult ministry of Jesus. The introductory prologue sweeps rapidly through the first chapters of the Gospel of Luke in order to reach that goal. Shot in Israel and claiming to be a documentary that reveals 'ab-solute truth' (see Staley and Walsh 2007: 96), the film does not signal its designation as a 'documentary' until after the Infancy Narrative has been summarily covered. After a shot of sheep in the fields, with the biblical resonance to Jesus as the Good Shepherd, Mary (played by Israeli actress Rivka Neuman) is seen by the well, where she has been washing clothes with other women from the village. She carries a pitcher of water on her shoulder as well as her basket (in an act of multitasking). The voice-over does not mention Joseph at this point but informs the audience that God sent his angel Gabriel to visit a virgin called Mary in Nazareth.

Mary enters a large room (with no attempt at historical accuracy in the setting) to be greeted by the sound of a wind and a bright light, two of the most common indicators of divine intervention in religious films. The angel (a man dressed in white and backlit) is standing squarely on the ground as he utters his greeting, and the angelic light that illuminates Mary is the only indication that she has been touched by divine intervention. As the angel and Mary are filmed only in shot/reverse shot, they never share the frame or noticeably interconnect. Most remarkably, Mary does not speak any words of acceptance and the narrative moves swiftly on. Mary figures as a catalyst rather than a protagonist whose individual response is considered significant.

Dayasagar

Similarly, the Annunciation and Nativity are also covered briefly in the opening few minutes of Bhimsingh's *Dayasagar*, which also serves as an evangelistic tool. The cast of Indian actors in the New Testament roles offers an important example of the theme of inculturation within Christianity.

Mary is sitting in a garden of flowers, reading from a scroll – an image familiar from Annunciation paintings but out of line with the historical reality – and her veil blows in a breeze that grows in intensity (announcing the presence of the Holy Spirit). When the angel appears through superimposition, the style initially appears to be a throw-back to the earliest days of silent cinema. Here the blond-haired angel (indicating a sense of foreignness amidst the Indian cast) wears a golden crown. However, the film returns to its cultural roots when the Annunciation is conveyed in song rather than spoken dialogue and Mary does not verbalise any questions. Mary remains seated and crosses her hands across her chest in a sign of agreement (as in *Mater Dei*). However, as in *The Jesus Film*, she does not personally utter the words of assent.

The Nativity Story

An important line of Lukan text is also missing in Catherine Hardwicke's *The Nativity Story*. Mary has been working in the fields when the messenger arrives, and she removes her veil, using it to wipe the sweat from her face, so that her long dark hair falls loosely around her face. There is the sound of wind in the trees, and the branches move visibly. A bird is seen flying in the sky, the only time that this accepted visual indication of the presence of the Holy Spirit is found in the filmic Annunciation scenes discussed here (although the chosen bird is a hawk rather than a dove, presumably for more visual impact). Mary looks around as if aware of a change in the atmosphere and the camera pans swiftly, taking up her point-of-view as her eyes dart around the space, as if searching for an explanation. She sees other villagers by a tree, as a sign of the normality of the world around her. Then a figure appears as a distant shape in white behind the trees, and there is a loud exhalation of breath as a male voice says: 'Hail, O favoured one. The Lord is with you.' As her eyes pan back to the tree where the villagers were gathered, they have disappeared and she is alone in the space as if ordinary life has stopped.

Mary gets to her feet, holding onto the tree for support (the need to cling onto something tangible is also seen in the Annunciation scene in Zeffirelli's *Jesus of Nazareth*) and takes refuge behind the trunk. The angel (whose vibrant white clothes shimmer at the edges to signal his other-worldly status) suddenly appears right in front of her, saying, 'Do not be afraid, Mary, for you have found favour with God.' They walk together in the same frame, emphasising an unusually close filmic connection between heaven and earth, given the traditional shot/reverse shot separation. However, when responding to the news that she is to give birth to a son ('How can this be, since I've been with no man?'), there is a shot of Mary's face alone as she asks this most human of questions.

During the angelic explanation, Mary and the angel are together in the frame, circling each other in a form of dance. But when Mary repeats the phrase 'Son of God', she is expressing confusion rather than making the words her own. It is at this point that she and the angel stop moving, and Mary's static position indicates her hesitation (unlike Mary in Delannoy's *Mary of Nazareth*, who responds to these same words with a joyful smile). The focus is on Mary's face as she hears the words spoken by the angel: 'Mary, even your cousin Elizabeth has conceived a son in her old age. For nothing said by God can be impossible.' The camera tracks in on Mary's face at this point, as if intensifying the message. Then Mary and the angel face each other in long shot (he is on the left as in traditional paintings) and she kneels down clasping her hands together. Ultimately, Mary responds: 'Let it be done to me according to your word,' and she bows her head. Mary looks upwards to see a bird flying away in the sky. However, she looks concerned throughout the Annunciation event and there is little sense that she has undergone a transformative action. Significantly, the vital 'handmaid' phrase is omitted completely. Although her physical posture indicates her obedience, the failure to speak her own penultimate line of the Lukan text makes Mary appear only half committed to her decision.

Fig. 2 Uncertain commitment in *The Nativity Story*

51

ACTIVE RECEPTIVITY

Within Catholic theology, Mary's response to the angel has been met by more positive interpretations. St Bernard of Clairvaux (1090–1153), whose writings had a great influence on Marian devotion, regarded the Annunciation as the site of freedom, with Mary as an active participant rather than a passive servant. Addressing his words directly to Mary, St Bernard said: 'The angel is waiting for your reply. [...] The price of our salvation is being offered you. If you consent, we shall immediately be set free' (in Boss 2000: 32). In the twelfth and thirteenth centuries, it was believed that Mary became the mother of Jesus 'through an act of her own free will, so that God did not force her to be the mother of Christ, but sought her consent' (Boss 2000: 31).

The question of autonomy indicates one of the key differences between the Annunciation scenes in the New Testament and the Koran, despite the obvious parallels. In Bohrani's *The Saint Mary*, Mary is by flowing water when Gabriel arrives and the tactic used to convey divine intervention in the Iranian film (with an actor in a white robe playing the part of the angel) obviously provides a visual link across cultural and religious divides. However, there are some notable distinctions in the *mise-en-scène*. The intensity of the light that surrounds the angel is more vibrant than commonly found in traditional New Testament films and it gives an additional sense of wonder that is frequently missing in Western versions.

The whole event is also described in voice-over rather than in direct dialogue between Mary and the angel, which increases the audience's distanciation from the episode. The narrator reports that Mary became frightened and the angel reassured her. 'He said, "Fear not Mary, for I am Gabriel. I am a messenger from thy Lord to announce to thee the glad tidings of a holy son." She said, "How shall I have a son seeing that no man has touched me and I am not unchaste?"' The scene is shot in slow motion and flooded with light to create an ethereal quality that is underpinned by the non-diegetic music.

There is a close-up of Gabriel's left hand as the voice-over continues. 'He said, "Even so, your Lord says, 'It is easy for me. Whenever God desires to create something or wishes something to be, he simply says, "Be", and it becomes.' God gives you glad tidings of a messenger from Him, whose name is the Saviour, Jesus son of Mary. He will be highly honoured in this world and the next and amongst the closest to God."'

The white light disappears and Mary faints (as in the Marian films by Kowalski and Costa). Bohrani's film clearly reflects the Koran's emphasis on the omnipotence of God and there is no question of Mary's consent: 'There could be no Muslim text equivalent to the homily of St Bernard where he imagines the heavens and the earth suspended, waiting for Mary to pronounce her *fiat*. God has merely to say to something "Be", and it is' (Fitzgerald 2007: 301).

In contrast, according to St Thomas Aquinas: 'The Annunciation asked the consent of the Virgin *in the name of all human nature*' so that 'the "Yes" of the Daughter of Zion recapitulated and brought to their maximum all the "yeses" to the Lord that preceded it and made possible, for its part, all those that would follow it' (see Bossard in Anon. 1997: 148 [emphasis in original]). Jesus himself asked 'let this cup pass' in the Garden of Gethsemane before accepting the will of the Father and going forward to be crucified (Mt 26:39), and Beaudin argues that Mary's 'state of grace' (as underlined by the dogma of the Immaculate Conception) does not mean that she would not have experienced tests. But she had the courage to accept God's will despite her own incomprehension (see Beaudin 2002: 9).

If Mary had the opportunity to say 'no', then her actions would have changed the course of Salvation history: 'This cannot be said of any other creature. Peter and Judas, to say nothing of countless later Christians, may reject Christ, be ambivalent about him, and in an extended sense, therefore, affect who Christ is. But their rejection would not bring about the withdrawal of the promise which Christ, crucified and risen, represents for us' (Endean 2007: 289).

Rejecting the notion that the Annunciation is an act perpetrated against an unwilling victim (as seen in the rape of the gods in pagan mythology), French philosopher and anthropologist René Girard maintains that 'the Gospels are always giving us a message exactly opposite to the one conveyed by mythology: the message of a non-violent deity, who has nothing in common with the epiphanies of the sacred' (1987: 220). Luce Irigaray regards the conception of Jesus 'as inaugurating a new relationship between the divine and women based not on the abusive violence of the gods of Greek mythology, but on the loving and fruitful encounter between Mary and the Spirit' (see Beattie 2002: 134).

It is in attempting to remove perceived distortions about power and autonomy at work in the Annunciation scene that late twentieth-century feminist exegetes have offered a more positive reinterpretation of Mary's response to the angel's message, remarking on Mary's bravery in questioning the heavenly messenger about her proposed pregnancy, despite the fact that the priest Zechariah was notably struck dumb for querying God's power in an earlier scene in the Lukan narrative (see, for example, Donnelly 1994: 123). Five films that offer this more pro-active response on the part of Mary are *Mary, mother of Jesus*; *The Nativity*; *Jesus of Nazareth*; *Maria, Daughter of Her Son*; and *Mary of Nazareth*.

Mary, mother of Jesus

Indeed, the young heroine (Melinda Kinnaman) of Connor's *Mary, mother of Jesus* is asking to serve God *before* the Annunciation takes place. Sitting by an open window with the rain falling outside and lightning in the background, the inclement weather reflecting her dissatisfaction with the political situation, Mary turns to God for answers: 'Why the suffering? I beg you for an answer. Am I not asking the right question? How can I ease this suffering? What can I do?'

The Annunciation, which takes place out in the fields, is signalled by wind, shimmering air, and the appearance of a male figure wearing diaphanous robes against the dramatic backdrop of the sun. When the angel utters the message (in an English accent), Mary immediately bows her head and her knee, like a servant responding to a royal command: 'Behold, the handmaiden of the Lord.' Then she raises her eyes to the angel: 'Let it be done according to thy word.' Mary has received an immediate response to her prayer to be an active participant.

The Nativity

Connor's visible angelic figure in *Mary, mother of Jesus* follows a well-trodden path. Bernard Kowalski (who is known as a director of episodes of the *Columbo* series) succeeded in bringing a sense of mystery to the Annunciation scene in *The Nativity* (produced for 20th Century Fox TV and ABC) where other directors had failed. By setting the Annunciation in a barren canyon, so that the rocks form a womb-like space, Kowalski visually draws parallels between the Creation story in the Book of Genesis and the Annunciation in the New Testament: 'As the earth at the dawn of the universe was "without form and void", so Mary is a virgin; nothing has yet been created in her' (Boss 2003: 4). In Kowalski's film, Mary (Madeleine Stowe) is standing by a river when she receives the angelic message, evoking an image in which Mary 'stands at the Annunciation in the same relation to God as do the waters of creation' (*Ibid.*). Her pink dress is damp around the edges, and she appears dazed (rather than afraid) as she sinks down by the water and looks at the light sparkling on the surface. There are a number of close-ups of her eyes in this scene (to stress the importance of vision) and one point-of-view shot of the water. The sunlight is dazzling through the trees so that Mary is simultaneously overshadowed and illuminated.

As in Franco Zeffirelli's *Jesus of Nazareth* and Raffaele Mertes's *Joseph of Nazareth* (2000), there is no visible angel and the audience hears only Mary's half of the dialogue. The scene would be unintelligible to an audience not familiar with the Lukan text. Natural forces of bright sunlight and wind are employed to indicate the divine. There is a low-angle shot as Mary looks towards the sky and asks: 'How can this be done? I know no man.' Then Mary utters the words: 'Behold, the handmaiden of the Lord. Be it done to me according to your word' and continues to gaze upwards while the camera contemplates her from below. When she is next shown from a different angle (the front), her right hand is slightly outstretched (a similar gesture is seen in *Jesus of Nazareth*). Then she lies down in slow motion on the ground in a foetal position, which may represent the moment of conception, and appears to sleep. A long shot reveals her as a small, isolated figure in the canyon, her response being one of peace.

Unusually, Mary has an opportunity to share her news immediately with Joseph, for he comes to find her, climbing across the rocks and wading through the water to reach her sleeping figure. Upon awakening, Mary seems afraid and runs away into the water, so that both protagonists undergo a form of baptism. When Joseph reaches Mary, she grasps him so that he literally and metaphorically loses his footing as his own life is upended by the revelation of the angel's message. Having found her initially asleep, Joseph rejects her report as a dream. However, avoiding any attempt at archaic dialogue, Mary retorts: 'I know how you have babies.'

Mary relates the angel's side of the dialogue (which the audience did not hear in the Annunciation scene). She also includes the information that the priest Zechariah has been struck dumb because he did not believe in his wife Elizabeth's forthcoming pregnancy, although this is specific information not included in the precise Lukan Annunciation dialogue but is recorded earlier in the gospel (Lk 1:18–20). The vernacular used by the protagonists lifts them out of the biblical setting as Mary asks: 'Do you think I'm crazy? Do you?', and Joseph replies: 'It's just something's made you hysterical, that's all.'[14]

However, Mary persists: 'I know I am [having a baby] and I know what he's coming into this world to do. He will be the Christ. He is here. I've been touched by God!' When she repeats the angel's message in her own words, it becomes her own project (see Popelard 2002: 27), and as she describes the future birth ('The Saviour, Joseph! My child!'), the use of the possessive adjective excludes Joseph from the equation but indicates her enthusiastic participation in God's plan.

Jesus of Nazareth

In describing his approach to the Annunciation scene in *Jesus of Nazareth*, Zeffirelli explained that he 'obviously rejected the idea of having an angel with wings and a halo. Instead, God's message comes in the form of a silent beam of light that passes through a high aperture in the little mud-brick room to fall on the face of the young Madonna. [Olivia Hussey] simply went into a trance and the effect was heart-stopping' (1986: 280).

The decision not to represent the angel or to record the dialogue met with ambivalent reactions from critics. Kinnard and Davis note that 'the episode attains an intense spiritual quality too often absent from other films of this type' (1992: 189). In contrast: 'From the point of view of physical representation, dialogue, and action, the annunciation sequence could have been anything from a 1960s visionary to a religious hysteric' (Stern *et al.* 1999: 223). The latter criticism would have some validity for an audience member who is unfamiliar with the Annunciation text, as only Mary's responses to the invisible messenger are heard (as in Kowalski's *The Nativity*). However, from the perspective of a Christian viewer, the scene makes perfect sense.

As in *From the Manger to the Cross*, Mary is lying down (although here there is a greater attempt at historical authenticity, as she is sleeping on a pallet on the floor). She is wearing a loose white garment and her long dark hair flows freely, in contrast to the nun-like clothing of Olcott's protagonist. Light suddenly streams through the open window and the flapping of the shutter is evocative of the wings of a bird (the Holy Spirit?) or an angel. Mary is woken by the disturbance and looks upwards, followed by a point-of-

FIG. 3 Divine intervention in *Jesus of Nazareth*

view shot of the window upside down to signal her disorientation. The shutter settles back and Mary leaps to her feet and runs away from the pool of light, knocking over pots as she backs into the corner. The intrusive sounds indicate everyday reality at a moment of divine intervention. The noise wakes her mother, Anne, whose bed is on the far side of the room.

Mary's fear is manifested by her tight grip on the wall (whose visible cracks might visualise the way in which the certainty of her existence is crumbling around her) and she asks an understandable (but biblically extratextual) question: 'Who are you?' In response there is a sudden breeze. The virginal conception of Jesus is 'a sign of the presence and work of the Spirit' (Anglican-Roman Catholic International Commission 2005: 18) rather than a symbol of the absence of the male, and this presence is frequently manifested in films by the light breeze that blows gently through Mary's hair, indicating that she is being touched by a divine presence.

Mary grasps the wall (the continuing sign of earthly solidity) but works her way closer to the light (with its heavenly connotations), so that the rays illuminate her face as a second sign of communion with the divine. There is no sound except off-screen animal noises, the barking dogs indicating that ordinary life is continuing in the world outside while this momentous event occurs. When Mary kneels, huddled by the wall, she demonstrates the most obvious sign of fear, but her subsequent responses closely follow the Lukan text in the questioning of angelic authority. She stands in front of the window, still close to the wall, as she asks, 'How can that be? No man has ever touched me.'

Unusually there is a diegetic witness to the Annunciation (as in Godard's *Hail Mary*), but Anne can see only the light streaming through the window and watches the scene in puzzlement, unable to hear the messenger's words. Lloyd Baugh regards Anne's presence as a 'domestication' of the event that undercuts the mystery, seeing her as the good Jewish (or Italian) mother who would 'insist on knowing what's going on' (1997: 75). But Anne also comes to the aid of the uninformed viewer, asking the questions that would fill in the gaps ('Mary, who are you talking to?'). Nevertheless, the viewers are closer to the action than Anne and see only occasional shots from her more distant point-of-view.

Indeed, Mary does not tell her mother about her own foretold pregnancy but reveals the information about Elizabeth (described here as her 'cousin'). Additional details, such as the exact date of conception on the nineteenth day of Tishri (September – October according to the Jewish calendar), are not found in the Lukan text but enhance the Jewish context, which was Zeffirelli's declared intention. Anne responds, 'What nonsense is this, child?' but Mary needs the confirmation of Elizabeth's impending motherhood in order to believe the angel's announcement (a theme that will be taken up by Catherine Hardwicke in *The Nativity Story*). As Mary relates the news of Elizabeth to her incredulous mother, the camera closes in on her face, as if to signal the truthfulness of her words.

Whereas Hardwicke's Annunciation scene appears hurried, Zeffirelli gives Mary the opportunity to absorb the message and make an active decision to take part. This extended Annunciation episode allows Mary to undergo a plethora of emotions until she reaches her *fiat*, creating the sense that Gabriel's message has had a transformative effect on the life of Mary. When Mary first kneels down, she is still clinging onto the wall as she says, 'Behold, the handmaiden of the Lord. Be it done unto me according to thy word.' Her physical posture remains one of humility. But at this point, she lets go of the wall (an indication of her movement towards the divine and her confidence to stand alone) and holds out her right hand (as Mary does in *From the Manger to the Cross*). The non-diegetic music does not begin until she speaks the words of assent, underlining the significance of this moment of acceptance.

Fig. 4 The moment of acceptance in *Jesus of Nazareth*

Maria, daughter of her son

Fabrizio Costa's *Maria, Daughter of Her Son* (starring the Israeli actress Yaël Abecassis) takes an original approach by drawing on the apocrypha for details of Mary's early life. There is also a replication of the two-stage Annunciation found in *The Protevangelium of James*. After the relationship with Joseph has been established (as in Zeffirelli's film), Mary walks to the stream as the sun is setting to wash clothes. The earth is bathed in a golden glow. Noticing a sudden breeze, she looks around in puzzlement and hears a male voice: 'Greetings Mary. Thou that art highly favoured. The Lord is with thee. Blessed art thou among women.' Some distance away there is a male figure sitting on the ground with his right hand raised. The figure mysteriously disappears (fading out).

Mary's first reaction is fear, and she picks up her basket and hurries home without speaking to the messenger, looking back anxiously over her shoulder to see if she is being followed. Now night is falling, and as she enters her own darkened room, a disembodied voice is heard: 'Fear not, Mary, for thou hast found favour with God. And behold! Thou shalt conceive in thy womb and bring forth a son.' There is a mysterious bright yellow light, which Mary turns towards so that she is partially lit by its warm glow. At the words, 'He shall be great, and shall be called the son of the Highest,' Mary crouches on her bed, raising her left arm to her face and nervously covering her mouth. The voice continues: 'And the Lord God shall give unto him the throne of his father David.' Mary glances around in panic at these words. 'And of his kingdom there shall be no end.' Mary looks towards the window, where the moon can now be seen through the grille. The light becomes brighter and streams through the window.

The moon has enjoyed symbolic value across the centuries, notably linked to the female menstrual cycle. As Marina Warner points out, 'the conception of a child depended on the fertility of a woman, and that in turn was, it appeared, governed by the moon, a nexus of images of water, moonlight, and birth bound together the Christian doctrine of the Redemption through an incarnate god with the relations of the cosmic galaxy and the earth' (1990: 260). There is an age-old belief that 'the light of the moon not only dispelled the shadows of night, but also had all-important life-giving powers' (Warner 1990: 259).

As in *Jesus of Nazareth*, the prolonged narrative allows the Annunciation to become a 'transformation scene'. Initially, a frightened Mary sits up on the end of the bed in *Maria, Daughter of Her Son*, and her body is huddled as she asks: 'How can this be since I have no husband?' The shadow of the grille creates a cage-like pattern across her body, so that she appears to be entrapped. A gentle musical soundtrack (of angelic voices) accompanies the message: 'The Holy Spirit shall come upon thee and the power of the Highest shall overshadow thee.' Mary raises her head at these words and looks upwards. 'Therefore also, that holy thing which shall be born of thee shall be called the son of God.' At this stage, Mary rises to her feet. 'And behold, thy kinswoman Elizabeth, she has also conceived a son in her old age and this is the sixth month for her who was called barren.' Mary now kneels down in the pool of light – so that the shadow of the bars has disappeared, indicating that she is fully embraced by the divine power. However, the washing basket is conspicuous in the background, reminding the viewer of the mundane world in the midst of angelic intervention.

On her knees, Mary holds out her arms, looking towards the light streaming through the window. As she speaks, she has her back to the camera. 'Behold!' Then the next shot focuses on her face as she gazes upwards. Her repetition of the word 'Behold!' underpins her sense of commitment. 'I am the handmaiden of the Lord. Let it be done to me according to your word!' Her face is noticeably joyful – a factor that is frequently missing from Annunciation scenes in which the chief facial expressions are confusion and fear. Then Mary faints, falling to the ground (as in Kowalski's *The Nativity*) and the light goes out. The fact that the Annunciation takes place in a darkened space (as in *Jesus of Nazareth*) ensures that the use of bright light to illuminate the gloom is an effective indication of the divine presence that is obviously more difficult to replicate in the daytime Annunciation scenes.

мary of Nazareth

Jean Delannoy also made use of light effects by setting the Annunciation in a cellar room in the house of Mary (Miriam Muller). In *Mary of Nazareth*, the scene takes place directly after Joseph's marriage proposal (see the following chapter). Here, Mary's domestic occupation also has a biblical overtone, for she is involved in the life-giving task of baking bread (rather than fetching water from the well). Pope John Paul II, in his letter 'On the Eucharist in Relation to the Church', wrote: 'At the Annunciation Mary conceived the Son of God in the physical reality of his body and blood, thus anticipating within herself what to some degree happens sacramentally in every believer who receives, under the signs of bread and wine, the Lord's body and blood' (in LaVerdiere 2007: 17).

As Mary puts the baked bread on the table and removes her apron (which is an indication that she is not in a servile role at the key moment), she looks up to be confronted by a bright light, wind and an authoritative male voice. However, when *Mary of Nazareth* was broadcast in a dubbed version in the USA in 1995 on Lifetime ('the cable network for women'), the French male actor voicing Gabriel was replaced by a woman (see Duricy 2000: 121), presumably as a nod to the predicted female spectatorship showing an interest in gender equality in Heaven.

The wind is particularly fierce, blowing out the lighted oil lamp and initially leaving Mary in darkness. Then a bright light appears from above, causing Mary to look up and shield her eyes as the angelic salutation is heard. The voice addresses Mary directly by name twice and also calls her 'full of grace'. Mary looks frightened and holds her hands clasped across her chest as she gazes upward. (There is non-diegetic music, in comparison to the silence chosen by Zeffirelli.) In contrast to the puzzled face of Mary in Hardwicke's *The Nativity Story*, Delannoy's Mary closes her eyes at the words 'Son of God' as if she truly understands the message at this point. She then opens her arms wide in a gesture of acceptance with a smile on her face as she proclaims that she is 'the handmaid of the Lord'. Indeed, the scene is very similar to a shot in the silent *The Life and Passion of Jesus Christ*, indicating that Mary's active acceptance on screen is not a post-feminist phenomenon.[15]

Although the screenplay later acknowledges that Mary is aware that repudiation by Joseph could lead to her punishment by death, her physical stance and smiling face indicate that she willingly takes part in this plan of salvation. More notably, the French film director – outwardly an exponent of tradition – incorporated a liberationist reading of the Annunciation simply by leaving Mary standing after the angel's visit (rather than in a crouched position or a dead faint). As Sally Cunneen describes, 'the more difficult thing for women is not the giving of self, to which they have been largely conditioned, but the necessary prior task of becoming a self able to give' (1996: 49). Mary's upright position at the centre of the frame confirms her self-confidence. In reading the Annunciation as 'the supreme act of a human person whereby she made a gift of herself to another (God)' (Bearsley 1983: 89), Delannoy re-flects the decisive action of a ratio-nal woman, rather than her capitu-lation within a patriarchal system. Brown claims that a more positive reading of Mary's response is in the Lukan tradition that Mary is one of those 'who hear the word of God and keep it' (Lk 11:28), and Mary's enthusiastic response is highlighted by the context in which Luke has placed it (see Brown 1993: 318–19).

Fig. 5 Mary's active response in *Mary of Nazareth*

Some feminist commentators have declined the negative readings of the Gospel story and reinterpreted the Virgin Mary's response to the Annunciation as an example of synergy between God and the human race in the cause of salvation. Instead of accepting a reductive treatment of the *fiat* – and, therefore, rejecting Mary as a symbol of women's passivity – feminist Mariologists have refocused the Lukan Annunciation scene as an act of free co-operation between God and Mary, thereby transforming the traditionally acquiescent handmaid into the subject, rather than simply the object, of this liberating action (see Ruether 1993: 155).

Liberation Mariology has taken the Gospel scene and translated it into an example of independent co-operation. Simone de Beauvoir understood Mary's response to the angel's message to be a sign of capitulation because it was only in accepting the 'subordinate role' that she would be glorified (1949: 283). (This is the approach adopted by Godard). But the revisionists offer a more positive interpretation, claiming that Mary's announcement that she is the 'servant of the Lord' frees her from earthly authority. Her *fiat* is a declaration of independence (see Makarian 1995: 93). Liberationist re-interpretations of the Annunciation scene reflect upon the actions of this woman of faith 'who actively and freely responds to God's invitation' (Cheah 1995: 72). Mary does not accept her *fiat* unquestioningly, as the Lukan verses confirm. The more expansive scenes in the films of Zeffirelli and Costa reflect this viewpoint.

In addition to the feminist perspective, the petition for a fifth Marian dogma that would see the Virgin Mary elevated to the position of 'Coredemptrix, Mediatrix of All Graces and Advocate for the People of God' has been regarded as 'a Catholic response to feminist theology' (Seifert 1996: 167). Joseph Seifert, a champion of the proposed fifth dogma, claims that it 'would counteract the idea that human beings in general, and particularly that women are mere passive vessels of divine grace and that the Virgin Mary was made Mother of God, freed from all sin, and extolled above all creatures, *solely* by the grace and election of God, *without any* great need for her own free choice' (1996: 167 [emphasis in original]).

THE VISITATION

During those days Mary set out and travelled to the hill country in haste to a town of Judah, where she entered the house of Zechariah and greeted Elizabeth. When Elizabeth heard Mary's greeting, the infant leaped in her womb, and Elizabeth, filled with the holy Spirit, cried out in a loud voice and said, 'Most blessed are you among women, and blessed is the fruit of your womb. And how does this happen to me, that the mother of my Lord should come to me? For at the moment the sound of your greeting reached my ears, the infant in my womb leaped for joy. Blessed are you who believed that what was spoken to you by the Lord would be fulfilled.' (Lk 1:39–45)

Following the Annunciation in Luke's Gospel, Mary visits her kinswoman Elizabeth (traditionally described as a cousin, but reconfigured as an 'aunt' in Kowalski's *The Nativity*). The Visitation is one of the most beautiful episodes in the New Testament as a celebration of female friendship and an exaltation of the blessedness of motherhood.

It is also a literal manifestation of Mary's interior pilgrimage, which she begins at the Annunciation and must travel through to the Resurrection. The sign at the petrol station in Godard's *Hail Mary* offers suitable commentary: 'Bonne route' ('Have a good journey').

The journey is initially inspired by the news of Elizabeth's unexpected pregnancy that forms 'the sign' in Gabriel's Annunciation message. Feminist interpretations of the Lukan episode stress Mary's courage when she makes the decision to travel to the hill country around Judea, for it is a substantial distance from Nazareth to Ein Kerem (near Jerusalem), which is accepted in the tradition as the home of Elizabeth and Zechariah. Tim Perry reminds us that a young Jewish girl 'would not normally have left her home without accompaniment – either to browse in her own home town or (especially!) to travel some seventy miles to the hill country around Jerusalem. Until she entered the bridal chamber, a girl lived in seclusion in her home' (2006: 73). In the fourth century, St Ambrose of Milan (d.397) made that very point: 'Committed to staying hidden inside her house, [Mary] never showed herself in public without being guarded by a trustworthy companion' (in Gambero 1999: 200). Yet St Ambrose also added, 'Her best guardian, however, was always herself' (*Ibid.*). In fact, in the films *Mater Dei*, *Mary of Nazareth* and *Joseph of Nazareth*, Mary appears to travel alone, underlining her sense of autonomy. Mary's self-determination is particularly emphasised by Delannoy, who makes great capital out of images of Mary riding into and out of town on a donkey with notable independence of spirit in *Mary of Nazareth*.

Further artistic licence comes to the fore in Connor's *Mary, mother of Jesus*. Although Mary follows convention by travelling in a caravan, she steps outside the traditional framework when she approaches Elizabeth's house and sees a woman being pursued by angry men who begin to stone her as an adulteress. Mary runs towards them, yelling for them to stop, but her cries come too late as the woman is already dead. The scene serves as a foretaste of her own possible fate (she may be accused of adultery when her pregnancy is known) and of Jesus's actions later in life when he prevents a similar execution (see Jn 8:1–11), but she personally intervenes in a manner that was unlikely behaviour for a young woman given the historical time frame.

However, while Elizabeth Johnson accepts that first-century Judaism 'had its patriarchal, androcentric mores and that many, even the majority of women, were legally disadvantaged and powerless,' she argues 'that no homogenous definition will fit all groups' (2003: 189). When St Ambrose praised Mary for 'her modesty, her domestic seclusion, her silence,' he revealed 'much about emergent ideals of Christian womanhood' (Beattie 2007: 99) rather than concrete evidence of Mary's character. By the fact that Jesus's family will later seek to hold him back (Mk 3:20–21) during his ministry, Johnson identifies 'the exercise of female power in the action of Miriam of Nazareth who, no stranger to Roman violence and the havoc it could wreak on human lives, goes to persuade her child out of the line of fire' (in Perry 2006: 40).

Mary's desire to see Elizabeth with her own eyes can be interpreted in various ways: as a confirmation of Mary's own miraculous pregnancy by proving that the angel's words are true, and as a manifestation of a sisterly bond. When the newly pregnant Mary cannot sleep in Hardwicke's *The Nativity Story*, she wonders in a voice-over: 'How is anyone to believe me? How are they to understand?' Returning the next day to the olive tree, the scene of the Annunciation, she remembers the words of the angel: 'Even your own cousin has conceived a son in her old age.' The desire to visit Elizabeth is partly fuelled by the need to see whether the angel's message was genuine (as she travels along, she prays, 'Please Lord, let Elizabeth be with child as the angel spoke'), but she also fits Elisabeth Schüssler Fiorenza's description of the frightened Mary of the New Testament who 'sought help from another woman' (in Boss 2007: 37).

In *The Nativity Story* the first sign of real euphoria on Mary's face within the diegesis is when she embraces the visibly pregnant Elizabeth; and the second occurs when the two women react elatedly as Mary feels her baby move. They stand out in the fields in the sunshine, each touching the stomach of the other and experiencing the joy of new life. The Visitation scene is particularly esteemed by the pro-life movement, whose adherents point out that Elizabeth's child (the future John the Baptist) responds in the womb to Mary's voice. Anti-abortionists stress the reverence for human life from the moment of conception and 'will regard Elizabeth's words to Mary,

FIG. 6 The joy of expectant motherhood in *The Nativity Story*

"Blessed is the fruit of your womb" as true in a real sense of every unborn child' (Buono in Anon. 1997: 127).

Zeffirelli's *Jesus of Nazareth* presents Mary travelling in a caravan to visit Elizabeth – her mode of transport more in keeping with the customs of the time. In the Visitation scene itself (whose colour palette evokes a Renaissance painting), Elizabeth hurries through the house, her body partially hidden behind banisters and pillars so as to create a moment of suspense for Mary (although presumably not for the bible-reading Christian audience) who is eager to know the veracity of the angel's message. When Mary's eyes fall upon Elizabeth's visibly pregnant stomach, her response ('So it is true!') relates also to the acceptance of her own miraculous pregnancy.

The scene also extols the joy of expectant motherhood. Mary places her hand on Elizabeth's stomach as she rejoices in her kinswoman's elation, and then she touches her own stomach as Elizabeth acknowledges Mary's own news: 'A thing even more wonderful?' Zeffirelli emphasises the connection between two women, separated by an age gap but united in the miraculousness of their respective pregnancies – Elizabeth because of her previous inability to conceive, and Mary because of her virginity. For the ancient Jews 'sexual power was considered as the most fundamental kind of political power because on it depended the survival of the nation. To be sterile was to be accursed of God. Yet at the same time it was acknowledged that this power of sexuality was a gift of God which could not have its effect without His active intervention' (Ashley 1985: 493).

While Elizabeth is the superior within a worldly ranking because of her age and status as the wife of a priest (see Green in Perry 2006: 74), Elizabeth kneels before her younger relative in Zeffirelli's scene. On one level, Elizabeth's gesture is a reversal of the earthly hierarchy – a first sign of honour paid to Mary, as Elizabeth says: 'You are blessed among women.' However, her next statement indicates that she genuflects in recognition of the child Mary carries in her womb: 'And blessed shall be the fruit of your womb.' (The words now form part of the 'Hail Mary' prayer.) 'I, too, am highly favoured that the mother of the Chosen should come to me. From the moment your greeting reached my ears, the child in my womb leapt for joy.' It is Mary's role as the mother of the Messiah that leads to Elizabeth's act of humility.

The Visitation is also regarded as the first missionary action of the New Testament (see Beaudin 2002: 11), for Mary travels to bring the news of the Messiah. Whereas the priest Zechariah is struck dumb because he doubts that his wife Elizabeth could conceive in her old age, Mary now expresses a confidence that finds its outpouring in *The Magnificat*, and its treatment (or curtailment) in the filmic narrative is significant for an understanding of the presentation of Mary's on-screen persona.

THE MAGNIFICAT

> *And Mary said:*
>> '*My soul proclaims the greatness of the Lord;*
>>> *my spirit rejoices in God my savior.*
>> *For he has looked upon his handmaid's lowliness;*
>>> *behold, from now on will all ages call me blessed.*
>> *The Mighty One has done great things for me,*
>>> *and holy is his name.*
>> *His mercy is from age to age to those who fear him.*
>> *He has shown might with his arm,*
>>> *dispersed the arrogant of mind and heart.*
>> *He has thrown down the rulers from their thrones but lifted up the*
>>> *lowly.*
>> *The hungry he has filled with good things;*
>>> *the rich he has sent away empty.*
>> *He has helped Israel his servant,*
>>> *remembering his mercy,*
>>> *according to his promise to our fathers,*
>>> *to Abraham and to his descendents forever.*'
>
> (Lk 1:46–55)

Exegetes have studied the similarities between *The Magnificat* and hymns of praise sung by Hannah and Miriam in the Old Testament (see Warner 1990: 13). *The Magnificat* is believed by some theologians to be a canticle placed on Mary's lips by the evangelist rather than her immediate response which, it is argued, would be 'well beyond the capabilities of an illiterate first-century Palestinian teenager' (Perry 2006: 76). However, whether or not *The Magnificat* is 'an on-the-spot poetic utterance' (see Brown *et al.* 1978: 139–40), the argument remains that the Lukan community regarded Mary as a suitable exponent of this message of liberation. Mary 'is clearly associated in that moving "Declaration of Independence" with, among others, its themes of joy, care for the poor and the powerless, and the reversal of people's status in life' (Cheah 1995: 85). Liberation Mariologists have embraced this canticle, remarking that it 'pinpoints Mary's keen mind, understanding spirit, joyous heart, concern for others, and love for God. It sets her apart as a woman of unshakeable faith, unwavering hope, and uncommon love' (Buono in Anon. 1997: 500).

However, some directors omit the canticle, even when they feature the Visitation scene. Given the professed desire for authenticity in Eric Till's film *Mary and Joseph*, the omission of the canticle (in favour of Mary's extrabiblical public declaration to be the mother of the Messiah before an uncomprehending crowd) is an odd choice, replacing the resonant verses of the New Testament with a dubious invention. Equally surprising is the exclusion of the canticle in *Maria, Daughter of Her Son*, when so much of the film is striving to find material in non-canonical sources. Costa's film also develops a markedly difficult relationship between Mary and Elizabeth, for Elizabeth's suffering at the execution of John will later work as a parallel narrative to the story of Mary and Jesus.

A similar approach is also adopted in Connor's *Mary, mother of Jesus*, in which *The Magnificat* likewise does not feature in the Visitation scene. As Elizabeth recounts Zechariah's encounter in the Temple, she walks away from Mary, clearly not rejoicing because she fears that there is 'something not natural' in her own pregnancy. Indeed, the film takes the unusual step of presenting Elizabeth's personal anxieties about the angelic message to Zechariah (arising from the fact that she did not see the messenger herself). Consequently there is no *Magnificat*, no rejoicing, and nothing that signals Mary as blessed. Instead, *The Magnificat* is read over the credits, together with a range of artistic images of the Madonna and Child that underline Mary's ongoing cultural significance.

When the canticle is reinstated, the editing of the text (because significant verses are frequently cut) has bearing on the overall treatment of Mary within the diegesis. When Mary arrives at Elizabeth's house in *Mater Dei*, dressed in a blue cloak, she strikes an iconic pose with her hands outstretched. As the actress playing Elizabeth is shorter than Mary, the older woman literally looks up to her as Mary recites only the first verses as far as 'all generations will call me blessed'. In this pre-Vatican II film, the focus is on Mary's personal status rather than any liberationist role.

In *Jesus of Nazareth*, Mary utters the first words of the Canticle: 'My soul doth magnify the Lord! [...] He who is mighty has done unto me a mighty thing.' The servants kneel down in front of her as she speaks, so that she is leading the assembly in prayer to God. However, in Zeffirelli's film, Mary does not complete *The Magnificat*, so that the more explicit political dimension is lost. After reciting the first verses, Mary goes to Elizabeth and raises her kinswoman to her feet, so that they stand on equal ground as two expectant mothers.

In the Visitation scene of *Mary of Nazareth*, Delannoy also does not conform fully to the 'liberationist' focus, for his use of the Lukan canticle offers a somewhat mixed message. Elizabeth initially kneels in front of Mary but her younger relative raises her to her feet and they embrace. Rather than expressing her joy directly to her relatives, Mary turns away from Elizabeth and Zechariah and stands on the open hillside with arms outstretched (a stance adopted by the Marian apparition at Lourdes, as the eponymous heroine testifies in Delannoy's earlier film about the apparitions at Lourdes, *Bernadette* (1988)). Furthermore, the presence of the dumb-struck priest Zechariah adds an additional resonance to Mary's prophetic voice.

Mary proclaims her sermon to the empty countryside (to the accompaniment of non-diegetic hallelujahs on the soundtrack) and then, with a change of camera angle, to the cinema audience (presumably embodying the generations 'who will call her blessed'). However, what is most noticeable is the editing of the biblical text, for she recites *The Magnificat* only as far as the line: 'His mercy is from age to age to those who fear him.' Delannoy's script centres on Mary herself – linking the protagonist with the spectator and focusing on her individual status. By cutting out the second part of the canticle, in which 'The hungry he has filled with good things; the rich he has sent away empty' (Lk 1:53), Delannoy offers a Mary 'who is liberated' but not the prophet Mary who is 'liberator'. Liberation Mariologists would require both (see Cheah 1995: 80). In contrast, Kowalski's *The Nativity* is again of note for giving Mary the space to recite the whole canticle. With an audience made up of Joachim, Elizabeth and Zechariah, Mary becomes a prophetess.

In Hardwicke's *The Nativity Story*, the canticle is delivered in Mary's voice-over during the final images of the Flight into Egypt, although it is notable that the first lines are missing (as if the filmmaker were uncomfortable with Mary's 'handmaid' status, given that such a reference was also omitted at the Annunciation). Removing the canticle from its original context (as in Connor's film) means that Mary's longest speech in the New Testament is withdrawn from its vital position within the narrative. However, the verses take on a different dimension, becoming the last spoken words that will accompany the audience out of the cinema and turning *The Magnificat* into a concluding prayerful message.

The Magnificat is regarded by liberation theologians as a prayer of social justice, and one presumably rejected by political dictators. In Latin American liberation theology:

Only God is strong [and] powerful; only God saves. [...] Today the different ideologies – from national security to Marxist socialism – present themselves as self-redeeming, as the only salvation; in that way, they are the "opium of the people." The *Magnificat* proposes God as the only Saviour and, through Christ, guarantees the "salvific being with the brothers," that is, the commitment with them in the struggle against all sorts of injustices, both economic and non-economic. (Javier Lozano Barragan in Margerie 1987: 50–1)

In interpreting this scene, Leonardo Boff claims: 'Mary shares the pain unjustly imposed on Jesus; she freely shoulders it all with Him, in order to bring about redemption, expiation and liberation. The powerful, the rich and the proud will be toppled from their places. Thus will they be able to cease their inhumanity' (in Margerie 1987: 55). Pasolini, who suggested that 'at the deepest level, Marxism and Catholicism had profound affinities' (see Greene 1990: 71) did not include *The Magnificat* because it is found only in Luke's Gospel, but responses to his film would have given support to his desire that 'Catholicism must be capable ... of taking into account the problems of the society in which we live; and so too must Marxism face the religious moment of humanity' (in Greene 1990: 71). Sandro Petraglia considers whether Pasolini 'began with Christ in order to arrive at Marx or, vice versa, if in fact his love for the story of the Passion took him ... to a version of the myth profoundly renewed by a populist, sub-proletarian, or Third World current' (in Greene 1990: 72).

Adopting a political angle, *Son of Man* (Mark Dornford-May, 2006) situates the story of the New Testament in an African township (in a fictional 'Kingdom of Judea') during a time of bloodshed. Pauline Malefane, who also contributed to the script in Xhosa and English, presents the audience with a black Madonna for the twenty-first century. The line in the *Song of Songs* ('I am black but beautiful') has provided 'the biblical justification for the many portraits of Mary that have shunned the conventional representation of her as Italian or North American in favour of the Black Madonna' (Pelikan 1996: 25). Indeed, Pelikan points out that Marvin Pope's analysis of the Old Testament verse 'has convincingly shown on linguistic grounds that "Black am I *and* beautiful" not "*but* beautiful," is the correct translation of the Hebrew of this verse' which overturns the 'all too widespread sense of contradiction between blackness and comeliness' (1996: 26).

Dornford-May combines the Annunciation and *The Magnificat*. Mary is a young woman fleeing from the soldiers, and she takes refuge in a school classroom. As she goes to hide in the corner by the door, she turns around to look at the room. The director plays with the hierarchy of knowledge, as the audience sees the horror on her face before its origin is revealed. A reverse shot shows the bodies of dead children on the floor. When the soldiers come to search for her, Mary finds refuge among the corpses by lying prone with the children, so that she is not caught. The Annunciation message brings life in the midst of death.

In *Son of Man*, the angels are played by young black children dressed in white loin cloths with white feathers stuck to their bodies and heads, making them attractive 'cherubs' who might lack the authority to convey such a momentous message. When the angel addresses Mary and tells her that she will be the mother of the Saviour, Mary does not utter any of the Lukan Annunciation dialogue and there is no 'handmaid' speech. Rather, Mary sings the words of *The Magnificat* in Xhosa, which therefore takes on its full political resonance amidst the carnage in the room.

Pope Benedict XVI describes Mary's acceptance at the Annunciation as 'the definitive moment, the moment of marriage, the establishment of a new and everlasting covenant. As Mary stood before the Lord, she represented the whole of humanity. In the angel's message, it was as if God made a marriage proposal to the human race. And in our name, Mary said yes' (2008). However, Mary was already betrothed to Joseph, who was also to be affected by Mary's momentous decision. In the Visitation scenes in *The Nativity Story* and *Jesus of Nazareth*, Mary and Elizabeth discuss the issues that awaken the curiosity of those writers trying to fill in the gaps. How will Mary cope with the change in her circumstances ('Are you frightened?' asks Elizabeth in *The Nativity Story*); and how will Joseph react?

In Zeffirelli's film, Mary turns to her older relative for comfort, and Elizabeth advises: 'When you get back to Nazareth, tell Joseph what you have seen and heard, what you know. The Lord God wills life where no life is possible. And one life shall be the Son of God and the other shall be His prophet. Go, tell all this to Joseph.' However, Mary asks the most poignant question of all: 'But will he believe me?' As the following chapter will demonstrate, scriptwriters have found Joseph's reaction to be a major source of creativity.

CHAPTER 3

Mary and Joseph

There are films that present Joseph as an unquestioning protector of Mary.[1] But the reaction of Joseph to Mary's pregnancy has fascinated a disparate range of directors, with Jean-Luc Godard being a particularly notorious example. The majority of the historical 'Infancy Narrative' scripts, as well as some of the allegories that update the story of Jesus to contemporary society, transform Joseph's response into one of the mainstays of the plot. The perceived 'power relations' between the couple have resulted in numerous filmic interpretations.

As Mary's on-screen portrait has evolved in tandem with developments in theology and gender studies, so the cinematic role played by Joseph is open to a range of readings. In *The Life and Passion of Jesus Christ*, Joseph is a figure in a silent tableau and there is no attempt to address the repercussions of the angel Gabriel's tidings. By the time of the release of Hardwicke's *The Nativity Story* in the twenty-first century, in which Joseph becomes the 'man of the hour' during a pilgrimage of faith, the dynamics of the couple had seen many more nuanced manifestations on film.

Joseph is described as a carpenter in Matthew's Gospel (Mt 13:55). This solitary New Testament reference to his trade has been accepted in the tradition and adopted consistently by scriptwriters, with the (predictable) exception of Godard. However, the Hebrew word *nagar* means a craftsman, while the Greek equivalent *tekton* means a builder (see Hazleton 2004: 132–3), and these variations are also demonstrated on screen. In

71

Delannoy's *Mary of Nazareth*, the gentle Joseph is engaged in delicate tasks (making a bird cage that will later be used for the Temple offering after Jesus is born), whereas the hero of Hardwicke's *The Nativity Story* is building a whole house out of stone. Perhaps Mertes's *Joseph of Nazareth* (one of The Bible Close to Jesus Series) gilds the lily by having the titular protagonist lauded by King Herod himself as 'the best craftsman in the world!'

In discussing *Hail Mary*, Godard remarked that Jesus had made many filmic appearances but that 'no one has told the story of Mary and Joseph' (in Locke 1993: 1). He claimed that his 1985 film would consider Mary and Joseph's conversations before having a child: 'What could they say to each other? It's a major problem because from the Bible we know of only two or three words that Mary spoke, and from Joseph absolutely nothing' (in Dieckmann 1993: 121). However, it appeared that two US television movies from the late 1970s had escaped Godard's notice. Kowalski's *The Nativity* (1978) focused on the pre-Nativity relationship of Mary and Joseph and was praised for its 'geographic authenticity [although it was filmed in Spain] and the sincere attempt by the producers to include appropriate ethnic types in the cast, which lends badly needed verisimilitude to the proceedings' (Kinnard and Davis 1992: 191). When it was shown on ABC on 17 December 1978, it was marketed as 'the greatest family story of all time' about 'a man, a woman, and the Child who changed the world' (in Campbell and Pitts 1981: 183). A year later, Eric Till's *Mary and Joseph* (1979) strove for credibility with its location shooting in Israel, but was ridiculed for the anachronistic portrayal of Jesus's earthly parents as two twentieth-century American hippies (Blanche Baker and Jeff East) wearing biblical clothes. Joseph's conspicuously unsuccessful attempt to be a freedom fighter as well as a trainee carpenter did not impress the critics. *The New York Times* review was memorably scathing: 'The art of meaninglessness has rarely been so well served' (in Campbell and Pitts 1981: 185).

These two films attempted to appeal to a younger audience by employing youthful actors in the key roles. Therefore, they rejected the Catholic tradition in which Joseph is depicted as an elderly man. He has often been portrayed as a widower to explain the status of the 'brothers of Jesus', who are presented in the apocryphal *Protevangelium of James* as Joseph's sons from a previous marriage: 'I have sons and am old; she is but a girl. I object lest I should become a laughing stock' (in Elliott 1993: 61). The Italian film *For Love, Only For Love* relates how an older, worldly wise Joseph has his life disrupted by his love for Mary, the extent of the age difference between them indicated when he first meets her as a little girl (Eliana Giua). Mertes's *Joseph of Nazareth*, Connor's *Mary, mother of Jesus* and Costa's *Maria, Daughter of Her Son* also maintain the age-determined hierarchy. In the latter film, Joseph remarks on this fact on several occasions: 'Why have you given *me* this child?' However, when the on-screen couple are closer in age (as in *Mary and Joseph* or *Hail Mary*), the balance is further disrupted by elements of adolescent jealousy.[2]

INDEPENDENCE OF MIND

From the late 1970s onwards, Mary on screen is not a reticent figure, despite the danger that her characterisation might be seen as anachronistic when viewed against the historical background within the diegesis. As the Catholic Church reflected changing attitudes to the status of women in two major publications (the US Bishops' letter *Behold your Mother* and Pope Paul VI's apostolic exhortation *Marialis Cultus*), so the filmic representations of Mary gradually took on a more self-determined angle. In Zeffirelli's *Jesus of Nazareth*, the villagers describe Mary as 'a bit strange, not like the others' but there is no sustained interest in her character's motivation. However, in subsequent films with a Marian element – and epitomised by Catherine Hardwicke's *The Nativity Story* – Mary's personality becomes more complex. In some cases, her filmic representation is identifiably 'Protestant', in the sense that the dogma of the Immaculate Conception does not inform the screenplay (see Greydanus 2006).

Bernard Kowalski's *The Nativity* presents Joseph as a particularly shy and hesitant suitor. He literally looks up to Mary as he walks up the hill to her house, where Mary is polishing *menorahs* as a sign of her Jewish culture. In their initial scene together, Mary speaks first and directs the development of their relationship, so she is later scolded for her actions (which are considered unbecoming for a woman of marriageable age) by her uncle: 'You've always been such a dutiful young girl. How do you manage to be such a disobedient woman?' The chastisement of Mary as 'disobedient' evidently runs counter to the belief that Mary is 'all holy' according to Catholic teaching.

Fabrizio Costa's *Maria, Daughter of Her Son* employs three performers for three stages in Mary's biography: her infancy, when she is dedicated to the Temple (as recorded in *The Protevangelium of James*); her (apocryphal) life in the Temple; and her womanhood from her engagement to Joseph onwards. The second actress (Sara Filizzola) stands out amongst the other girls in the Temple because of her height. When the girls sing a hymn of joy, Mary responds enthusiastically ('Rabbi, it's lovely!') only to be reproached for her intervention ('Mary, we don't need your comments'). However, Mary continues to smile despite the reproof and then begins to dance. When she is further reprimanded for her actions by the rabbi, she initially returns to her place and bows her head, but she soon begins to dance again and the other girls follow her. When it comes to an opportunity to praise God, the Mary of *Maria, Daughter of Her Son* refuses to be restricted by patriarchal control. The music heard in the Temple sequence subsequently becomes her *leitmotif* at moments of happiness during the remainder of the film.

The younger Mary in Kevin Connor's *Mary, mother of Jesus* is even more notably spirited, pulling a beggar woman from out of the path of the Roman army on horseback, and defending one of the Nazareth villagers in front of the soldiers: 'Captain, he showed courage. A soldier, as you are, may honour courage in another man without dishonour to himself.' Indeed, the Roman captain appears to take notice of her wishes and responds: 'You're a brave girl. Let him go.' Given the historical timeframe, Mary demonstrates proto-feminist characteristics that earn the rebuke of a village elder: 'Well, if you want a forward woman for your wife, Joseph, that's your affair.' Such events and mutterings about marital gender relations are a considerably fresh departure from the traditional image of Mary and Joseph. While Godard explicitly updated the story to the twentieth century in *Hail Mary*, Connor's film also attempts to engage with contemporary society despite the historical trappings.

When Mary learns of the arranged marriage to Joseph in Hardwicke's *The Nativity Story*, she shows a certain petulance as she walks out of the family home ('Why do they force me to marry a man I hardly know, a man I do not love?') that made some Catholic viewers uncomfortable (see Greydanus 2006). Indeed, the dogma of the Immaculate Conception was clearly not in the mind of the Protestant director, who explained, 'I wanted them to see Mary, as a girl, as a teenager at first, not perfectly pious from the very first moment' (in Geiger 2006).

Critics of Hardwicke's approach might also note the anachronism. As Leslie Hazleton indicates in *Mary: A Flesh and Blood Biography of the Virgin Mother*, there were no 'teenagers' as the term is currently understood in Mary's time. In *The Nativity Story*, Mary is seen finishing her domestic tasks, regretfully aware that childhood is now behind her, but her attitude belongs to a Western viewpoint that takes 'for granted the idea of childhood, and of the teen years as a kind of older childhood, a slow adaptation to adulthood' (2004: 24). In fact, a thirteen-year-old girl would already be considered a woman in a society where the lifespan was short.

THE COURTSHIP

However, Hardwicke was in harmony with Hazleton's rejection of the Hollywood idea of Mary and Joseph as 'two teenagers under the olive trees, under the stars, under the full moon...' because 'marriage was arranged by others, and became an arrangement between husband and wife' (Hazleton 2004: 136). Many directors are not so restricted by that presumed historical situation. Indeed, while arranged marriages remain the order of the day in *Jesus of Nazareth* and *The Nativity Story*, Hollywood instincts come to the fore in a number of films, presenting the relationship of Mary and Joseph as a love story.

Nevertheless, Madeleine Stowe is not a simpering heroine in the key role in Kowalski's *The Nativity*. She plays one of a number of on-screen Marys who actively express a predilection for their marriage partner. When Kowalski's female protagonist finally elects her bashful suitor, she holds his arm in a gesture of possession and discusses ways to circumnavigate the Law so that they can be married more quickly. When Joseph later explains to Mary that it would be a sin to marry before the year is out – for they would have to run away to another place – he is rather relieved when she agrees that they should follow the Law.

While St Augustine believed in 'the authority of the *paterfamilias*' in the marriage of Mary and Joseph, despite Mary's special privilege as the mother of God (see Beattie 2002: 177), many directors refute this traditional hierarchy. Indeed, in *Mary of Nazareth*, Joseph is in awe of Mary *before* the Annunciation, providing evidence that Delannoy's film is markedly 'Catholic' in approach despite the director's own Protestant faith. On one level, Delannoy's Mary would initially fit the ideal of St Ambrose: 'Never an agitated movement, never a hurried step, never a raised voice. The very appearance of her person reflected the holiness of her mind and expressed her goodness' (in Gambero 1999: 200). But the filmic protagonist also shows a self-confidence that does not fit into any patriarchal stereotype. In fact, Mary makes the marriage proposal herself in *Mary of Nazareth*, realising that the terminally shy Joseph is too nervous: 'Do you want to ask me if I will be your wife?' As he replies happily in the affirmative, she says, 'I will marry you, Joseph', and she holds out her hands towards him.

Consequently, when she then tells him, 'Go now', and he leaves without question, the order of command is firmly established.

Costa's *Maria, Daughter of Her Son* takes inspiration from the apocryphal account in which Joseph is chosen by divine intervention. It is recorded in *The Protevangelium of James* that the rods [staffs] of all the potential suitors for Mary are gathered together in the Temple: 'Joseph received the last rod, and behold, a dove came out of the rod and flew on to Joseph's head' (in Elliott 1993: 60). In Costa's film, Mary laughs as she watches with her friends as the prospective husbands are gathered together. Although Joseph is standing humbly at the back of the crowd, he is slightly taller than the other men, illuminated by the beams of sunlight, and the camera centres him as Mary catches his bashful gaze. While Mary claims, 'I could never be in a man's arms' (an apparent early vow of virginity that will later become an element of the plot), Joseph picks up his staff and the celestial choir on the musical soundtrack prepare the audience for the heavenly sign: his staff miraculously blooms and the engagement to Mary is confirmed.

In a Hollywood narrative, the betrothal might be the finale, the happy ending. Reflecting on Mary's response at the Annunciation, Benedict XVI remarks: 'In fairy tales, the story ends there, and all "live happily ever after". In real life it is not so simple' (2008). One of the inevitable complications is the effect of the news of Mary's unexpected pregnancy on Joseph.

Elizabeth Johnson has complained that the focus on Mary's handmaid status has promoted the view of every woman 'as a vessel of passive receptivity, a receptivity moreover to the primary activity of males, be they divine or human, God, fathers, husbands, or priests,' with the problem 'compounded by the thoroughly masculine character of the deity' (1985: 127). However, Beverley R. Gaventa argues that 'if Mary is *God's* slave, then she cannot at the same time be the slave of human beings' (1999: 54 [emphasis in original]), so that Mary is not subject to traditional patriarchal power relations. By accepting Jesus as his son, Joseph 'is being asked to say "yes" to what Mary has already said "yes"' (Buby 1994: 54).

POST-ANNUNCIATION REPERCUSSIONS

Now this is how the birth of Jesus Christ came about. When his mother Mary was betrothed to Joseph, but before they lived together, she was found with child through the holy Spirit. Joseph her husband, since he was a righteous man, yet unwilling to expose her to shame, decided to divorce her quietly. Such was his intention when, behold, the angel of the Lord appeared to him in a dream and said, 'Joseph, son of David, do not be afraid to take Mary your wife into your home. For it is through the holy Spirit that this child has been conceived in her. She will bear a son and you are to name him Jesus, because he will save his people from their sins.' (Mt 1:18–21)

In the Gospels of Matthew and Luke, the evangelists use the Greek verb 'to be betrothed or engaged' (*mnēsteuein*) to describe the status of the relationship between Mary and Joseph at the time of the Annunciation. The couple had gone through the first step in the Jewish matrimonial procedure, which involved the formal exchange of consent before witnesses. With Zeffirelli's desire to promote the authentic Jewish background of Jesus's family, the betrothal is a key scene in *Jesus of Nazareth*, although the participants are not arranged in a traditional circle (as in *The Nativity*) 'but in a precise horizontal composition, with Mary, Joseph and the rabbi in the centre as if they were posing for a photographer' (Baugh 1997: 75).

The New Testament Mary would have continued to live with her family until the second stage of the marriage was completed. However, even during the betrothal period, the man had rights over the woman, so that any infringement of those rights could be punished as adultery. The importance of knowing whether Mary and Joseph lived under Judean or Galilean law is disputed by exegetes, for in parts of Judea marital relations were not absolutely condemned in the interim.

While the Marian focus of Luke's Gospel does not reflect on Joseph's reaction to the angel Gabriel's tidings, the Gospel of Matthew takes up Joseph's perspective. However, from the narratological perspective, Matthew has ensured that his readers initially know more than Joseph (for they have already been informed in a preceding line of the intervention of the Holy Spirit). As most screenwriters conflate the Gospels of Matthew and Luke, so that the audience has already witnessed the Annunciation scene, Joseph is left in a position of inferiority in the hierarchy of knowledge.

Matthew describes Joseph as a righteous (*dikaios* in the original Greek) man who, 'unwilling to expose [Mary] to shame, decided to divorce her quietly' (Mt 1:19). Exegetes have put forward a number of hypotheses in seeking to explain the description of Joseph as *dikaios* in his initial decision to divorce Mary informally: i) the suspicion hypothesis, in which Joseph thought that Mary had been unfaithful but showed himself to be upright when he chose not to enforce the law on adultery; ii) the fear hypothesis, in which Joseph knew that Mary was pregnant through divine intervention and consequently drew back from Mary in awe (a theory that has no biblical support, as there is no evidence of a previous revelation to Joseph); and iii) obedience to the law, indicating that Joseph thought that Mary had committed adultery and so wanted to follow the law in this matter (see Brown 1993: 126–7). The dilemma comes to the fore in Hardwicke's *The Nativity Story*, in which Joseph expresses his confusion: 'Do you know the reason why I chose you, Mary? I believed you were a woman of great virtue. I have lived my life seeking honour, honour, Mary. So how am I to answer this? [His eyes are filled with tears.] If I claim this child is mine I will be lying. If I accuse you…'

When Joseph's reaction to Mary's news becomes a filmic plot device, it is the 'suspicion hypothesis' that frequently comes to the fore. After the intertitle in *From the Manger to the Cross* informs the audience that Joseph decided 'to put [Mary] away privily' (although the reasons for this decision are not clarified), Mary is seen passing by Joseph, carrying her water pitcher. The breakdown in the relationship is emphasised by the lack of communication between them. Joseph is in the foreground, deep in thought (as his hands clasped beneath his chin indicate), and the viewers are left to imagine the inner workings of his mind as he leans against his carpenter's work bench. However, his doubts are quickly assuaged as he immediately receives the angelic message that 'it is through the holy Spirit that this child has been conceived' (Mt 1:20). The action mirrors the earlier Annunciation sequence: Joseph is shown lying down, the angel is once again indicated by a bright light and, in response, Joseph stretches his arms upwards towards the messenger as Mary did. The parallel gesture underlines the connection between the couple. The next scene shows Mary and Joseph on the journey to Bethlehem for the census, and confirms that the betrothal has not been broken.

In later films, Joseph's ponderings become a central concern. Pasolini's *The Gospel according to St Matthew* begins with a moment of relationship crisis that is revealed without words. As the film's title indicates, it is Matthew's Gospel (and, consequently, Joseph's viewpoint) that is exploited here. But it is unusual for a cinema audience to witness Joseph's confusion without having already seen the Annunciation and understood the context. Readers of Matthew's Gospel will know by this point that Mary is with child 'through the holy Spirit' but Pasolini's spectators have been given no such background information.

An initial close-up of Mary's unsmiling face from Joseph's perspective is followed by a series of shot/reverse shots that demonstrate the tension between the couple. Mary (Margherita Caruso) lowers her eyes, looking down at her body which is initially off-screen. Another shot of a visibly unhappy Joseph is followed by a shot of Mary that reveals the cause for concern: the first visibly pregnant Mary shown in film.[3] Mary's arms are covered by her veil, so that her obviously pregnant stomach becomes the focus of the audience's gaze and provides one of the director's 'classic reverential compositions' (Fraser 1998: 69). Stéphane Bouquet identifies the influence of the painter Giotto in these early images of the Virgin (2003: 40). Although Pasolini tends to avoid classical symmetrical framing because Christ's arrival in the world makes the ordinary world extraordinary (see Bouquet 2003: 46), the audience is presented here with the calm before the storm.

FIG. 7 Humanity and spirituality in *The Gospel according to St Matthew*

FIG. 8 Pasolini's pregnant Virgin Mary

Margherita Caruso's countenance in this opening scene has elicited a variety of reactions. Naomi Greene maintains that Mary 'is not the pious and luminous Madonna of Renaissance paintings but a very pregnant, bewildered young peasant woman who might well have stepped out of a neo-realist film' (1990: 75). In opposition, Adele Reinhartz claims, 'This Madonna could as easily belong in any church or art museum, so beautiful and expressive is her face. As she stares out at us, and then at her betrothed husband Joseph, we cannot but believe in her purity and spirituality, and we can well imagine why the divine spirit chose her over all other women' (2007: 70). This difference of opinion signifies that Pasolini has done his job well. He has manifested spirituality in the very human young woman of Nazareth.

While Joseph turns and moves away, Mary initially remains stationary with her back to the stone grotto, as if trapped. When she eventually follows Joseph, she stops behind the garden wall, which forms a physical barrier between the couple. In the background, two women appear in a doorway (one is carrying a child as an indication of Mary's future role), but they stand at a distance, offering no comfort to the young girl.

Joseph is seen walking slowly through the empty landscape. Mary's house is set apart from the rest of the community, underlining the impression of her own isolation at this moment. The increasing spatial distance between the couple reflects their emotional separation, and the stone walls along the side of the narrow road symbolise Joseph's refusal to yield. Although Mary's eyes follow Joseph, as if she wishes to maintain the bond between them, he never looks back. At one point Mary humbly lowers her gaze, but then she appears to gather her strength and looks up, continuing to watch Joseph as if refusing to lose hope.

Having reached the village, Joseph watches a group of young boys playing. One child is standing slightly apart in a pale robe, perhaps foreshadowing the 'different' son that Mary will bear. Joseph sits down on the ground, resting his head on his arm against a rock and presumably falling asleep. When he opens his eyes with a start, the children's place has been taken by an androgynous angel dressed in white with shoulder-length hair, who utters the very first dialogue of the film: 'Joseph, fear not to take Mary as your wife for she has conceived by the power of the Holy Ghost. She will bear a son whom you will call Jesus for he is to save his people from their sins.' At these words there is the first shadow of a smile on Joseph's face and the non-diegetic music is triumphant. Greene remarks that 'Pasolini's matter-of-fact style only heightened this believability: for example, the angel who appears "in a dream" in Matthew's text becomes, in the film, a totally real, albeit androgynous, being' (1990: 73). There is a view of Mary's house from the distance and Joseph returns along the same path that he trod earlier. This time the eerie silence that accompanied his abandonment of Mary is replaced by a voice-over reciting the joyful words of the prophet Isaiah: 'the virgin shall be with child and bear a son, and shall name him Immanuel' (Isaiah 7:14).

As discussed in Chapter 1, the prophecy in Isaiah (used by Matthew as a fulfilment citation) is one of the most contested verses in the history of exegesis, with regard to the translation of the original Hebrew as 'virgin' or 'young girl'. Julia Kristeva claims, 'Western Christianity has organised that "translation error", projected its own fantasies into it and produced one of the most powerful imaginary constructs known in the history of civilisations' (1986: 163). Yet, for Christians, the status of Mary as both virgin *and* mother is at the heart of their beliefs. Pasolini does not present any dilemma here. When Mary stands at the top of the steps in *The Gospel according to St Matthew* and Joseph ascends to meet her, she is restored to a position of honour with all doubts alleviated. Mary responds to Joseph's faint smile with an increasingly happier smile that obliterates the need for verbal expression.

Interestingly, while he succeeds in offending the Catholic Church from a whole variety of angles in *Hail Mary*, fellow Marxist Jean-Luc Godard does not shy away from Mary's physical virginity, as Mary's visit to the doctor confirms. This theme is underpinned with the film's repeated use of moon imagery (see Askren 1989), with the full moon betokening the unbroken hymen. Countering the controversial view of some Christians that the virginal conception is a contradiction of the full humanity of Jesus (see Ashley 1985: 493), *Hail Mary* reflects the Lutheran idea of Mary (underlined by the music of Bach on the soundtrack) as an ordinary human being who fulfilled an extraordinary role.

The narrative suspense depends on the rapidity with which Joseph is informed of the fact (and then the origin) of Mary's pregnancy. Zeffirelli creates tension in *Jesus of Nazareth* by interrupting the focus on the Visitation event and returning to Nazareth, where some villagers are commenting to Joseph on Mary's unexpected departure. At the description of Mary as 'a remarkable girl', Joseph looks decidedly pensive, and the interweaving of Joseph's troubled expression into the ongoing Visitation scene increases the sense of apprehension, as the audience is fully aware of the details concerning Mary's absence.[4]

In the extended version of *Jesus of Nazareth*, Mary's anxious question to Elizabeth ('Will he believe me?') is immediately answered in the negative in the following scene. There is a cut to Joseph shaking his head and saying, 'That's too much for any man to believe.' The audience joins a conversation between the betrothed couple (Anne is a silent witness as she was at the Annunciation) after Mary has evidently explained that she is miraculously pregnant. The fact that Joseph has his back to Mary accentuates the atmosphere of rejection. Although she tries to encourage Joseph ('But you're not "any man". You too are chosen'), he maintains a spatial distance on the far side of the room that indicates his feelings: 'I am sick at heart. You're to be my wife. The wedding vow has to be broken.' His response makes him initially a formalist who is concerned for the letter of the law and his personal reputation. Indeed, he puts his hand on Anne's arm and insists: 'I swear I've never been with her.'

In Kowalski's *The Nativity*, Joseph's confusion over the revelation of Mary's pregnancy (the unfinished shell of the marital home that he had been building indicates the uncertain state of his relationship with Mary) is also accentuated by the threat to Mary's life. As his friend Zephora later points out, 'It is a matter, Joseph, of if you love her. On that she'll live or die.' As Mary's father (troubled by doubts himself) explains: 'If you still love her, there must be a room in your heart for trust.'

Joseph's moment of truth also occurs in the open air as did the Annunciation, using natural symbols of divine intervention and no audible angelic message. When he climbs to the top of a hill, breathing heavily, and looks out across the barren landscape, he has a vision of Mary's face in the brightness of the sun. Stumbling back down the hillside, Joseph explains to his friends in one of New Testament films' more romantic declarations: 'I love her! And a place opened up inside me that I never knew. And I saw and I heard and I knew. She *has* conceived by the Holy Spirit and she will have a child. And his name will be Jesus.' Joseph hurries to the door of Mary's house and tells her, 'We'll be married. I've come to take you home,' and he leads his now visibly pregnant fiancée outside, collecting her on a donkey.

The forcefulness of Joseph's reaction varies from one screenplay to another. In Delannoy's *Mary of Nazareth*, Mary offers no explanation of her pregnancy to her parents nor to Joseph, but simply smiles enigmatically at their confusion. (In Kowalski's *The Nativity*, Mary also maintains an outwardly calm confidence, despite her father's distress at her apparent predicament.) Such an approach reflects the biblical exegesis that concludes that the Virgin Mary 'is never portrayed as subject to Joseph or under control of any man, but in a unique way as free from parental and connubial control' (Johnson 1985: 133).

However, while Delannoy's protagonist does not ask any questions ('Not his name, nor where, nor when') in *Mary of Nazareth*, many of the other on-screen Josephs demand clarification.[5] One of the most forceful reactions occurs in Connor's *Mary, mother of Jesus*, in which Joseph's physical aggression against tangible objects in the room is compounded by his final rejection of Mary: 'You are dead to me.'

In *Maria, Daughter of Her Son*, Joseph cries: 'Who did this to you? Who brought this infamy?' believing that someone has taken advantage of her innocence or raped her. Jane Schaberg focused on this possibility in her inflammatory book *The Illegitimacy of Jesus* (1987), in which she examined the ancient heresy that Mary had been raped by a Roman soldier. The subject is addressed in Denys Arcand's *Jesus of Montreal*, where the narrators of the Passion Play recount the rumours of Jesus's illegitimacy as 'the son of Panthera' (one of the reasons that the play is banned by the Catholic authorities within the diegesis).

The danger of assault by the Romans is a central theme in a number of films. The first meeting of the young protagonists in *Mary and Joseph* is at a wedding, whose cheerful musical festivities are cross-cut with shots of approaching Roman soldiers and a more dramatic orchestral soundtrack. When the two narrative lines interweave and the soldiers on horseback burst into the feast, the budding romance between Mary and Joseph is interrupted. Mary has to flee from the attentions of a soldier, thereby allowing Joseph to come to her rescue.

In Mertes's *Joseph of Nazareth*, one of the young women of Nazareth is actually raped by a soldier, giving Joseph the opportunity to speak words of mercy that will later be put to the test when Mary herself becomes pregnant. And the threat receives a tangential allusion in Hardwicke's *The Nativity Story*, when a soldier looks closely at Mary as he rides by; and an explicit reference when Joachim expresses his belief that Mary must have been raped: 'Was it one of Herod's soldiers? Was it?' The legend is also given an oblique nod in *Monty Python's Life of Brian* when Mrs Cohen confesses that Brian's father was a Roman Centurion named Naughtius Maximus (see Lang 2007: 227). Although Brian's mother is evidently *not* the Virgin Mary (the mother of Jesus appearing only briefly in the initial Nativity scene happening next door), she is hailed as the mother of the Messiah ('Behold his mother! [...] Blessed art thou!') by the confused crowds who follow her son by mistake. However, none of the New Testament films enter into heretical territory and the truth of Mary's pregnancy is soon clarified.

SOCIETY'S REACTION (DREAM AND REALITY)

In the shorter version of Zeffirelli's *Jesus of Nazareth*, the audience does not witness the verbal exchange between Mary and Joseph. The action cuts directly to Joseph's conversation with the rabbi, in which the punishment for Mary's apparent sin is clarified: after Joseph has written a bill of repudiation delivered in the presence of two witnesses, Mary will be stoned to death with her supposed 'lover'. According to the Book of Deuteronomy, the law demands that Joseph 'purge the evil from [the community's] midst' (Dt 22:24). However, Zeffirelli's Joseph cannot bear to expose Mary's shame and decides to send her away in secret, as described in Matthew's Gospel. The rabbi's advice is: 'God knoweth the secret of the heart, trust in Him. And accept. Accept it Joseph. The Lord will not abandon you.'

However, a dream sequence is used to visualise the punishment for Mary's purported adultery. The stoning is shot using a red filter – an indication of bloodshed – that distinguishes the scene from 'reality'. When Joseph falls onto the ground and wakes up, he receives an angelic message (this time in the form of a disembodied male voice that is also audible to the audience). Joseph looks towards the empty courtyard and (just as during the earlier Annunciation to Mary) the animal noises reveal that everyday life is continuing during this moment of divine intervention.

The filming of the second stage of the marriage ceremony that subsequently follows is reminiscent of Pasolini's approach in the opening scene of *The Gospel according to St Matthew*. The uneasy relationship between Mary and Joseph is also captured by facial expressions rather than words. When Mary is carried into the celebration, the villagers are enjoying the feast and there is no sign of condemnation of the pregnant bride. However, when Anne lifts her daughter's veil, Mary's smile fades away as she notices her bridegroom's solemn countenance.

Variations on the punishment episode also occur in Connor's *Mary, mother of Jesus*, Hardwicke's *The Nativity Story* and Till's *Mary and Joseph*. In *Mary, mother of Jesus*, Joseph is in bed, with an oil lamp close by his head (the flames evoking the fires of hell as he lies in torment) and he dreams that Mary is being stoned. He utters Mary's name in his sleep and, in his dream, rejects the chance to throw a stone as Mary asks him to 'have faith' and calls his name. His eyes are open as he turns towards the flame and hears a disembodied male voice: 'Joseph, son of David, don't be afraid to take Mary for your wife. Her child is of the Holy Spirit.' Joseph stares into the flame, which may now be reread as the light of illumination and a symbol of the fire of the Holy Spirit.

Playing with the expectations of her audience, Hardwicke leads the spectator to believe that the stoning scene is actually part of the present diegesis in *The Nativity Story*. Joseph is cutting beams of wood and carries his load towards the village (a foreshadowing of Jesus's Crucifixion), where he sees a crowd gathered. While Joseph is a bystander in Zeffirelli's film, Hardwicke's protagonist accepts a stone to cast at Mary. It is at this point that Gabriel (the same actor from the Annunciation scene) intervenes and bars his path, speaking Joseph's name out loud. There is a cut to Joseph lying in bed at night, only now informing the audience that they have been misled and that the event was a dream sequence. The viewers do not hear the whole angelic message, but there is a clear reference to the Holy Spirit. As Joseph sits up, his body covered in beads of sweat, a bird (as already seen in the Annunciation scene) is flying away.

Eric Till's *Mary and Joseph* takes the issue of punishment a stage further by incorporating the actual stoning into the narrative, adapting incidents from the adult life of Jesus in the New Testament to propel the action forward. Mary (who has announced publicly that she is to be the mother of the Messiah) is charged with blasphemy rather than adultery. On the day of the trial there is a storm, which evokes the Good Friday weather conditions (Mk 15:33), and Mary prays for the strength to follow God's will as Jesus did in Gethsemane (Mt 26:39). Mary walks through the jeering crowd (a foretaste of Christ's journey to Calvary that is a staple of New Testament films) with only her mother to support her. The mother of Mary's friend denies that she knows her, which would remind a Christian audience of Peter's rejection of Jesus (Lk 22:54–62). When Mary is condemned to death by stoning, she replies: 'Into God's hands I commit my spirit,' with its Old Testament (Psalm 31:6) and New Testament (Lk 23:46) resonance. The framing ensures that Mary looks very small down in the pit, and the man who initiated the prosecution hesitates 'to cast the first stone' (Jn 8:7). It is at this point that Joseph dons the 'action hero' mantle (which he had previously worn with uneven results) and arrives to accept a punishment (flagellation) in Mary's place. After Joseph has been beaten, Mary holds his injured body in a *pietà* gesture, using her blue veil to bathe his wounds. As the *New York Times* correctly pointed out, the film 'distorts all known Biblical facts surrounding the pre-Nativity' (in Campbell and Pitts 1981: 185).

Even when Joseph himself believes Mary's word and accepts her as his wife, the filmic narratives still consider the wider repercussions on the couple's standing with the community. While Joseph is restored to a position of strength in both *The Nativity Story* and *Mary, mother of Jesus*, his relationship with Mary changes his status within the community, as Mary openly contravenes Galilean law by which 'the wife had to be taken to the husband's home as a virgin' (Brown 1993: 124). Once Mary's pregnancy is visible in *The Nativity Story*, a blue filter is cast over the proceedings to emphasise Mary's ostracisation within Nazareth. When Joseph tells Mary that he will declare her unborn child as his own, Mary reminds him of the tensions that lie ahead ('People... they will not look at you the same. They will not look at us the same'), to which Joseph replies: 'You are my wife, I am your husband. That is all anyone need know.' But at the harvest festivities, the couple receive condemnatory glances from their former friends. When they eventually leave for the journey to Bethlehem, Joseph humorously remarks, 'They'll miss us,' as the villagers will now have to find a new target for their reproach.

Delannoy's Joseph is visibly a cuckold in *Mary of Nazareth* when a noticeably pregnant Mary returns home after her visit to Elizabeth, and the director later makes some play of the fact that Joseph takes a visibly pregnant Mary to his house in full view of the villagers. In *Mary, mother of Jesus*, Mary is also clearly the topic of gossip at the Nazareth market, and when her blue shawl falls down and reveals her pregnant stomach, she meets the reproachful gaze and condemnation of a stall holder ('It's true isn't it? You've been with a man!'). But when the abuse continues and there is a call for Mary to be stoned, Joseph appears (having now been informed in a dream of the true situation) and puts a protective arm around her shoulders. 'Silent! Be silent! Mary is my betrothed. Tomorrow I will make her my wife. Any man or woman who dares say scandal against her – even a whisper – will have to answer to me.' He then walks through the crowd, shielding Mary with his right arm, and takes her to his house. As well as emphasising the 'uprightness' of Joseph, the film illustrates a second issue: 'All gossip aside, by taking Mary into his home, [Joseph] has guaranteed that this child who is not his own will nevertheless be his heir, and if his heir then David's heir, and if David's heir then possibly the Davidic Messiah' (Perry 2006: 57).

CHASTITY

In the biblical setting of Till's *Mary and Joseph* and the twentieth-century environment of Godard's *Hail Mary*, Joseph walks a lengthy path of doubt and renunciation. Till's protagonist initially decides to marry Mary *despite* his belief in her infidelity: 'Please, let me live with you, let me be a father to your child. I don't care what you've done, it doesn't matter any more.' In the re-working of the story into a twentieth-century setting in *Hail Mary*, Godard's Joseph will shout angrily on screen, 'Tell me who you did it with! I don't care, if you stay with me, if I stay with you, sleep with you, wake up with you.' But while Joseph will learn the truth in a dream in *Mary and Joseph* ('Dear God, thank you for saving me. I've been so sinful and so full of pride. Now I know why you have humbled me…'), Godard's Joseph is literally beaten into submission by a return visit from the thuggish Uncle Gabriel. Joseph eventually responds, 'I'll only be your shadow' and 'Yes… I'll sacrifice myself'.

Godard's Joseph in *Hail Mary* suffers from a failure to enter into co-herent dialogue, his first words in the film to Juliette (who is Mary's rival for his affections) being: 'Stop talking', followed by: 'Can't you see I'm not listening?' But his subsequent comments lead into one of the key themes of the film: Mary's chastity and Joseph's sexual frustration. The first time that the audience sees Mary and Joseph together is during the Annunciation at the petrol station, when the shot of the traffic signal turning from green to red will indicate that Mary is now off limits to Joseph.

Most controversially, Godard breaks with the artistic tradition in which the sole access to the body of the Virgin Mary is a glimpse of the breast – a tradition to which New Testament film directors have constantly adhered. The filming of the actress's naked body in *Hail Mary* not only 'touches the raw nerve that female sexuality represents for patriarchal religion' (Mulvey 1993: 39–40) but simultaneously epitomises patriarchy's traditional mastery of the gaze. Consequently, some of the customary tools that are used for an analysis of the female body on screen (which would normally be inappropriate for a study of the Virgin Mary) came into play in critical reviews.

Godard stresses that he 'was trying to make the audience see not a naked woman, but flesh, if that's at all possible' (in Dieckmann 1993: 120). But that comment presents one of the film's problematics. Joseph's frustration and Mary's suffering lead to a focus upon the carnality of her struggle, making the very sexuality that is renounced the object of vision. The use of high-angled shots of Mary as God/Godard's victim, visualise Mary's lament: 'I am a soul imprisoned by a body.'

Therefore, Godard's avowed interest in flesh leads his protagonist to focus on the giving of her body to God and turns Mary's virginity into a purely physical concept. The outwardly radical approach to the biblical narrative is transformed into an ultimately reductive treatment of both the female protagonist and the Incarnation narrative. Laura Mulvey argues that 'the camera, essentially destined to be voyeur rather than lover, has unlimited access to the carnal joy of the image' (1993: 39). Yet the image is frequently joyless – a fact underlined by Mary's vocalised resentment: 'God is a vampire who suffered me in him... because I suffered and He didn't, and He profited from my pain.' A struggle might be perfectly feasible, given that a sacred vow of virginity should allow 'the soul to reign fully over the body and live a spiritual life in complete peace and freedom' (Go 1976: 16). But the visualisation and interpretation of that struggle in Godard's film runs wholly counter to the Catholic vision of Mary as a uniquely immaculate individual.

A fusion of images of Mary's body with projections of nature in *Hail Mary* may promote a vision of the Marian cult in which the Virgin Mary is not an icon divided from her flesh, but a person who is 'linked, like every woman, and much more than any other, to the procreation and mystery of life' (Bingemer 1991: 105). However, when Mary proclaims:

'I rejoiced in giving my body to the eyes ... of Him who has become my Master forever,' and glanced at this wondrous being,' her celibacy is not a private vow to God. Mary shuts the bathroom door on Joseph's vision of her nakedness, but the camera follows inside and turns her moment of private contemplation into another physical performance. The spiritual dimension is lost as Mary/Myriem Roussel writhes on her bed, for she is the servant of Godard rather than any Supreme Being, and the power relations are mortal rather than divine: 'More than ever the essential question has become that of the attack in and on the shot, of the body of the film reduced here to its simplest and most naked expression, that of the actress's body simultaneously offered and refused' (see Bellour and Bandy 1992: 69).

There is relevance here in the fact that *Hail Mary* developed from aborted projects on incest (in which Godard would have played the father and Myriem Roussel his daughter) and on the Freud/Dora relationship. Rather than drawing on the uniqueness of the Virgin Mary's place in sacred history and her position as Mother/Daughter of God and Bride of Christ, thereby actualising 'the threefold metamorphosis of a woman in the tightest parenthood structure' (Kristeva 1986: 169),[6] the female protagonist of *Hail Mary* comes to epitomise what Mulvey describes as the 'despairing obsession with the enigma of femininity' and the split between feminine beauty 'and either deceitful or mysteriously unknowable essence' that has been a recurrent theme in Godard's films since Patricia's betrayal of Michel in *Breathless* (see Mulvey 1993: 40–1).

Godard's preference for collage is seen in his borrowing of dialogue from Catholic playwright Paul Claudel's *The Tidings Brought to Mary* (the definitive version being first staged in 1948). Claudel's play, which was filmed by Alain Cuny under the English title *The Annunciation to Marie* (1991), offers a perspective on the Annunciation story that sets out the Mariological issues of power and sacrifice, and the awakened interest in Mary as an active participant in the plan of salvation rather than an empty vessel/vassal. The setting is medieval France and the play tells the story of a young woman named Violaine (played in the film by Ulrika Jonsson) who sacrifices her own happiness to save her sister from suicide, and later undergoes a metaphorical virgin birth on Christmas Eve.

There are obvious parallels in the interaction between Claudel's protagonists Violaine and Jacques (in Act II, Scene 3) and Joseph and Mary (in shots 144–47 of *Hail Mary*), where the discussion hinges upon questions of possession and jealousy:

The Tidings brought to Mary	*Hail Mary*
Jacques: I do not understand, Violaine.	Joseph: I don't understand, I don't understand, Mary.
Violaine: My beloved, do not force me to tell you my great secret.	Mary: It's a big secret.
Jacques: A great secret, Violaine ?	
Violaine: So great that all is consumed, and you will not ask me to marry you any more. [...]	Joseph: My love...
Violaine: Why do you want to marry me? Why do you want to take for yourself what belongs only to God? The hand of God is upon me, and you cannot defend me!	Mary: We don't know how to say it. So immense that all is consumed and you'll leave me. [...]
	Mary: Know what? The hand of God is upon me and you can't interfere.

(Claudel 1965: 172 [My translation])

The women may be in a servant's role, but the protection of 'the hand of God' frees them from male authority, leaving Jacques and Joseph as impotent figures in the divine plan with opposing reactions to their situation. In both the Cuny and the Godard films, the men are reduced to the passive, uncomprehending role in the face of the 'great secret' to which they are not privy. De Beauvoir's criticism of Claudel's female characters is that the woman is the instrument of salvation for the man, without the act being reciprocated (1949: 364); but the woman's role also supports the theory that the religious principle is 'expressed through woman, through the *anima*. [...] Man had no share in the Incarnation as a male element, only woman was involved, through Mary' (Beaumont 1968: 94–5).

Both directors present female characters whose ascendancy comes at a price, as indicated by Mary's repression of her physical desires in *Hail Mary*: 'It will always be horrible for me to be the Master, but, there'll be no more sexuality in me.' Salvation is bought at the cost of sacrifice in *Hail Mary* and *The Annunciation to Marie*. Literal martyrdom is freely accepted in the case of Violaine. Physical chastity is reluctantly borne by Godard's Mary.

Jacques and Joseph reach out to touch the flesh of their virginal partners in each film, seeking confirmation of their emotional exclusiveness. However, both discover that the female body has become the guarded temple of the sacred. In Cuny's film, Violaine's admirer Pierre de Craon asks, 'Who are you, young girl, and what part in you has God reserved to himself, that the hand which touches you with fleshly desire should that same instant be withered, as if it had approached the mystery of his dwelling place?' And these words evoke one of the notably controversial scenes in *Hail Mary*, when Mary remains both the vassal and the vessel as the Lord's handmaiden, whose half-naked body is the object of the camera.

In the relevant scene in *Hail Mary*, which is set in a bedroom, Joseph reaches out towards Mary's naked stomach in a gesture of possession that is rebuffed verbally by Mary. At the sudden reappearance of the brutish Gabriel, Joseph is physically forced into submission. But he gradually comes to understand that love is expressed by non-possession and the withdrawing of his hand from Mary's body. When Jacques renounces Violaine at the realisation that he cannot possess her fully in *The Annunciation to Marie*, the medieval mysticism and biblical tones do not disguise the selfish heart of Jacques in Cuny's film. Godard's film stands in contrast, for the very act of non-possession becomes Joseph's demonstration of love. Unfortunately, Godard succeeds in obscuring the Christian message by focusing the camera on Mary's naked body.

The scene in *Hail Mary* contrasts markedly with an analogous episode in Jean Delannoy's *Mary of Nazareth*, shot in the open air in the sunlight.

Fig. 9 The bond between Mary and Joseph in *Mary of Nazareth*

When Joseph learns the truth of the virginal conception in *Mary of Nazareth*, he walks towards Mary through the stream in which she is washing clothes. Joseph kneels down in the water before Mary, underlining the act of reverence, and Mary touches her pregnant stomach and then Joseph's hands, symbolising the bond between the couple and the child she carries in her womb.

EVER VIRGIN

While Mary Daly underlines the fact that a female virgin 'is being defined merely by what she does *not* do sexually – which is still a kind of inverse sexual and relational definition,' the acceptance that 'a virgin is not defined exclusively by her relationship with men' (1986: 84 [emphasis in original]) leads to the ambivalent reaction of feminist theologians to the status of virginity. Theories about the freedom and power of virginity are adopted in certain versions of liberation Mariology, where Mary appears to escape earthly male authority, echoing the view of St Thomas Aquinas that the woman who is consecrated to God is 'freed from subordination to men' and 'immediately united with Christ' (see Ranke-Heinemann 1990: 190).

In Matthew's Gospel, it is stated that Joseph did not have sexual relations with Mary 'until she bore a son' (Mt 1:25). Mary remained 'ever virgin' in the opinion of Catholic theologians, but Protestant exegetes argue that this verse infers that the couple enjoyed conjugal relations after the birth of Jesus. Debates over the grammatical use of 'until' continue. Perry claims 'that Matthew's point is not to allude to Mary and Joseph's assumption of a normal sexual relationship after Jesus's birth, but to explicitly affirm one of chastity prior to it. It thus reemphasises that Jesus can in no way be biologically connected to Joseph' (2006: 57).

The term *Josephite* now relates to a marriage in which the 'spouses voluntarily and for supernatural motives follow the precedent of Mary and Joseph in practising total abstinence, either from the beginning or only later' (Pelikan 1996: 122). Catholic theologians regard the marriage of Mary and Joseph as a true marriage even though it was not consummated. St Augustine considered such a marriage as the ideal expression of continence and the best expression of love between a husband and wife (see Warner 1990: 77). The image of a woman who 'was worthy of [...] love precisely because she was too pure to reciprocate it' became a symbol of courtly love in the Middle Ages (Warner 1990: 137).

The Catholic view that Mary remained 'ever virgin' is generally not actively contested in New Testament films. La Marre's *Color of the Cross* and Serge Moati's French TV movie *Jésus* (1999)[7] are notable exceptions, for Jesus's siblings play a visible role; and the final scene in *Hail Mary*, in which Mary puts on the red lipstick that she had earlier rejected, may be an indication that she has now renounced her virginal state. However, it is uncommon for explicit reference to be made to Mary's perpetual virginity and to Joseph's attendant personal sacrifice: 'I'll stay. I'll never touch you', says Godard's protagonist.

Therefore, it is notable that this issue becomes the focus in Costa's *Maria, Daughter of Her Son* in a rare 'bedroom scene'. The moonlight through the small window bathes the marital bed in cold white light (a reminder of Mary's virginal status) and Mary is also dressed in white. Mary kisses Joseph on the lips and lies down with her back towards him to go to sleep. When Joseph leans on his elbow and reaches out to touch her, she puts the back of her hand against his mouth, saying 'no'. When Joseph asks for forgiveness, Mary responds: 'No, I'm the one to beg your pardon. I love you but I just can't… It seems that I can be nothing more than a mother. I feel that I'm consecrated to my son. Do you understand?' While Joseph (who has already shown his befuddlement at the Annunciation, wandering around in the dark shouting, 'Lord, I am confused!') admits that he finds it 'a little too complicated,' he continues: 'I love you. And this is the way I have to prove it. The only way,' and he accepts his celibate role. There is only one other occasion, when he is troubled by the actions of the young Jesus, that he cries out in frustration, 'I have a wife who's not my wife at all! I have a son who's not my son!' Nevertheless, on his deathbed, he tells Mary: 'My love will be yours forever, forever. You know, Mary, I can't complain, I have no regrets. The Lord has been good.' As Christopher O'Donnell makes clear, Scripture does not reveal whether Joseph would have wanted to have children by the mother of the Messiah, 'but merely to raise the question brings us into wider considerations of spirituality' (2007a: 31–2). Costa is one of the few directors prepared to raise those wider considerations.

UNIQUENESS

The birth of a child without male assistance is regarded as the most matriarchal of images. One feminist response to the Annunciation has been to laud the *absence* of a mortal father and use this fact to promote the significance of a woman in the plan of Salvation. Nor is this view attributed only to a second-wave feminist response to Mary's liberation. The belief that Mary was not under the authority of any man (meaning her husband) was expressed by Pseudo-Augustine in the 11th century, *De Assumptione*, c4, PL 1143, and this was a theme taken up by Thomas Aquinas in the *Summa theologica 3*, q30, a1, ad2 (see Laurentin 1989: 100).

In *Woman and the Salvation of the World*, Paul Evdokimov reports that 'the giving birth of the *Theotokos, without a human father*, also announces the end of the kingdom of the male, the end of Patriarchy' (1994: 203 [emphasis in original]). Consequently, some Christian feminists see the virginal conception of Jesus as an act of resistance against patriarchal society, following the line that Mary's virginity in her motherhood means that 'she achieved her full realization as a person *independent* of any man' (Ashley 1985: 543 [emphasis in original]).

Godard's *Hail Mary* is inspired by psychoanalyst Françoise Dolto's *L'Évangile au risque de la psychanalyse* (see Laugier 1993: 27–38), which reminds the reader that fatherhood is not restricted to the moment of conception – it takes 'three seconds to be a begetter'– but represents a lifelong commitment to the child (Dolto 1977: 25). Yet Godard's outwardly controversial approach to the New Testament, with scenes of a half-naked Mary in conversation with Joseph ('the familiar Godard sulking adolescents' (Warren 1993: 11)), succeeds in undercutting the distinctive dimension to the Marian narrative.

It is easy to strip away the biblical elements from Mary's narrative and still retain a discernible storyline: a young woman experiences an unplanned pregnancy and, although her boyfriend knows that he is not the father, he decides to marry her and they raise the child together. Ralph Howard and Katharina Otto make that fact explicit in the parodic *The Second Greatest Story Ever Told* when Joey and Mary (the latter dressed coincidentally in the Papal colours of yellow and white) sit on a park bench in 1960s Brooklyn and discuss their relationship. Joey is the hesitant, humble suitor ('I realise that I'm no Montgomery Clift') with a plea for acceptance ('But I'm going to have the best prefabricated home construction business in Brooklyn') and an eye on gender equality ('Not that I wouldn't respect your career goal. I think a woman's place is any place she wants.'). When Mary confesses that she is pregnant and affirms that the father is 'up there,' pointing awkwardly at the sky, Joey naturally assumes that the man is dead. After a pause for commiseration, Joey says, 'Mary, you know, I would be proud to raise your baby with you, if you'll have me. I'm really not good at the initial stages. I need a chance to show you. I really do love you, Mary, so much, so much.' As he takes her hand, the sound of Bing Crosby singing the song 'True Love' becomes the accompaniment.

Clearly, the issues of trust raised in the New Testament story have echoes in human relationships that reach beyond the confines of the Bible, as the attempt to reconfigure the story within a contemporary setting indicates. But the life of Mary and Joseph does not simply create a plot in which a kindly man generously accepts the role of stepfather in unusual circumstances. Rejecting the binary opposites that reign in patriarchal society, Mary's virginal motherhood is 'an affirmation that in Christ opposites are reconciled without loss of distinction' (Beattie 2002: 125). To rework the narrative simply in line with traditional sexual power relations, as Godard does in *Hail Mary*, is to undermine its uniqueness.

As Dolto points out in *L'Évangile au risque de la psychanalyse*, 'the human density of every couple is found in the story of the couple formed by Joseph and Mary. But, in return, this extraordinary couple helps us to discover the depth of any encounter between an ordinary man and woman' (1977: 26 [my translation]). The problem is how to demonstrate on film that Mary and Joseph form an *extraordinary* couple, as Dolto rightly indicates. Their marriage not only rises above the common relationship problems of possession, phallocracy and dependence (see Dolto 1977: 24), but it also creates the human family into which the Son of God was born.

CHAPTER 4

virgin and mother

By transposing events from the Infancy Narratives and apocryphal passages onto the screen, directors encounter theological issues with a Marian dimension. The traditionally impoverished status of Mary and Joseph links to liberation theology; and the birth of Jesus raises questions about Incarnation theology and the second Marian dogma of the Perpetual Virginity. While every woman influences the course of history by bringing a child into the world, Mary has a unique place because of the world-changing importance of the birth of her son.

Bruce Babington and Philip Evans argue that 'the greatest constraint on the Hollywood Christ narrative is its requirement at least formally to accept Christ's divinity' (1993: 99). But Christ's divinity is not a 'constraint' but rather the impetus of the narrative, without which the New Testament is reduced to the biography of a prophetic man of peace. The same questions confront all filmmakers, regardless of the scale of the budget, and ranging from George Stevens's 'wonderful failure' (see Lang 2007: 169) *The Greatest Story Ever Told* to independent productions such as Mark Dornford-May's *Son of Man*, struggling to gain recognition via film festivals.[1]

The Nativity scene provides an opportunity for filmmakers to reflect the human/divine interconnection, with the virgin birth, angelic announcement to the shepherds, the visit of the Magi, and the shining star. There are a small number of films in which the birth of Jesus forms the climax, as the title often indicates (*The Nativity, Mary and Joseph, The Nativity Story*); and in the Life of Christ films that omit the Annunciation, the Nativity is the initial event that launches the action. A number of feminist commentators have pointed to apparent contradictions within the Marian cult, arguing that some Christian women have abandoned 'a virgin-mother model that seems to make no sense' (Donnelly 1994: 107–8). But Anne Carr has argued that Mary's virgin motherhood 'need not be understood as an impossible double bind, an inimitable ideal, but as a central Christian symbol that signifies autonomy *and* relationship, strength *and* tenderness, struggle *and* victory, God's power *and* human agency – not in competition but cooperation' (in Donnelly 1994: 108 [emphasis in original]). The Nativity setting remains one of the richest sources of inspiration for theological and artistic reflection on the significance of Mary within the New Testament narrative.

JOURNEY TO BETHLEHEM

> *In those days a decree went out from Caesar Augustus that the whole world should be enrolled. This was the first enrolment, when Quirinius was governor of Syria. So all went to be enrolled, each to his own town. And Joseph too went up from Galilee from the town of Nazareth to Judea, to the city of David that is called Bethlehem, because he was of the house and family of David, to be enrolled with Mary, his betrothed, who was with child.* (Lk 2:1–5)

From the days of silent cinema onwards, Mary and Joseph have travelled on screen to Bethlehem for the Nativity, a distance described variously in films as a four-day trip (*Mary and Joseph*) or a hundred miles (*The Nativity Story*) to complete a census whose precise existence is now generally discounted by historians (see Perry 2006: 81).[2] It is the destination that is usually more important than the trek. As Joseph clarifies in *Jesus of Nazareth*, the location of the birth relates to the Messianic prophecy in the Book of Micah (Mi 5:1). Sometimes the journey is covered perfunctorily on foot (as in *The Life and Passion of Jesus Christ* and *Mater Dei*). In many cases, it passes relatively swiftly via the editing. Mary and Joseph usually appear in extreme long shot as solitary figures against an immense vista (in Ray's *King of Kings*, for example), frequently in a desert setting and often cross-cut with the voyage of the Magi.

In addition to giving the Magi a comedic incarnation in *The Nativity Story*, Catherine Hardwicke took a fresh approach by markedly expanding the 'road movie' aspect and devoting a third of her film to Mary and

Joseph's own pilgrimage of faith. The extended journey allows the relationship between the couple to develop, and they confess mutual fears that both reflect and exceed those of any prospective parent. Sharing a fish by the Sea of Galilee (without realising the future significance of that location or its food supply for the ministry of their unborn child), they wonder how to cope with their miraculous baby. Mary worries, 'Do you ever wonder when we'll know? When he's more than just a child... Will it be something he says, a look in his eye?' Joseph adds, 'I wonder if I will even be able to teach him anything.'

Mary's admiration for her husband grows as she observes his courage and generosity (he secretly goes hungry for her sake); and she bathes his bloodstained feet in a foretaste of her future maternal role, although the Crucifixion lies beyond the film's diegesis. During the trip, a fortune teller reads Mary's palm and makes a prediction about her pregnancy ('You carry him like a son. To see yourself in a young face, there is no greater joy'),[3] and Mary clasps Joseph's hand, knowing that the words will hurt him because he is not the baby's father. When Joseph later asks God to bolster his spirits ('If I am doing your will, I pray you, give me a sign'), his prayer seems to be heard only by the audience. But the astrological signs followed by the Magi are visible behind him in the night sky, offering an indication of the divine blessing that he seeks.

The perils in the path of Mary and Joseph attempt to add a dramatic tension not found in the two verses that describe the journey in Luke's Gospel (Lk 2:4–5). Indeed, such tension is difficult to inject, given that most viewers know the outcome of the events. Nevertheless, the moment of imagined potential disaster, when Mary is almost swept away by the waters of the river Jordan in Hardwicke's film, also offers a theological message. As it is a snake that causes the danger by unnerving the donkey, Mary survives a visible confrontation with a manifestation of the Devil that links her and her unborn baby to the verse of Genesis 3:15 – a theme that Mel Gibson also explores in *The Passion of the Christ*.

NO ROOM AT THE INN

While they were there, the time came for her to have her child, and she gave birth to her firstborn son. She wrapped him in swaddling clothes and laid him in a manger, because there was no room for them in the inn. (Lk 2:6–7)

By filling in gaps in the biblical text, screenwriters imagine the various events and emotions that lie behind the short verses that Luke provides. The popular image of the stable traditionally serves as the backdrop for the Nativity, emphasising the poverty of the scene that finds an echo in Latin American liberation theology, where 'Mary is not only the glorious Mother of God, but also the Mother of all men, the Advocate of the Poor, a Woman of the People, who has known, with the People, suffering and oppression' (Codina in Margerie 1987: 48).

The exact location of Jesus's birth continues to trouble biblical historians, with discussions over Palestinian ethnography leading to disputes over whether Jesus was born in a cave or main family dwelling room (see, for example, Tilby 2001: 6–8). However, a belief in the lowly surroundings is generally maintained because Luke specifically states that Jesus was laid in a manger. LaVerdiere points out that in ancient Palestine 'mangers were usually made of stone, either freestanding or hewn from the bedrock. Jesus's manger could have been in an open courtyard, corral, a kind of stable, or in a cave' (2007: 48).

The Greek word *katalyma* 'refers to a place of hospitality for people on a journey' and the translation of this noun as 'inn' may be 'too restrictive unless the context calls for it' (LaVerdiere 2007: 52–3). Nevertheless, Nativity scenes from *The Life and Passion of Jesus Christ* onwards often feature an unwelcoming innkeeper who rejects Joseph and Mary and, therefore, her unborn child. In Delannoy's *Mary of Nazareth*, Mary asks, 'O Lord, where are you? Why do you leave us alone on this winter's night?'; and in Hardwicke's *The Nativity Story*, a crane shot of Joseph, holding Mary in his arms, reveals their isolation and vulnerability when they can find no shelter in Bethlehem.

Throughout film history, Joseph's failure to find a room at the inn has been met by Mary's quiet acceptance of their situation. Here there is a focus on what Bertrand de Margerie describes as the 'Divine Motherhood in the concrete and historical form that God has given to it: inside a small, despised people, the people of Israel, in poverty and in insignificance, in a marginalized powerlessness' (1987: 50).

Schalom Ben-Chorin notes that the New Testament Nativity story reminds him of Jewish mothers throughout the ages who have given birth in exile or in concentration camps (2001: 91). When Ray's *King of Kings* opens with the portentous (uncredited) voice of Orson Welles introducing the theme of crucifixion under Herod's reign, the pile of Jewish corpses may well remind the viewer of the Holocaust.

Indeed, in writing the script of *Mary of Nazareth*, Jean Delannoy linked his film to twentieth-century history, claiming that the story transcends its biblical time frame and has resonance for contemporary homeless couples, as well as any man who weds an unmarried mother and embraces the child as his own. He goes on to compare the New Testament setting with the situation of the Jews in World War II, identifying Berlin as Rome and Hitler as Caesar (Delannoy 1998: 245). In his study of the Virgin Mary, Jaroslav Pelikan asks whether there 'would have been an Auschwitz, if every Christian church and every Christian home had focused its devotion on icons of Mary not only as the Mother of God and Queen of Heaven, but as the Jewish maiden and the new Miriam?' (in Cunneen 1996: 58).

St Francis of Assisi played an important role in developing the traditional image of the Christmas crib, with the ox and the ass being part of the Franciscan legacy dating back to 1223. Consequently, there is generally a call for animal wranglers on the sets of Nativity films, which adds to the complications. Catherine Hardwicke remarked: 'Being there, it felt very gritty. We had all the real animals right there in the cave, in the grotto with us. They didn't care about the filmmaking process' (in Lytal 2006). Perry points out that Christmas card nativities do not reveal 'how noisy this scene is' (2006: 83) but films also often play down this feature. In Ray's *King of Kings*, shots of the lambs, oxen and donkey are accompanied by gentle non-diegetic music that drowns out any raucous animal sounds. Nor can films (without the benefit of 'odorama') fully convey the aroma of the scene. Anyone who has experienced a 'Living Christmas Crib' (in which live animals add to the authenticity of the *tableau vivant*) will testify to the pungent smells. When Mary looks around the stable in Delannoy's *Mary of Nazareth* and claims, 'My son could not have wanted a more beautiful palace for the place of his birth,' she is both leaving Joseph out of the picture with her use of the possessive adjective (as Mary initially does in Kowalski's *The Nativity*) and taking a very optimistic approach to their situation.

The focus on the human woman of Nazareth also links with aspects of liberation Mariology, in which the domesticated handmaiden is reassessed as a woman of courage who survives personal trials, leading to the writing of feminist litanies in which Mary is addressed 'as unwed mother, refugee woman with child, widow, and mother of a son executed as a common criminal' (Johnson 1985: 130).[4] Codina claims that the Second Vatican Council of the 1960s was more interested in the ecumenical dialogue with Protestants than with devotion to the Virgin Mary. But he stresses that post-conciliar Mariology regards Mary as 'the sign and sacrament of the motherly mercy of God towards the Poor, of the tenderness of God who loves and defends the Poor' (in Margerie 1987: 49). Although the film's time frame ensures that the female protagonist of *Mary of Nazareth* is not a material model for contemporary Western Catholics, she embodies the view of Mary of the New Testament as 'a universal model on the level of her deep commitment in faith to God's will' (Sean 1969: 35). Rather than focusing upon the privileges of Mary, this is a vision that embraces the Holy Family as a part of humanity. The material poverty of the Christmas crib scene is 'the outward sign of the metaphysical poverty of the assumed human nature. Without losing the riches of the divinity, God the Son takes on our humanity with all the limitations intrinsic to what is created and bodily' (Saward 2002: 162).

THE VIRGIN BIRTH

One of the most delicate questions for directors (at least if they are respectful of Catholic sensibilities) comes in the staging of the birth itself. Evidently, there are issues of sensitivity to consider in the filming of any birth, let alone that of the Messiah. Indeed, in the days of the Hollywood Production Code, birth scenes were strictly banned.[5] But in the case of Mary, there are additional theological matters to examine. Does Mary suffer labour pains? How does a filmmaker take into account the human/divine nature of Jesus at the Nativity?

In the first millennium, when the Church was faced with the threats posed by Docetism (which refused to acknowledge the full humanity of Jesus) and Arianism (which denied the full divinity of Jesus), the virgin birth confirmed the humanity and divinity of Christ and 'was the key to orthodox Christology' (Warner 1990: 64).

In the apocryphal *Protevangelium of James*, Mary says, 'Joseph, take me down from the she-ass, for the child within me presses me to come forth' (in Elliott 1993: 64), indicating that she is in discomfort, and Joseph goes away to find a midwife. However, when he returns, the cloud that had overshadowed the cave where Mary lay disappeared 'and a great light appeared, so that our eyes could not bear it. A short time afterwards that light withdrew until the baby appeared, and it came and took the breast of its mother Mary' (in Elliott 1993: 64). The details of the birth itself are bathed in a mysterious light.

However, the theology of Mary's *in partu* virginity, as symbolised by the unbroken hymen in the apocryphal *Protevangelium of James*, was not supported by all the Church Fathers. Tertullian, for example, maintained that 'there is no nativity without flesh, and no flesh without nativity' (see Beattie 2007: 97). Pelikan argues that the apocryphal works 'may implicitly have represented as well a hesitancy to ascribe total humanity to her divine Son' and that the Gnostics had asserted 'that Jesus had not been "born" of the Virgin Mary in the usual sense at all, but had "passed through Mary as water runs through a tube," not only without birth pangs but without the involvement of the mother except in a purely passive sense' (1996: 47–8).

Within this equation, the virginal body represents wholeness and, consequently, holiness. Critics of the Marian cult point to the identification of women with the dangers of sexual conduct, stressing that Mary's virginity 'has functioned to impede the integration of women's sexuality into the goal of wholeness' (Johnson 1985: 128). Uta Ranke-Heinemann claims that if Mary is the *mater inviolata*, all other mothers must be considered '*matres violatae*', women who have been in some way 'desecrated' by maternity (1990: 345). In fact, some Catholic women have preferred to drop the titles 'Mother inviolate and Mother undefiled' from the official Marian Litany of praise because they consider 'the implications of such invocations insulting' (Cunneen 1996: 286). The Catholic Church has been criticised for assuming 'that natural bodily processes are not worthy of the Creator, as if womb and breasts, flesh and bleeding are outside the sphere of the sacred' (Johnson 2003: 277).

This factor is particularly notable in the comparisons made between Marian devotion and the worship of the ancient mother-goddesses, where Mary has been denounced as 'the very antithesis of the fruitfulness borne by her predecessors' and not a symbol of 'the prestige of real women which seems to have coexisted with the lauding of the goddesses of fertility in a period of complementarity' (Haskins 1993: 53). In their investigation into theology and film, Deacy and Williams Ortiz maintain that natural female functions have been 'long connected with negative concepts of flesh, the earth, physicality that subordinate women in religious, cultural and social contexts' (2008: 101).

Until the 1970s, filmmakers responded to such issues with a relatively consistent approach. The location of the birth was a stable, albeit of varying size and comfort; Mary was tired but not in labour pain; and no exact details about the delivery of the baby were presented. However, *The Life and Passion of Jesus Christ* offers the clearest example of a supernatural birth. Mary and Joseph kneel in prayer in the stable, and Joseph's hands are raised and open as if to receive a gift. Through the wonders of stop motion, the baby appears miraculously in the manger. There is a slight time delay before Mary and Joseph realise that the baby has arrived but they then express joy in their faces and body language. Mary does not immediately touch the baby but continues to pray by the manger. Such a representation would seem to offer an argument for the divinity of Jesus rather than his humanity. But when Mary holds up her naked son to be adored by the assembled crowd in a subsequent scene, the baby's humanity is clearly recognised.

Interestingly, another film that offers such a wondrous birth is the Indian evangelical film *Dayasagar*. While there are elements of a normal pregnancy (Mary is visibly in pain), the birth itself defies natural laws. As there is no room at the inn, Mary lies down in straw in a stable in the conventional manner of Christmas Nativity scenes. But when Joseph looks up to the heavens and sees a star, a bright beam of yellow light shoots forth from the star towards the earth – and at the end of the beam there is a baby. Joseph strokes Mary's forehead and they both smile, to the accompaniment of 'Silent Night' on the soundtrack.

These two examples from 1905 and 1978 are very unusual filmic approaches to the Nativity. In most cases, the birth happens off-screen. The shift of focus may be horizontal to another event in the world outside (the arrival of the shepherds or the Magi) or vertical (to the shining star, with its heavenly connotations). In *From the Manger to the Cross*, Mary and Joseph are lying down in a stable, with Mary in the foreground and the empty manger on the left of the screen. Joseph is asleep but Mary's eyes are open, as if she is waiting. As she closes her eyes, there is a cut to the shepherds, and then the audience is told that Mary 'brought forth her first-born son, and wrapped him in swaddling clothes, and laid him in a manger' via the intertitle. The birth itself is not visualised. In the following scene the baby is sleeping peacefully in the manger with Mary and Joseph at his side. Their hands are crossed across their chests in a similar gesture of reverent humility.

While Ray deals with the matter via voice-over in *King of Kings* ('Now, when this Holy Child was born in Judea, three Wise Men came from the East'), George Stevens also avoids the act of childbirth. Baugh describes Stevens's Nativity scene as tender and static, in the *style sulpicien* of holy cards (1997: 29) and points out the main intention is not to offend. The film's first image is of a fresco of Christ (with the face of Max von Sydow) on the ceiling of a chapel. Von Sydow's voice announces: 'I am he' and the opening verses of John's Gospel are intoned by a narrator. At the words:

'And the life was the light of men,' an image of a star turns into a flame, which introduces the line: 'And the darkness lasted not.' A shadowy figure carries a lighted candle through a stable, and then a baby's cry is heard. There is a shot of an infant's hand and forearm as the narrator says: 'The greatest story ever told.' The actual birth of the 'Word made flesh' remains oblique.

However, Christian art countered this tendency to ignore the humanity of Jesus 'by its portrayals of the pregnant Mary' (Pelikan 1996: 48), and this aspect gradually became a feature of New Testament feature films, with Pasolini's young virgin leading the way in *The Gospel according to St Matthew*. There are also paintings of *Madonna lactans*, in which Mary nurses her child at the breast, an image that receives particular attention in Veronesi's *For Love, Only For Love* and Delannoy's *Mary of Nazareth*. The fact that a virgin would not normally produce milk is an additional theological danger zone.

The virginal birth of Jesus is also recorded in the Koran. Mary 'retired to a far-off place. And when she felt the throes of childbirth she lay down by the trunk of a palm-tree, crying: "Oh, would that I had died before this and passed into oblivion!"' (19:22). In Bohrani's film *The Saint Mary*, Mary verbalises her anguish and then her pain is manifested by the close-up shot of her hand grasping at a date tree, while her cries are audible. Her own cry is overlaid by a baby's cry. The camera pans upwards and to the left towards the daytime sky. (In Christian filmic Nativity scenes, the same effect is usually represented by a shot of the star in the night sky.) God comes to Mary's aid with words of comfort: 'Do not despair. Your Lord has provided a brook that runs at your feet, and if you shake the trunk of the palm-tree it will drop fresh ripe dates in your lap.'[6] There is no Joseph to support Mary in the Koran and she is reliant on God alone. Mary's isolation is depicted in the wide vistas of a desert landscape in the sunlight that are a noticeable contrast to the darker enclosed space of the traditional Christian stable.

Although there are some post-1970 films that avoid the issue of labour pains, they are markedly different in style. In Kowalski's *The Nativity*, Mary says specifically that she does not feel pain.[7] Therefore, despite the earlier reference to Mary as 'disobedient', the Nativity scene is in keeping with Catholic doctrine. Although Mary is in slight discomfort during the journey in *The Jesus Film*, the prologue does not present the birth itself and the 'school Nativity play' tone is maintained when Mary and Joseph are next seen with Jesus in the stable.

Notably, the re-workings also avoid the birth scene. In *Hail Mary*, there are images of a snowy countryside[8] and a donkey (which may also remind the audience of Robert Bresson's *Au hasard Balthazar* (1966)), but no direct depiction of the birth event. It is remarkable that Godard circumvented at least one controversial issue when he had already embraced so many. In Howard and Otto's parody *The Second Greatest Story Ever Told*, Jake ('Jesus's little brother') is born at Christmas. A van delivering crisps from the 'Wise' food company pulls up outside the house and three men carry large containers of products up the steps to the front door, which is illuminated by an electric light in the shape of a star. They join the group of friends and family gathered around Mary and her baby. Although a mysterious glow emanates from the mother and child, Joseph maintains a sense of earthly normality by standing at their side with a cigar behind his ear as the proud father.

Francisco Suárez claimed that the 'troublesome weariness with which all pregnant women are burdened, she alone did not experience who alone conceived without pleasure' (in Warner 1990: 43). However, rather than portraying this more ethereal Virgin, the on-screen Marys from the 1970s (including Mary of the Koran in *The Saint Mary*) usually suffer during the journey while heavily pregnant and cry out in pain during their labour.

Zeffirelli's *Jesus of Nazareth* is the first to make a compromise between Mary's discernible labour pain and a birth whose mystery remains hidden. When Joseph helps Mary from the donkey and she rests by a pillar, she is clearly in pain, indicating the kind of natural birth that had previously been circumnavigated in filmic representations. In the stable, there are several shots of Mary's agonised face, her hand grasping a blanket or clutching Joseph's shoulders, and then she falls back exhausted. However, the camera lingers on Joseph's face until a baby's cry is heard. The audience do not see *how* the baby is born. Mary is lying on the ground, with her head turned to one side, and the baby's crying continues, followed by a shot of the star. In the next shot, Joseph picks up the child (who is now 'wrapped in swaddling clothes') and gives him to Mary. The couple are assisted by an extrabiblical character named Abigail, who arrives after the birth, calling for water as if to suggest that Mary needs a midwife's care but without giving any particulars. Her presence clouds the issue, leaving the scene open to an interpretation that might be satisfactory to both Protestants and Catholics.[9]

In her *Flesh and Blood Biography of the Mother of Jesus*, Hazleton relates in explicit detail the difficulties and mortal dangers of childbirth in the environment in which Mary lived, with stories of women howling in pain for days 'until it takes three women to hold you down' (2004: 2). There is an effort to reflect the contemporary conditions in the scene of the birth of John the Baptist in Hardwicke's *The Nativity Story*, with the shots of the holding rope onto which Elizabeth clings in labour, the presence of the midwives, and the ululating cries of the women as they greet the newborn baby. (None of these aspects feature in the presentation of the birth of Jesus in the same film.) The graphic realism of labour pain is also strikingly illustrated in Veronesi's *For Love, Only For Love*, in which Mary stands upright, holding onto the walls of the cave and screaming loudly. However, even after such patent on-screen agony, the birth itself is discreetly handled. As the focus returns to Joseph (who looks helplessly for assistance), a baby's cry is heard. When Joseph returns to the cave, the suffering is over (the specifics of the birth remaining unclear) and Mary is nursing the baby at her breast.

Maria, Daughter of Her Son maintains a fictional hierarchy between the expectant parents, in which Joseph panics and mops his brow while Mary comforts him despite her labour pains: 'Keep calm, Joseph. Everything will be fine.' However, the narrative continues to reflect the apocryphal literature which is evidently a key source text for the script. In *The Protevangelium of James*, Joseph himself recounts the event: 'I, Joseph was walking, and yet I did not walk, and I looked up to the air and saw the air in amazement. And I looked up at the vault of heaven, and saw it standing still...' (in Elliott 1993: 64). As the on-screen Joseph runs off for help in *Maria, Daughter of Her Son*, the focus returns to Mary who is illuminated by a bright light as she gives a sigh, presumably indicating the moment of birth. The film goes into slow motion and a choir singing the words 'Sanctus, Sanctus' is heard on the soundtrack.[10] There is a crane shot that signals the isolation of Joseph in the landscape as well as his confusion. He gazes around, looks upwards (towards the eye of God) and asks: 'What is happening to me?' At this point he hears a baby's cry. When he runs back, he finds the baby wrapped in a blanket in Mary's arms. 'He's so beautiful,' says Mary, the adjective 'beautiful' being (not surprisingly) the consistent choice of all comments on the appearance of the baby Jesus in cinematic Nativity scenes.

At one time, expectant fathers paced up and down outside the hospital delivery room waiting for news, while now they are encouraged to be present at their children's birth. Both Jean Delannoy and Catherine Hardwicke go a stage further by adding a 'new man' dimension to Joseph and giving him the midwife role. Indeed, Delannoy admitted that he cast Francis Lalanne as Joseph knowing that the actor had already assisted at the birth of his own child in real life (1998: 254). In *Mary of Nazareth*, Joseph prepares the water and brandishes a knife, but the audience does not see him actually use either. The camera focuses safely on Mary's upper body as Joseph grasps her hand, and her cries lessen and she turns her head. The audience do not see the birth itself, and there is a cut to a scene with the shepherds.

In contrast, the camera remains in the stable during the moment of birth in *The Nativity Story* and initially frames the couple in long shot rather than conventionally focusing on Mary's face. The scene combines dimensions of the supernatural and the natural. As predicted by the Magi, the planets Venus, Jupiter and an astral body converge, and the cave is flooded with light. But the expectant mother, who is illuminated by the starlight, is also covered in sweat and obviously in pain. More controversially, Joseph is shown kneeling at Mary's feet, evidently ready to act as the midwife. Although the camera subsequently returns to focus on Mary's face in the more accepted treatment of the event, the reaction shots of Joseph (still on his knees) and a further long shot of the two protagonists indicate that the baby is to be born in the ordinary manner.

Nevertheless, despite the consternation (and outrage) expressed by some Catholic commentators at Hardwicke's handling of the Nativity scene (see Greydanus 2006), the moment of delivery retains its mystery. Mary looks up towards the starlight before the moment of birth; Joseph gives a cry (off-screen) and there is a shot of the star that is transformed into a light of divine proportions (although criticised for its 'super trouper' dimension) that whites out the screen. The non-diegetic music reaches a crescendo. At this moment, a baby's cry is heard. When Joseph holds up the baby, crying tears of joy himself, there is no visible umbilical cord and only a small smear of blood on the baby's skin.

Amongst the issues that Cognet attributed to the decline in Mariology in the 1960s (including a difficulty with accepting apparitions and suggestions of idolatry), he identified the doctrine of the Incarnation. In particular, some Christians argue that for Christ's humanity to be realised, his birth must not be distinguishable from the birth of ordinary human beings, and regard the special privileges accorded to the mother of Jesus as unhelpful (see Cognet 1967: 41). However, the Catholic Church responds that the physical motherhood of Mary asserts the humanity of Jesus, while the special nature of his birth confirms his divinity. The film director who wishes to represent the humanity and divinity of the baby Jesus is, therefore, faced with a dilemma.

Consequently, it is no surprise that most directors have taken a binary route, choosing to present slight labour pains[11] and to leave the mechanics of the birth itself shrouded in mystery off-screen. Tina Beattie argues that there is a challenge 'to find a way of refiguring the Marian narrative in order to accommodate a symbolics of childbirth that represents the reality of birth, without completely reinventing the story of Mary and its eschatological significance' (2002: 101). But theologians meet this challenge in dialogue and published texts. For a filmmaker, this task is considerably more demanding.

MADONNA AND CHILD

Maurice Hamington claims that Mary represents 'contradictory religious imagery for men and women,' pointing out that there is a 'paradox of devotion to Mary coexisting with the cultural *machismo*' in Latin America (1995: 16). While Freudians see in the Marian cult 'a sublimation of male oedipal urges,' the Jungians argue that Mary's appeal is located 'in society's corporate need to express the archetypal feminine and maternal images of the collective unconscious' (Shinners 1989: 163). Jungians claim that all men want a virgin mother, and that there is an unconscious feminine element in men which reflects the mother at an infantile stage, 'but with maturity it develops (or should) into what Jung calls the anima, with the mother element still present but less to the fore. [...] Obviously the anima – with the maternal element in the background – is at least closely related to ideas of the Goddess' (Ashe 1976: 234).

There are purported parallels between the narrative of the Incarnation and the virgin births found in classical mythology. One line of defence (used by Origen (d.254) and the twentieth-century theologian Hugo Rahner, among others) is that God prepared his people for the birth of Jesus through previous symbols that made the ultimate reality more accessible, while Justin Martyr made the distinction between parthenogenesis and divine impregnation (see Warner 1990: 35–6). However, it is the *differences* between the goddess myths and the New Testament Infancy Narratives that shed light on the unique nature of Mary for Christians. Mary is the opposite of a goddess because she is the woman who has given Christ his humanity, humility and the capacity to suffer and die (see Laurentin 1989: 97). Mary could not be a goddess in the pagan sense because her motherhood supports the humanity of Jesus. René Girard maintains: 'There is no more telling feature than the inability of the greatest minds in the modern world to grasp the difference between the Christian crib at Christmas-time and the bestial monstrosities of mythological births' (1987: 222). The concrete reality of the film set and the evident humanity of the actress who incarnates Mary ensure that the traditional trappings of goddess imagery are circumvented. Nevertheless, as the Nativity scene relies chiefly on visuals rather than dialogue, the representation of Mary within the frame as the faithful worship the baby Jesus is an additional aspect for consideration.

Dorothy McGuire in *The Greatest Story Ever Told*, her head covered by a white veil, offers the traditional iconography of the mother of Jesus, sitting high up in the stable loft and illuminated by light. Yet the black African Mary in Dornford-May's *Son of Man* (in which the birth of Jesus takes place in a shed in a contemporary African township), with a round electric fan behind her head to create a halo effect, is an equally recognisable Madonna. Despite the differences in presentation, the image of a mother holding her child in warm embrace is understood across all cultural divides and, according to Benko, the reverence for motherhood and childbirth remains 'the basic principle of Mariology' (2004: 5). Andrew Greeley alleges that people are attracted by 'the marvellous possibility that God loves us the way a mother loves her baby' (1990: 252). In his Nativity play *Bariona* (1940) Jean-Paul Sartre considers the dichotomy of the mother who can wrap God in swaddling clothes and hold him in her arms: 'For the Christ is her child, flesh of her flesh and the fruit of her womb [...]. No other woman has had God to herself in this way, a God so small that he can be taken in her arms and covered with kisses...' (in Laurentin 1984: 276–77 [my translation]).

Simone de Beauvoir famously criticised the Virgin Mary in *The Second Sex*, claiming: 'For the first time in human history the mother kneels before her son; she freely accepts her inferiority' (in Cunneen 1996: 285). However, this image has been reinterpreted by Julia Kristeva, who admits that she has never understood de Beauvoir's negative assessment of the Virgin's 'humiliation'. In examining the painting by Piero della Francesca to which de Beauvor reportedly refers, Kristeva argues that Mary appears happy and 'confident' rather than defeated (see Clément and Kristeva 1998: 100).

In Matthew's Gospel, the evangelist refers on a number of occasions to 'the child' (Mt 2:9) or 'the child with Mary his mother' (Mt 2:11), whereas Joseph is not mentioned in the same breath. Therefore, of particular interest is the framing of the family within the Nativity scenes. In *From the Manger to the Cross*, Joseph stands at the head of the manger and raises an arm to Heaven, so that he is a reverent protector who is set slightly apart. When the family is depicted sleeping, Mary is always close to the baby with Joseph lying at a discreet distance (perhaps indicating the future course of his celibate marriage to Mary according to Catholic doctrine).

Jane Schaberg asserts that Christian iconography 'can communicate, as well as female mothering power, the failure of male partnering and parenting, a loss for woman and child, as well as the imbalance in parenting and the heavy burden placed on the woman' (2005: 20). Therefore, it is notable how much the fatherly role is actually stressed in a range of New Testament films. The actors playing Joseph gently touch the baby Jesus in *The Jesus Film*, *Joseph of Nazareth* and *For Love, Only For Love*. The point is made explicitly in *Maria, Daughter of Her Son*, when the hesitant Joseph is afraid to take the baby in his arms to bless him. Mary asks, 'How can you hurt him? You're his father, Joseph.' After witnessing the 'new man' who acts as a midwife in Hardwicke's *The Nativity Story*, there is no surprise at the kindness of Joseph when he poignantly takes off his cap to make a pillow for Jesus's head. When Joseph asks how Mary is feeling, she replies, 'I have been given the strength I prayed for. Strength from God. And from you.'

In fact, in Zeffirelli's *Jesus of Nazareth*, it is Joseph who takes on the role of revealing Jesus to the shepherds, for Mary is lying exhausted on the ground under a blanket. There are tears in Joseph's eyes as he draws back the curtain to exhibit the baby, and the shepherds kneel down and look beyond Mary towards Jesus, so that she is not honoured in any particular way. Her immediate job is done, and Joseph has clearly adopted the parenting role at this point.

It is particularly notable in *The Life and Passion of Jesus Christ* that Mary does not touch the baby herself, as if in awe, until the shepherds and Wise Men have arrived. The assembled crowd (including Joseph) bow down before the mother and her baby. However, given the manner in which Mary lifts her son up high, it is Jesus who receives the adoration and she who makes him visible. The Church's feast of the Epiphany, which commemorates the visit of the Magi, celebrates the manifestation of Jesus to the Gentiles, and it is only when the kings appear that Mary is ready to present Jesus to the wider cinema audience. In Albert Serra's *Birdsong* (2008), a minimalist film that charts the epic journey of the Magi across a barren landscape, the baby Jesus is mysteriously absent from the shots of the home life of Mary (played by Montse Triola) and Joseph. However, there is a moment of pure reverence, highlighted by the film's only instance of non-diegetic music, when the three men finally prostrate themselves before the mother and child, and the family's private life takes on monumental significance.

In *From the Manger to the Cross*, Mary turns back the covers to reveal the baby to the shepherds, but they maintain a reverent distance, standing behind Mary, who has her eyes raised to Heaven. The shepherds' attention is on the baby not on her, so that she leads their homage of the Christ-child. When the Wise Men arrive on camels, Mary holds the baby in her lap, acting as a throne for him.

Given its intentions as a visual hymn to Mary, it might be expected that Cordero's *Mater Dei* would be in greatest danger of the Mariolatry label in the Nativity scene. Strikingly, this is not the case, and Mary is presented as a proud mother with her newborn baby rather than the object of personal adulation. When the shepherds (notably including women amongst their number) come to the stable, the camera remains at the back of the crowd so that the audience is initially placed in the role of a late arrival, unable to see what is happening at the front. Then the viewers are offered the first close-up of the baby Jesus, but only Mary's hand is visible within the frame. In a subsequent shot, it is clear that the shepherds are bowing down to the baby, but Mary looks towards the people who are honouring her child while their gaze is fixed on him. When the Magi arrive, Mary and Joseph kneel on the same side of the manger as the kings, so that Jesus remains the object of adoration.

In Ray's *King of Kings*, there is a particularly unusual framing of the figures within the scene. Mary is in the background in a private space, shielding Jesus from inquiring eyes as she nurses him. Joseph sits in the foreground with the shepherds – all of them distanced from the Madonna and child and not engaged in any act of worship. The scene is notably low-key and there is no sense that the child in the corner is the Messiah (a complete contrast to the Christmas card Nativity scene for which Hardwicke was criticised in *The Nativity Story*). When the Magi appear, they are understandably confused because the setting is so humble and the child they seek is not centre stage. Although Mary and Jesus remain in the background, they are illuminated by light from a lamp, and the kings' attention is finally caught by a baby's cry. Without introduction, the kings move past Joseph (he rises to meet

FIG. 10 Ray's unusual framing in *King of Kings*

them but they pay him no heed) and walk towards the baby with their gifts. It is only at this point that there is a shot of Mary in the centre of the frame, holding the baby in an iconic pose. More importantly, she pulls back the blanket in which Jesus is wrapped so that the kings can see his face more clearly. Mary looks

FIG. 11 Madonna and child in *King of Kings*

down at her child, to indicate that her baby is the object of contemplation rather than herself.

Stéphane Bouquet comments on the significance that Pasolini gives to Mary in the Nativity scene in *The Gospel according to St Matthew*, in which the baby is initially hardly visible in her arms (2003: 14). However, this protective stance changes when the Magi arrive, ironically accompanied on the soundtrack by the music 'Motherless child'. The young Mary stands up and looks to Joseph uncertainly, wondering how to react. When the Magi kneel in front of her, she hands Jesus to the central king and he holds him up, while another king kisses the baby's feet. It is clear, therefore, that it is Jesus who is the centre of attention, and it is Mary who gives him to the king to present to the world. The scene is notably reduced in dramatic scale by Rossellini in *The Messiah*, and the stable has an outer wall that serves as an additional barrier for the visitor. Holding the baby, Mary (Mita Ungaro) is sitting outside in shadow, rather than illuminated, when the kings pay homage.

Mariologists stress that Mary's key role is to point the way to Jesus. This function is made explicit in the icon called the *Hodegetria* that is found in Orthodox churches. This icon of the incarnation 'depicts the Mother of God holding her Divine Son on her left arm, while with her right hand she is gently pointing towards Christ, who is the Way (John 14:6)' (Craciun 2002: 45). Indeed, one of the few lines that Dorothy McGuire speaks aloud in *The Greatest Story Ever Told* is when Mary introduces her baby to the kings ('Jesus will be his name') and holds him out for them to see. Mary admits to Joseph in Till's *Mary and Joseph*, 'I know that [Jesus] can never only be ours alone,' and when a shepherd arrives, she turns the baby towards him and he grasps the child's finger. The theme is taken further in *The Nativity Story*, when the reticence of the faithful is overcome by Mary. As the elderly shepherd (who had helped Mary and Joseph on their journey) kneels down and reaches out towards the baby, he hesitates and withdraws his hand in fear. But Mary holds Jesus towards him, saying, 'He is for all mankind.' The full meaning of the Nativity is realised as the humble man literally touches the Son of God.

THE TRUE IDENTITY OF JESUS

One of the most difficult issues that screenplay writers have to contend with is the manifestation of the human/divine identity of Jesus in his childhood. How is this uniqueness conveyed through the dialogue and *mise-en-scène*?

When Mary returns from the desert with her child in the Koran, she is rebuked by the people, but she has taken a vow of silence and refuses to answer questions. In the film *The Saint Mary*, the camera adopts Mary's point-of-view as she walks through the crowds, emphasising that she is an outcast as she sees the hostile faces.

In the Koran, when Mary points towards Jesus in her arms, the people ask, 'How can we speak with a babe in the cradle?' But it is the little baby himself who responds. When the people speak out against her in *The Saint Mary*, Mary is holding the baby Jesus in her arms and she looks at him, as if she wants him to answer. In response, the newborn baby speaks (in voice-over), 'I am Jesus, the Messiah, a servant of God. He has given me a book and honoured me with Prophethood.' The crowd of Mary's accusers are filmed in slow motion as they gasp in terror, while Mary looks down in wonderment at the baby in her arms. Three men come forward and kneel at the feet of Mary, who is holding the baby, and the narrator says, 'And thus we chose Mary and her son as a miracle, and a sign for all the world.' Although Muslims revere Jesus as a holy prophet rather than the Son of God, it is notable that the faces of the prophets are not seen on screen in *The Saint Mary*. The face of the baby Jesus is covered by a circle of bright light that obscures his features but highlights his significance in a manner that is not adopted in Christian filmic representations. Filmmakers of New Testament narratives must find other techniques to convey the special nature of Mary's child.

Information on Mary's personal response to the birth of her son is not provided in the Gospels, despite the belief of some Christians (particularly Catholics) that Luke had a direct Marian source. Luke tells the reader that 'Mary kept all these things, reflecting on them in her heart' (Lk 2:19), but the details of her ponderings are not provided. However, 'the great Doctors of the Church have all taken for granted that Mary had knowledge of her Son's Divinity' (Buono in Anon. 1997: 229); and in the Orthodox tradition 'Mary not only knows what is to happen to her infant son, but she offers him up to that fate in obedience to the Father and for the salvation of mankind' (Morris 1998: 46). Luke 'portrays Jesus as knowing his own identity as Son of God from his early years, while to others, especially his mother Mary, this was also made known by revelatory signs, but signs whose full significance was still obscure to them' (Ashley 1985: 495–6). As a visual medium, cinema is ideally suited to indicate those revelatory signs.

LaVerdiere points out that 'Mary laid Jesus in a manger, a feeding trough for the animals. In this context, Mary offers Jesus, her son, the firstborn of God, as nourishment for the flock' (2007: 6). This symbolism reaches its fulfilment in the Eucharist. (As the cross is raised in Gibson's *The Passion of the Christ*, there is a flashback to the Last Supper, reminding the audience that Jesus is the bread of life.)

Evidently, the humble location of the Nativity is important in itself. The Messiah is a king who is born 'not in glory but in humility,' as Gaspar remarks in *Jesus of Nazareth*. However, the choice of a cave rather than a wooden stable (as indicated in the films by Zeffirelli, Kowalski, Till, Veronesi and Hardwicke) has an added relevance, for it is also the traditional setting for the resurrection of Jesus: 'Thus the new life offered by Christ, individual and communal, comes forth not only from the actual womb of the Virgin, but also from the cave-womb of the tomb, that ancient underground cinema [Plato's cave] in which the dream of another life, another way of living this life – in the face of death – is projected' (Loughlin 2004: 54). Pope Benedict XVI argues that in the sixth chapter of John's Gospel 'the theology of the Incarnation and the theology of the Cross come together; the two cannot be separated' (2007: 269). Mary is the only witness to be present at both these moments in Salvation history. While LaVerdiere argues that, in looking at the Christmas crib, Christians do not necessarily 'associate the figure of Jesus in the manger with the figure of Jesus on the cross' (2007: 3), a number of filmmakers have tried to make this connection explicit.

Costa's *Maria, Daughter of Her Son* has a reverse temporal structure, beginning with the Crucifixion. When Mary swoons as Jesus dies, the film takes up her childhood narrative in an effect/cause pattern. Therefore, when Mary talks to her baby in the stable and uses words that the audience has already heard her say at the Crucifixion ('Little baby, great love of mine. Little baby, great gift of mine. Little baby, great gift of God'), the affinity between the two events is categorically created in the mind of the viewer.

Sometimes the links are left to be made by the spectator, requiring further knowledge of the details of the New Testament. For example, the connection between the birth and Resurrection is signalled in similar incidents in *The Greatest Story Ever Told* and *The Nativity Story*. When Herod sends out a command to kill the newborn babies, the soldiers are seen entering the empty stable in Stevens's film and one of them stabs at the manger with his spear (as the centurion will stab Jesus's body on Calvary). In both films, there is a shot of a white cloth hanging over the empty manger that evokes (in the minds of the 'informed' viewer) the burial shroud that will be left behind in the empty tomb after the Resurrection.

There are a number of foreshadowing incidents of the Crucifixion during the on-screen depiction of the childhood of Jesus. In *From the Manger to the Cross*, the young Jesus is shown carrying a plank of wood, and the shadow cast by the plank creates the shape of a cross upon the ground, at the sight of which Mary raises her hands to her heart in distress. On the journey to Bethlehem, Mary and Joseph pass scenes of crucifixion in *For Love, Only For Love*, *Mary of Nazareth* and *The Nativity Story*, offering a presentiment of the destiny of the baby Mary carries in her womb. This same device is used in *The Greatest Story Ever Told* on the return journey after the flight into Egypt (and in Young's *Jesus* it occurs in a flashback as the family returns from Jerusalem after the Finding in the Temple). In Stevens's film, the family is confronted by multiple crucifixions along the side of the road – a literal Stations of the Cross – and the image is accompanied by a chorus of women chanting 'My God, my God, why hast thou forsaken me?' When the parents pause, the dark-haired child in Mary's arms is sitting upright and his eyes witness the dying men. There are women in dark clothes (one standing and another bent over in grief) who present a foretaste of Mary's own future along with her son.

The question of exactly how much Jesus and his parents know about his future life is left unclear. Before the birth of Jesus in Kowalski's *The Nativity*, Joseph consoles Mary with the words: 'God has chosen the child in your womb to save his people. And he's got to give him some time to do it. He can't just let him be born and die.' His confident statement indicates that he is aware of Jesus's identity as the Messiah, but it is not certain whether he comprehends that Jesus will be executed (at some point in the future) in order to bring salvation.

BIBLICAL SCENES

There are a number of biblical scenes with Marian content that are often incorporated into the narrative of New Testament films: the Presentation in the Temple; the Slaughter of the Innocents; the Flight into Egypt; and the Finding in the Temple when Jesus was aged twelve.

The Presentation in the Temple is significant for a number of specific reasons. The scene shows Jesus's Jewish heritage, although some theologians argue that Luke was incorrect in his description of the Jewish law, revealing his own Hellenistic background (see Ben-Chorin 2001: 97–8); it reveals the relative poverty of Mary and Joseph, who could afford only the smaller offering of two pigeons (Lv 12:8) rather than a lamb and a dove (Lv 12:6); and it provides a premonition of the suffering that lies ahead in Mary's life, following the prophecy of Simeon that a sword will pierce Mary's heart.

> 'Behold, this child is destined for the fall and rise of many in Israel, and to be a sign that will be contradicted (and you yourself a sword will pierce) so that the thoughts of many hearts may be revealed.' (Lk 2:34–35)

'Popular imagination tied Simeon's sword to the death of Jesus' (Perry 2006: 85) but Perry argues that there is textual evidence to support 'the view that Simeon's sword is the eschatological divine judgment that will pass through not only Israel but Mary's own soul' (2006: 87). Edward Yarnold suggests that Simeon's words indicate 'that Mary, like everyone else, will find her Son a challenge which can be either accepted or rejected – a test which she passed, being the woman who heard the word of God and kept it' (2002: 233).

In *The Jesus Film* the Presentation scene is included because it forms part of Luke's Gospel (which is the source of the narrative). However, Simeon blesses the baby without mentioning 'the sword', so that the question of Mary's future suffering is circumvented. In *Jesus of Nazareth*, Mary and Joseph make no response at Simeon's declaration, but as they walk away with the baby, both parents turn their heads to look back silently towards the priest. In *Mary of Nazareth*, Mary is visibly troubled by Simeon's words and urges Joseph to leave the Temple quickly. More dramatically, *Maria, Daughter of Her Son* offers the most sudden manifestation of the difficulties that face the couple. Immediately after Simeon's words, King Herod makes an extrabiblical appearance in the Temple with his soldiers. He kills Zachariah with a lance (a strikingly quick re-reminder of the sword prophecy), proclaiming that he will now slaughter the children.

The Massacre of the Innocents is one of the most troubling of the bloody images in the Bible. Consequently, it is an opportunity for film directors to flex their muscles and for Herod to do his worst ('Kill! Kill! Kill them all!' screams the king in *Jesus of Nazareth*). The scene features in *The Life and Passion of Jesus Christ* where the women with their long dark flowing hair are similar in appearance, as if representing all the ordinary women whose children were killed. In an interview published in 1976, Rossellini admitted that the slaughter had the potential to be 'a major dramatic scene, in the sadomasochistic style of film-making so in vogue today' (in Baugh 1997: 90), but he chose a less dramatic approach himself. Mike Rich, who wrote the screenplay of *The Nativity Story*, referred to the difficulties of creating a family-friendly film without having a scene of slaughter 'that was so family-friendly that it lost its impact' (in Greydanus 2006).

Strangely, Mary in *Mary, mother of Jesus* is one of the few on-screen Marys to express a response to the events: 'I'm thinking of Bethlehem, of all the mothers who have no child to hold in their arms today.' Later she says, 'We'll never be safe. As long as I have breath in my body, God help me, this child shall live.' This theme was expanded into a TV mini-series entitled *A Child called Jesus*, which focused on the efforts of a fictional character named Sefir (played by Pierre Clémenti, who had once incarnated the role of Jesus himself in Philippe Garrel's *The Virgin's Bed*) to pursue the one child who had escaped Herod's massacre. Here Mary (Carmen San Martin) also laments: 'Those children, all my children, died so that my son might live.'

THE FLIGHT INTO EGYPT

> .... the angel of the Lord appeared to Joseph in a dream and said, 'Rise, take the child and his mother, flee to Egypt, and stay there until I tell you. Herod is going to search for the child to destroy him.' Joseph rose and took the child and his mother by night and departed for Egypt. (Mt 2:13–14)

The special nature of Jesus is seen in 'The Flight into Egypt' tableaux in *The Life and Passion of Jesus Christ*. The manger is surrounded by visible angels, who are now standing on the ground (for this is where heaven and earth meet in the presence of Jesus) forming a heavenly host with harps, pipes and incense. The angel who appears to Joseph and gives a warning message has golden wings that are much more impressive than those belonging to Gabriel in the first Annunciation scene – so the protector of the baby Jesus is more magnificent than the messenger of his birth.

As the soldiers arrive in pursuit, a sword-bearing angel wards off the enemy, timed to coincide with a visual effect in which the Holy Family fade out from the screen (into an invisible place of protection) and reappear when the danger is over. The images of the Sphinx and the Pyramids are a reminder of the importance of Egypt in the Old Testament, when another character named Joseph played a significant role in the lives of the Jewish people. Exegetes note that Joseph in the Book of Genesis was a dreamer – and that Mary's husband receives divine messages in dreams (see Ben-Chorin 2001: 89). However, the painted backdrop in the French silent film was outclassed in Olcott's *From the Manger to the Cross*, where location shooting incorporated the actual Pyramids into the shot.

In Ray's *King of Kings*, Joseph has a dream in which he is told that the family must flee to Egypt. Without complaint, Mary, holding the baby in her arms, utters her very first words in the film: 'Then we will go.' However, in *The Gospel according to St Matthew*, Mary climbs onto the donkey with the baby in her arms but she looks back sadly towards her home as they travel along. Pasolini saw the wider resonance of the New Testament events, claiming that 'Joseph and the Virgin Mary in flight were suggested by so many similar dramas of flight in the modern world (for example, in Algeria)' (in Greene 1990: 76), and the sorrow of a woman in exile is shown in Mary's face.

The family's life in Egypt is covered in a few brief shots in many films. In both *The Gospel according to St Matthew* and *The Greatest Story Ever Told*, the event is turned into a moment of family intimacy. Pasolini presents Mary smiling as the child Jesus walks across the sand and is picked up by Joseph. After Mary and Joseph flee 'into Egypt' in Stevens's film (their tiny figures set against a grandiose landscape that is recognisably North American), they set up camp amidst a small group of palm trees. Mary, dressed in white, is sitting on the ground and holding the baby while Joseph stands and reads from the ninth chapter of Isaiah ('Unto us a child is born...'). It is at this point that they hear the news that Herod is dead, and when Joseph says, 'Home', Mary adds, 'Nazareth' (one of the very few words that she speaks in the film).

In Dornford-May's *Son of Man*, the African family flees from brutal soldiers who are capturing young children, covering them with a blanket and then butchering them to death – a reminder of the ongoing brutality throughout the world today. Initially, Mary covers the child Jesus's eyes to try to protect him from the scene – and this action also has a foreshadowing element, for Jesus is beaten to death (rather than crucified) in Dornford-May's updated retelling of the New Testament narrative. However, after a few moments, Mary turns Jesus's head so that he sees the savagery, as if she is aware that he has a wisdom beyond his years.

AN EXTRAORDINARY CHILD

Most of the events of Jesus's childhood remain in an obscurity that has come to be called The Hidden Years. There are a number of apocryphal texts that expand the biography with stories of youthful miracles, but they have not become part of the established tradition, unlike incidents from the life of Mary (such as the names of her parents) in *The Protevangelium of James*.

Although the story of the exile is obviously the focus of the expansive *A Child called Jesus*, it is unusual for the period in Egypt to be extended in extrabiblical detail, as in *Mary of Nazareth* and *Maria, Daughter of Her Son*. In the latter film, there is a pause in the action as Mary raises some key theological issues about her baby: 'When I nurse him, I wonder who am I giving my love to. And when I wash him and clean him, I wonder whose son am I giving my love to. Could God have possibly hidden himself in this child?' She looks to Joseph for an answer in wonderment, and he is unable to oblige.

The confusing nature of the parent/child hierarchy is demonstrated in a number of film scenes. On the one hand, Mary is shown reading to Jesus in *From the Manger to the Cross* as if she is teaching him the Scriptures. This theme will later be expanded in *Mary, mother of Jesus*, when Mary tells the (bedtime) story of 'The Good Samaritan', as if suggesting that she was the source of one of his later parables. On the other hand, when Joseph berates Jesus in *Maria, Daughter of Her Son*, the boy raises the issue that stands at the heart of the Holy Family: 'You are not the father who can instruct me.' At these words, Joseph slaps Jesus across the face and he falls to the ground (an action that Joseph will spend the rest of his on-screen life repenting). However, it is striking that Mary sides with Joseph: 'Don't be too upset, Joseph. A father may punish a child who deserves it. [...] God entrusted him to you. That makes him your son, too.' In a later scene when Mary and Jesus are sitting outside under the night sky, the fierce wind that is blowing disturbs the sweet image of the mother and child. Jesus looks at the stars and says, 'If the sons of men fall, they can't get up and start again.' Mary hugs him but clearly does not know how to respond.

A film that draws heavily on the apocrypha, *Maria, Daughter of Her Son* also offers variations on stories of a wondrous child (whose activities are described in *The Infancy Gospel of Thomas*), and one who causes his parents some concern. When Jesus cures a sick donkey, his father stresses,

'Look, I know he's no ordinary child. But we have to treat him as though he were.' Further supernatural powers are suggested when the young Jesus is disturbed by the polytheist Egyptian society around him, and he writes in his book in Hebrew 'God is one'. When he goes to the market and sees people worshipping an Egyptian god, a sand storm brews up and everyone runs for shelter. Jesus stands in the centre, unmoved, as if he might have instigated the inclement weather. Indeed, the locals blame Jesus for the destruction and tell Joseph: 'We believe that your son is possessed by an evil spirit.'

Evidently, the child actor chosen to incarnate the young Jesus is the opposite of the traditional 'dangerous child'. Theologians have argued that Jesus must have resembled Mary: 'For in the union of God and humanity, it is Mary who imparts the humanity' (Boss 2007: 52). However, casting directors frequently ignore this proposition, choosing boys with blond hair (*King of Kings*; *Jesus of Nazareth*; *Maria, Daughter of Her Son*) and often with startling blue eyes that appear alien to both their birth mother and their surroundings. The idea that blondness is connected to goodness is presumably a motivation for their selection for the role, contrasting with the dark-haired demonic child Damien of *The Omen* (Richard Donner, 1976).[12]

In Young's *Jesus*, the apocryphal stories are also evoked when Mary is reminding her adult son of his childhood. In a flashback, the young Jesus is playing with some boys, and as they throw stones at a tree, they hit a bird and kill it. Jesus picks up the bird's body and runs with it to the house to show Mary (Jacqueline Bisset), crying that he does not want it to die. Mary explains, 'O, my sweet boy. Death comes to everything. All things must die. All things of this earth.' But Jesus takes the bird outside and turns his back (like a magician) and when he turns around, the bird is alive in his hands. Mary gasps in amazement. In the present, Mary remembers, 'I was worried the authorities would hear of it. Your father said that the bird was just stunned but I was so frightened.' Jesus replies enigmatically, 'There was nothing to be frightened about, was there mother?'

Obviously, on one level, Mary and Joseph are facing the difficulties encountered by any parent of an intelligent, inquisitive child. In *Mary, mother of Jesus*, the twelve-year-old Jesus asks, 'Why do they say "an eye for an eye, and a tooth for a tooth"? [...] If God makes the sun shine on both good and bad people... then shouldn't we also love our enemies and pray for those who do us wrong?' His parents exchange glances, with Joseph making a gesture as if to say, 'You can't argue with that.' When Jesus is beaten up by another boy (because he is 'stuck up and superior'), Jesus does not fight back and his look seems to unnerve his aggressors. When Mary sees her son with his bloody nose, he says, 'I know God doesn't want that, I know it. [...] Why is it that I see these things and no one else does?' But the extraordinary nature of Jesus is indicated when Mary takes him to the location of the Annunciation and, holding his hand, she tells him what happened. He understands that he is also on the same difficult journey and says, 'I'm not afraid because you're with me. You'll always be with me, won't you?' 'As long as I live,' replies Mary.

Ray replaces the biblical Finding in the Temple scene with an extra-biblical incident when Jesus is aged twelve. Mary is seen dressed in brown, the only time in Ray's film that she is not wearing iconic colours (perhaps because this scene belongs to the Hidden Years and she is not a public figure). When the Roman soldier Lucius arrives (an invented character who will later appear at the trial and crucifixion of Jesus) to check a census, it is clear that he is surprised that a boy born in Bethlehem some twelve years ago is still alive. The camera closes in on his face as he realises the significance of the date. But he decides to leave the family in peace. The scene creates an imaginary danger, but the exclusion of the Lukan Temple scene means that the presentation of Jesus as a child of great intellect is ignored.

THE FINDING IN THE TEMPLE

The Finding in the Temple, after Jesus has gone missing in Jerusalem, is the last key event of the Infancy Narratives.

> *After three days they found him in the temple, sitting in the midst of the teachers, listening to them and asking them questions, and all who heard him were astounded at his understanding and his answers. When his parents saw him, they were astonished, and his mother said to him, 'Son, why have you done this to us? Your father and I have been looking for you with great anxiety.' And he said to them, 'Why were you looking for me? Did you not know that I must be in my Father's house?' But they did not understand what he said to them.* (Lk 2:46–50)

When this scene is included, its potential significance and the extent of the parental reprimand vary from film to film. For example, Mary and Joseph smile when they find Jesus in *Jesus of Nazareth*, while Mary looks concerned at her son's behaviour in *Jesus*. During the silent era, Mary appears to briefly remonstrate with Jesus in *The Life and Passion of Jesus Christ*, but he gestures her away, and when they leave Mary has her arm across his shoulders. In *From the Manger to the Cross*, Jesus rides the donkey to Jerusalem while Mary and Joseph accompany him on foot (a sign of the child's elevated status and a foretaste of Palm Sunday). When Mary and Joseph return to the city to find their missing son, they are travelling against the direction of the crowd, a manifestation of the difficulties that they face in coping with their child. When Joseph enters the Temple to collect Jesus, Mary is visible through the window as she watches Jesus indicate heaven – his father's business. At the reunion outside, Mary embraces her son and the three of them walk down the steps together, the parents with their arms around Jesus.

There is an interesting angle in *Mater Dei* when Jesus is teaching potential future Marian theology, for he refers to the serpent in Genesis (which evokes Mary's role as the Second Eve). As Mary listens, there is gratification on her face, and there is no reproach from Joseph about 'my father's business'. By contrast, in *Maria, Daughter of Her Son*, Joseph feels again that his authority is questioned.

All the mothers are preparing their sons to go to the Temple in Rossellini's *The Messiah*. The camera zooms in on Mary and Jesus to enclose them within the frame, and Mary makes a long speech about the importance of the day and the significance of the *tallith* [prayer shawl]. 'As of today you are also a man. And having become a man, with your head covered by your *tallith*, you will be able to speak with doctors and teachers who have studied the Holy Law' (in Reinhartz 2007: 73). However, when the camera zooms out, the audience is reminded that another mother is engaged in the same process on the left, which indicates the humanity rather than the divinity of Jesus.[13]

Ben-Chorin sees Mary's reaction to the missing Jesus as incompatible with the sentiments of Mary of *The Magnificat*, wondering if her attitude has been changed by life's experiences (2001: 128). But Perry defends Mary's reaction:

> Some may be embarrassed that the mother of Jesus – after having heard the angel's message [....] should now erupt with such a worry-laden declaration. But this is not warranted. Although Jesus' identity and destiny are described in these instances, the timing and nature of his mission are not. [...] Mary's anxiety is one that every parent experiences when a child goes missing. (2006: 89)

This conflict between a normal parental reaction and the response of Mary, who knows that her son is the Messiah, will come into play when Jesus begins his mission. And Mary will face her greatest test when Jesus arrives on Calvary.

CHAPTER 5

mother and disciple

Beyond the Infancy Narratives, there are three scenes that bring Mary into focus in the New Testament: the miracle at Cana, when Jesus turned the water into wine; the 'mothers and brothers' pericope; and, evidently most importantly, the Crucifixion. In the Gospel of John, Mary is standing by the cross during the execution of Jesus. What role does she play in the Passion of her son? What are her emotions as she watches her son die? Screenwriters must draw on creative inspiration and theological reflection to fashion a biography of Mary that links the biblical episodes and brings her to Calvary.

BETWEEN THE LINES

As the evangelists were concerned with the ministry of Jesus rather than his relationship with his mother, scriptwriters must read between the lines in order to develop Mary's story. Some exegetes have argued that Mary remained at home with the family during Jesus's ministry (see Brown *et al.* 1978: 11), and this theme is addressed in the filmic Marian narratives. In *Mater Dei*, Mary accompanies Jesus in spirit (rather than physically) through his adult preaching. There are insert shots of Mary's anxious face set against a rocky landscape, interspersed with scenes from the ministry and the first incidents of the Passion. The matter is discussed explicitly in Costa's *Maria, Daughter of Her Son*, when Mary is told by her adult son that she will not follow him on his travels: 'You'll be there, mother, but not the way you wish.' At this point, Mary turns back and walks under a dark archway, as if signifying her return to the background. After the entry into

Jerusalem in Connor's *Mary, mother of Jesus*, Jesus talks to Mary: 'When I was born, we began on our journey together. For the last three years I've travelled alone. It's been hard but it's been much harder for you.' Explaining that his journey is about to end, and indicating that there is tragedy ahead but without giving the specifics, he tells her not to lose faith. 'Never, my son. Never,' Mary replies, with tears in her eyes. The door closes on Jesus and leaves Mary alone outside in a passageway. At this moment she is imprisoned by her fears, as indicated by the shadow of the blinds creating a pattern of bars across her body. The following day she will look through the bars of a real prison as she attempts to see her son after his arrest.

Notably, Mel Gibson also denies Mary an appearance during the public ministry of Jesus (seen in the flashback sequences) in *The Passion of the Christ*, but he draws on his own imagination to develop her role within the private sphere of the home. As Jesus remembers his earlier life as a carpenter, with the flashbacks to Nazareth being signalled by brighter lighting, there is a moment of relief during the film's graphic brutality. Mary is inside the house, pouring a drink of water for Jesus, and she shouts his name twice – like a mother calling in a recalcitrant boy – and will later remind him to 'take off his dirty apron' and 'wash his hands' (both being orders that he obeys). She observes with some scepticism the 'tall table' that Jesus has built and bends down to look at him through the table's wooden side pieces, which form a little *mechitzah* between them.[1]

Gibson's imagined scene presents a loving and caring relationship, as evidenced by Jesus's laughter when Mary hovers by the table on an imaginary tall chair to experience the new dining experience. Mary's dismissive appraisal of Jesus's carpentry efforts ('This will never catch on!') shows humorously that the Messiah has a better understanding of the future of furniture design than his mother, but also points to the affectionate familial relationship.[2]

Reflecting on the original Gospel text, Elaine Storkey sees the close affinity between mother and son as reflecting 'the dignity, love and affirmation which Christ gives to all women' (in Carroll 1994: 61). One of the women to whom Jesus gave such dignity is Mary Magdalene [henceforth named Magdalene for the purposes of clarity].[3] The relationship (and contrast) between Mary and Magdalene is a repeated theme in New Testament films, leading to a number of invented on-screen encounters, and reaching an apex at the biblical scene of the Crucifixion.

Within popular culture, the name of Magdalene has been ascribed to a reformed prostitute, sometimes equated with the adulterous woman whom Jesus saved from stoning, or the woman who anointed the feet of Jesus and dried them with her hair in the house of the Pharisee (see Lk 7:36-50). In the twenty-first century, her character then came under renewed scrutiny because of the preposterous assertions in Dan Brown's novel *The Da Vinci Code*, which was subsequently filmed by Ron Howard (2006). In fact, the concrete details in the New Testament introduce Mary of Magdala as a woman from whom seven Devils had been cast out (Lk 8:1-2) and there is no reference to adultery or prostitution. She became a follower of Jesus and witnessed both the Crucifixion and the Resurrection. Derek Hayes's *The Miracle Maker* (1999), a film using model animation to tell the story of Jesus, is one of the few attempts to give Magdalene her true biblical role.

Only a small number of filmmakers fail to make a visible distinction between Mary and Magdalene. One notorious example is the iconoclastic Philippe Garrel, whose self-indulgent allegory of the New Testament, updating the narrative to the 1960s, features a Jesus-figure who is unable to make an impression in an uncertain world. Garrel muddied the waters by having Mary and Magdalene played by the same actress (Zouzou) in scenes shot in Brittany; and then confused the audience even further by having a second actress (Valérie Lagrange) incarnate the two roles when Zouzou chose not to complete additional shooting in Morocco. There are inevitable uncertainties as to which part Zouzou is playing at any one time, although the woman who collects stones in exchange for sexual favours is evidently Magdalene. Rather than being the woman who was stoned (as in Jn 8:1-11), Magdalene wishes to 'throw stones' – an action that evokes the revolutionary fervour of May 68 in which Zouzou had played a part.[4]

Twenty years later, the two women who feature in the twentieth-century Passion Play in Arcand's *Jesus of Montreal* both manifest Mary/Magdalene characteristics. Within the narrative that encases the fictional production of the play, Constance (Johanne-Marie Tremblay) is an unmarried mother having an affair with a priest; and the younger Mireille (Catherine Wilkening) is mocked for wanting to escape from an exploitative career in modelling to take on a serious acting role ('And you'll play the Virgin Mary?', jeers her lover). Mireille bathes Daniel (who incarnates the role of Jesus in the play) like a child in the bath, but she also kisses him on the lips. In the final 'real-life' *pietà*, when Daniel collapses in an underground station, Constance is by his feet (in the traditional position allotted to Magdalene), while Mireille holds his head in the Madonna role.

However, from the first on-screen representations, including *The Life and Passion of Jesus Christ*, Mary and Magdalene are usually easily identifiable. Mary is often traditionally veiled while Magdalene's long hair flows freely. Although there is no interaction between the two women in the Calvary tableaux in this early silent film, in later productions, such as DeMille's *The King of Kings*, this contact is developed.

Indeed, *The King of Kings* offers one of the most marked initial contrasts between Mary and Magdalene. The screenplay, written by Jeanie McPherson, extended the role of Magdalene and surrounded her with admirers in the film's opening 'Pleasure Palace' scene. When Magdalene learns that her lover Judas has abandoned her charms to follow Jesus, she sets out to meet her opponent.[5] Scantily-clad, in a chariot drawn by zebras, she is evidently the antithesis of the mother of Jesus, to whom the audience is subsequently introduced. Therefore, when Magdalene is cured of the Seven Deadly Sins, she wraps her cloak around her body to cover her revealing dress, and veils her head, so that her appearance more closely resembles that of Mary.

In traditional religious painting, Magdalene is associated with the colour red while Mary is often dressed in red or her iconic blue. From the twelfth century, the blue becomes more luminous and reflects the colour that is found in the stained glass windows of the cathedrals of St Denis and Chartres in France. With the advance of colour film, this time-honoured colour scheme is sometimes embraced on screen. In Stevens's *The Greatest Story Ever Told*, Magdalene retains her red cloak as she travels with the apostles (so that she stands out amidst the group in long shots) while Mary is dressed in pale blue. Mary is also 'dressed in the rich red-and-blue-dyed clothes of the elite, in keeping with her portraits in later Christian art' in Young's *Jesus* (Staley and Walsh 2007: 204).

However, as the historical Mary of Nazareth is unlikely to have worn the expensive colour blue, most wardrobe designers dress the actress playing her role in more muted shades, with only occasional nods to the artistic heritage. The first sighting of Mary in Connor's *Mary, mother of Jesus* presents her in a white dress with a blue shawl, as if she takes on her traditional colour symbolism from the start. In some films, Mary adopts an item of blue clothing after the Annunciation (Elizabeth hands her a blue shawl in Hardwicke's *The Nativity Story*), as if to signal that her iconic image is now developing. Therefore, it is notable in *The Passion of the Christ* that Mary and Magdalene are clothed in similar fashion, initially 'robed like Dominican nuns' (Levine 2004: 204). They are not visibly separated by issues of atonement for sin, although in Gibson's film the hierarchy is maintained through age, framing and positioning.[6]

Magdalene is identified as the adulteress whom Jesus saves from death by stoning in Ray's *King of Kings* and Stevens's *The Greatest Story Ever*

Told. When Magdalene later goes to visit Mary in *King of Kings*, she has changed her style of clothing and covered her once exposed flesh. However, she hesitates by the door, afraid to enter the home of Jesus's mother, who is holding bread in her hand (a Eucharistic symbol). When Magdalene protests her sinfulness and stops by a pillar that acts as a barrier between the two women, Mary responds in her one expression of individual sermonising in Ray's film: 'Child, God knows that evil exists as well as good. Just as there is light and darkness.' Rather inevitably, the light from the window illuminates the half of the room in which Mary stands, while Magdalene remains in shadow. The two women are initially separated by shot/reverse shot editing, and when Magdalene eventually accepts the invitation to share Mary's table, she enters the frame with her, and therefore comes into the light.

In Costa's *Maria, Daughter of Her Son*, Magdalene takes a dominant role amongst the followers of Jesus, while Mary herself remains in the background. It is Magdalene who leads Mary to Jesus with the words: 'Mary, are you hiding? You're the Master's mother, your place is at his side.' While Mary is hesitant and explains that she feels rejected by Jesus, Magdalene encourages her with the words: 'He'll always be with you. Mary, you should be terribly proud of your son, the son you carried here inside you. Being his mother makes you the most important woman in the whole world.' (There are shades of *The Magnificat*'s 'all generations will call me blessed' that were missing in the film's earlier Visitation scene). In this case, Mary does not accompany Jesus during his ministry, but begs Magdalene: 'Stay near him. Love him for me, too, if you can.'

In comparison, Jean Delannoy includes Mary in the 'sisterhood' of female followers of Jesus in *Mary of Nazareth*, some of whom are presented as former prostitutes (including Magdalene). The director regarded this entourage as proof that Jesus was 'the world's first feminist' (see Delannoy 1998: 248). Delannoy's titular heroine accompanies Jesus, reflecting the re-visioned Mary within a Jewish patriarchal culture as a woman of courage who follows her son as one of the disciples, and a prominent figure in early Christian history. In *Mary of Nazareth*, Mary becomes the central figure amongst the women, often slightly raised above them as they sit together as an indication of her elevated status. One of her more sustained speeches, occasioned when the other female followers ask about the conception of Jesus, is an apparently superfluous narrative for the audience (for she recounts the Annunciation episode that has already been depicted without adding any additional perspective). However, the image of Mary relating her life story to the women provides evidence for the 'eyewitnesses and ministers of the word' who are mentioned as Luke's sources for the writing of his Gospel (see Pelikan 1996: 18). Presumably Mary would have been too old to recount her memoirs directly to Luke, as some biblical historians claim, but Delannoy depicts the kind of oral tradition that would have provided such material (see also Larrañga 1991: 27).

CANA

While the episodes involving Mary and the female followers of Jesus are created in the imagination of the directors, the wedding at Cana places Mary in a key role that has a solid biblical foundation. Cana is one of the key scenes in 'the Judean story' in the silent epic *Intolerance* (Griffith, 1916) (see Grace 2009: 24), and the presence of Mary (Lillian Langdon) is highlighted via an intertitle, although her exact contribution to the instigation of the miracle is unclear.

The scene raises its own Mariological questions, given Jesus's response to his mother when she observes the wine shortage. In the New Testament, Jesus's words have been variously translated: 'Woman, what concern is that to you and me?' (*New Revised Standard Version*); 'Dear woman, why do you involve me?' (*New International Version*); 'Woman, why turn to me?' (*New Jerusalem Bible*); 'Woman, how does your concern affect me?' (*New American Bible*). The common factor in these various renderings is that Jesus addresses Mary as 'woman', which was uncommon in Hebrew or Hellenistic culture. Perry argues that this word may have been used by John 'to downplay motherhood as the key to her presence in the story' (2006: 99–100). While St Augustine regarded the response as a sign 'that Jesus refuses here to perform a miracle at his mother's request,' St Thomas Aquinas saw the scene as evidence 'that we need only place our needs before God, without inquiring how he may help' (see McHugh 2002: 3).

Notably, Cordero's *Mater Dei* avoids this line: Jesus remains silent until he tells the servants to fill the water jars and the issue is circumnavigated. Nevertheless, the position of the Cana scene in the last section of the film, which deals with Mary's role as an intercessor, clearly pins its colours to the mast. McHugh argues that 'Mary's words do not of themselves imply that she is hinting that Jesus should intervene, much less that he should perform a miracle' but that, given the context, 'it certainly looks as if it was in the hope or expectation that Jesus would do something to relieve the embarrassment of the newly-wed couple' (2002: 4). However, filmic interpretations generally indicate Mary's significance at Cana as being 'to point the way to Jesus by preparing the acceptance of signs' (Prévost in Anon. 1997: 56).

Mary and Jesus are located in the centre of the frame in the silent *The Life and Passion of Jesus Christ*, engaged in conversation when the wine runs out. Mary rises first and points towards Jesus, then points around the room. After the miracle, the guests raise their hands in gestures of surprise but Mary sits down quietly. While the commotion visibly continues in the background, she calmly continues to converse with Jesus, apparently not astounded by her son's powers. The 'background' role is even more clearly indicated in Olcott's *From the Manger to the Cross*, in which Mary is standing outside the room and tells Jesus of the wine situation through the bars of a window. Mary also retreats into the background at the moment that the miracle is performed in Delannoy's *Mary of Nazareth*. She instructs the servants to follow her son's command, despite Jesus's apparent rebuff, and the camera focuses upon her face as she closes her eyes in prayerful gratitude as the new wine is placed before her. Variations on this theme are adopted in *Mary, mother of Jesus* and *The Gospel of John*.

However, the traditional pattern of Mary as initially discreet (and subsequently silent) intercessor is broken in Costa's *Maria, Daughter of Her Son*, when Mary hurries after her son and questions her own actions: 'It's my fault, isn't it? [....] You've begun your journey and I was the one who ordered you to take the first steps.' Jesus assuages her concerns with the response: 'Remember when I was little and you taught me how to walk? It was right then, and so it is now.' Mary's role becomes substantially more overt in Young's *Jesus*, when she hears the first disciples disputing whether Jesus is really the Messiah. Coming to her son's defence, she encourages them to follow him, and when the wine runs out, she is very clear in her request to Jesus: 'Perhaps you could provide?' When Jesus responds that his 'hour has not yet come,' Mary will accept no refusal. She takes him firmly by the arm, saying, 'It is time. [....] Andrew needs to know. The world needs to know.' The film offers an explicit presentation of the psychoanalytical interpretation of Cana as the moment when Mary, the mother of Jesus, gives birth to the Christ (see Quéré 1982: 164).

WHO IS MY MOTHER?

Scorsese's *The Last Temptation of Christ* is based on *The Last Temptation* (1955) by the Cretan writer Nikos Kazantzakis rather than the Gospel, as is emphasised in the film's opening credits. In the novel (which was placed on the index of forbidden books by the Catholic Church), Mary is unsupportive of Jesus, and Scorsese's adaptation maintains this characterisation in his film. The one occasion that Mary (Verna Bloom) offers public encouragement is in an early scene when Jesus carries a cross beam to a crucifixion site. When the crowd abuse Jesus for helping the Romans, Mary comes to his defence. In private, Mary sees Jesus tormented by dreams and wrestling with his confusion over God's love for him, and she grasps his convulsing body and strokes his hair. But the next day, as Jesus prepares to leave the house, Mary asks, 'Are you sure it's God? Are you sure it's not the Devil?' Scorsese's Mary offers a blatant example of a woman who does not understand her son's mission. Therefore, it is not surprising that she plays no part in the miracle of Cana, although this event is included in the film.

In a subsequent scene in Nazareth, Mary runs after Jesus and asks him to come back with her. Jesus brushes her hand away and asks, 'Who are you?' When she replies in astonishment, 'Your mother,' she is rebuffed again by Jesus: 'I don't have a mother. I don't have any family. I have a Father, in heaven.' When Mary is upset by his reaction, he asks her again, 'Who are you? I mean, really.' He kisses her forehead and turns away, leaving Mary to fall to her knees, sobbing. Another woman tries to console her with the conviction that Jesus is blessed: 'When he spoke to you, there were thousands of blue wings behind him. I swear to you, Mary, there were armies of angels.' Yet this vision brings Mary no comfort: 'I'd be happier if there weren't,' she replies.

Scorsese's confrontation between Mary and Jesus is a reworking of one of the more difficult episodes in the Gospel for Marian scholars: the 'Mothers and brothers' pericope. Pasolini, Costa and Connor deal openly with these biblical verses and attempt to address the adult relationship between mother and son. In *The Gospel according to St Matthew*, Jesus is preaching when he is told that his mother and brethren are looking for him. He turns his back and continues to talk about 'the unclean spirit'. Two women, linking arms and dressed similarly in black, arrive below and look up to where Jesus is speaking. At this juncture, it would not necessarily be clear to the audience which woman is Jesus's mother. But Mary (played by Susanna Pasolini, the director's own mother) is in the centre of the frame with her left hand across her heart.

Another apostle repeats: 'Your mother and brethren are here,' and Jesus turns around. There is a close-up of Mary gazing up at Jesus, her face marked by age, and he stares down at her (given their respective positions) without smiling. The slight smile that was initially on Mary's lips disappears. There is a shot of one of the other apostles, waiting in anticipation for a reaction, and then Jesus says: 'Who is a mother? Who are brethren to me?' Mary lowers her head sadly at these words and draws her veil around her face, as if in pain. There are several shots of the apostles (singularly and in a group of five) and then Jesus continues, 'Here are my mother and my brethren! If anyone does the will of my Father in Heaven he is my brother and sister and mother.' At these words, there is a shot of Mary looking upwards again, now with a slight smile on her face, as if she understands that she is part of this new extended family and has not been rejected.

Fig. 12 'Who is my mother?' Susanna Pasolini in *The Gospel according to St Matthew*

In a later scene, the apostles walk in the vicinity of Mary's home but on the other side of the valley. Mary is carrying a heavy basket outside her house and Jesus looks in her direction but does not stop. But when the eyes of the mother and son meet, the proximity of their faces in the shot/reverse shot editing is not feasible given the actual spatial distance (see Bouquet 2003: 18) indicating that there is a link between Mary and Jesus that goes beyond physical proximity. Swiss theologian Hans Urs von Balthasar regards Mary as a servant of the Lord and as a 'hearer *par excellence*' who was pregnant with the Word: 'Even after she has given him birth, she continues to carry him within her; she only needs to look into her heart, to find him' (in Heft 1980: 54). Before the Crucifixion scene, Pasolini's Mary (who never utters a word in the film) would fit this description of the perfect contemplative with a silent bond with her son.

Fabrizio Costa deals most openly with the theme of rejection in *Maria, Daughter of Her Son*, interweaving a second narrative thread that sheds light on the challenge to Mary's courage: the story of John the Baptist. In an extrabiblical episode after John's imprisonment, Elizabeth and Mary go to the palace to plead for John's life. They arrive to see blood being washed away from the floor and a body in a shroud.[7] For Mary, the scene is a foretaste of her own fate.

Costa's narrative expands to cover Mary's homeward journey (her solitary travels being an unlikely event, as noted in Chapter 2). When Mary stops at an inn and hears her son's reputation being disparaged by a group of strangers, she intervenes in Jesus's defence. A man retorts: 'So the fool that calls himself a prophet actually has a mother. Didn't your son ever tell you not to meddle in the affairs of men?' Mary responds, 'A woman must tell the truth, just like everyone else.' Her words offer elements of a discipleship role but also indicate how the public censure of Jesus causes her own suffering.

At this point Jesus arrives and asks Mary to sit at the table with him. Taking some bread, he creates an early Eucharistic meal, saying, 'Whoever eats my body will become part of me.' (Mary is not actually present at the

Last Supper in the New Testament or in most filmic adaptations, *The Last Temptation of Christ* being a notable exception.) But Mary does not understand Jesus's words in *Maria, Daughter of Her Son* and can think only of John's death: 'When I saw Elizabeth's pain… Her scream still rings in my ears.' Jesus refuses her plea to return home to Nazareth with him and criticises her lack of belief. 'Where's your faith gone, woman? When you talk like that you speak like a mother not like one who's opened her arms to God. Your fear is blinding you. Don't tempt the will of the Almighty.'

When this scene is later followed by the 'mothers and brothers' pericope, Mary believes that Jesus's words are a further rejection. She returns to the location of the Annunciation to ask for guidance and speaks her prayer aloud: 'You said to me, "Mother Mary, rejoice!" Now tell me what I have to rejoice about? I'm no longer his mother. I am nothing. But he's still my son and I'm afraid for him.' [She kneels down.] 'Please protect him.' But there is no divine intervention to console her. Costa's Mary suffers the longest and most difficult pilgrimage of faith of any of the on-screen Marys analysed in this study, only truly expressing her understanding of her role (and, therefore, of the title of the film) at her own death.

In contrast, in Connor's *Mary, mother of Jesus*, Mary is able to explain Jesus's words in the pericope more positively to James, one of the disciples: 'He wasn't casting his own family aside. He was asking those people to enter into a new kind of family. What he teaches – love and peace – comes from God and it's for all the world.' At this point Jesus comes up to his mother and embraces her, confirming her position in his affections.

THE FIRST DISCIPLE

Psychoanalyst Julia Kristeva argues that Christianity 'is focused on *Maternality*' (1986: 161 [emphasis in original]). However, feminist theologians have argued that account should be taken not only of Mary's maternity (which, Johnson complains, has limited the options available to women) but also of 'the gospel proclamation that Mary's blessedness consists in hearing the Word of God and keeping it' (Johnson 1985: 128), which encompasses a discipleship role. It is also possible to draw on the works of the Church Fathers for support: 'Indeed, Mary was "both Mother and Disciple" in the words of Saint Augustine, who added that her discipleship was even more important for her than her motherhood (Sermon 25)' (Buono in Anon. 1997: 61).

The first sighting of Mary in DeMille's *The King of Kings* combines both the maternal and discipleship elements, for she is introduced as

'Mary... the mother' after the presentation of the disciples, so that she is listed alongside them. There is a white dove on the windowsill near her which may indicate both her own purity and the presence of the Holy Spirit (the white dove will later be seen at the Last Supper and the Crucifixion in DeMille's film). Mary stops her work at the loom (a popular Marian occupation that has a source in the apocrypha) for the onset of the Sabbath (as a reminder of her Jewish faith).

An intercessory dimension is then introduced. When a blind child climbs onto the windowsill, Mary reaches out to her and responds to the girl's plea ('Please, I have come to find Jesus') by taking her to Jesus, whom the audience have not yet seen. With her right hand stroking the child's hair, Mary stretches out her left hand towards Jesus and says (via the title card): 'My Son, this little one hath need of Thee.' Then she turns away and retreats into the background, her work of intercession over, as Jesus cures the girl's blindness. Mary's actions are also made explicit in Ray's *King of Kings* when Magdalene asks Mary to introduce her to Jesus. Kneeling down, ostensibly to fetch a plate, Mary's position becomes an act of prayer as she quietly utters, 'Intercede.'

The power dynamics of Mary's relationship with Jesus in Ray's film were the cause of some irritation to critics. Baugh maintains that Mary 'is gifted with an almost divine omniscience about her son's mission; she seems to know more about it than he does, and she annoyingly keeps dropping hints to this effect' (1997: 19); and Staley and Walsh claim that Mary 'knows more of Jesus's purpose than Jesus does' (2007: 36). Perhaps the situation is exacerbated because there is no Annunciation scene in Ray's film: a young woman who had received an angelic pronouncement that her child would be the 'Son of God' would presumably not be surprised that her child did not lead an ordinary life. The omission of the Annunciation makes Mary's certainty about Jesus's future ('Someday he will leave me, but someone else will call him. My son will know him when he comes') appear unsupported.

Certainly, Mary in *King of Kings* is aware of her son's purpose (which is not always the case in filmic interpretations) but her role is less determined than some critics suggest. While Mary is present at the Baptism in the Jordan, she is one of the observant crowd. Although the camera centres her in the frame (she is wearing a pale blue veil that underlines the traditional iconography), she is mainly in the background and often indistinct because of the shallow focus. There is a reaction shot of Mary when John touches the head of Jesus, but she is a silent witness rather than a protagonist. When Jesus heads towards the shore, he is walking straight towards Mary, but the scene is cut before he reaches her.

Baugh describes Ray's Mary 'as a much sought-after spiritual counsellor' (1997: 20), presumably referring to the scenes with John the Baptist and Magdalene, who both visit her home. Yet, when Mary's words are analysed closely, her utterances are more limited. When John the Baptist asks, 'How could I baptise [Jesus]? He is without sin,' Mary does not offer any answers but continues with her work (kneading dough) and the camera keeps its distance from her. In comparison, it is Mary in Connor's *Mary, mother of Jesus* who explicitly tells her son that he 'should go to John and receive baptism from him'.

In *King of Kings*, Mary does, however, seem aware that Jesus will be travelling to Jerusalem 'to deliver the word'. She informs John, 'When his time comes, he will be there,' an event that she anticipates with both sadness 'and joy'. In the later scene with Magdalene, Mary precedes her comments on the Lost Sheep with the phrase, 'Has not my son said....', so that she is clearly signalled as a 'first disciple' rather than a prophet.

At the Sermon on the Mount in *King of Kings*, a scene that Martin Scorsese particularly praised for its filming as 'a modern press conference' (in Baugh 1997: 21), Mary is also present. She stands on Peter's left, her position placing her with the disciples. At the question from someone in the crowd about Jesus's identity ('Are you the Messiah?'), there is a shot of Mary (with Magdalene standing further in the background). As Jesus replies, 'I am the Good Shepherd. The Good Shepherd lays down his life for his sheep,' the camera continues to focus on Mary and she casts her eyes downwards at her son's words as if understanding their significance. However, when the sermon ends, Mary and Magdalene form a separate unit a small distance away from Jesus and his disciples, indicating that they are not part of that central grouping.

When Jesus visits Nazareth, Mary senses his presence before she sees him with a natural (rather than supernatural) mother's intuition. Jesus is mending a chair when Peter and John enter and urge him to leave for Jerusalem, leading Jesus to say, 'The chair will have to wait until I return.' It is clear at this point that Mary is aware that Jesus will never come back home,

Fig. 13 Mary's intuition in *King of Kings*

for she replies, 'The chair will never be mended.' But it is uncertain whether she knows exactly how her son's life will end. There is a shot of Jesus's face as he pauses – perhaps indicating his own confusion or his acknowledgement of his future. Mary's face is in the foreground so that the audience's attention focuses upon her pained expression as she delivers her line, but she does not speak 'almost smugly, directly into the camera' as Baugh suggests (1997: 23).

Critics complained that Jesus looked weak and ineffectual in this scene in *King of Kings*. But such a comment would be considerably more apt in an analysis of Philippe Garrel's strange allegory *The Virgin's Bed*. The opening image of Jesus emerging from the sea to join his mother on a floating airbed indicates that he is already somewhat adrift. Zouzou's first appearance is identifiably in the role of Mary and she is a decidedly more forceful character than her son. Amidst a number of odd declarations, Mary tries to calm Jesus's fears, attempts to dry him with a towel, places a crown of thorns upon his head, and sings him a song about going to school, 'carrying his cross on his shoulder'. As far as it is possible to deduce from the film's first bizarre scene, Mary is vigorously encouraging Jesus to go out and preach a message (for which purpose she gives him a megaphone) but he is a most unwilling prophet.

Back on *terra firma* in Rossellini's *The Messiah*, Mary is 'the source of the idea' of the kingdom of God. Mary says, 'The kingdom of God is here, but people have forgotten, because they have forgotten how to do good' (in Lang 2007: 221), and she travels with Jesus, teaching children and the disciples: 'When everyone remembers to love, this will be the kingdom of God and fulfilment of the Law' (in Reinhartz 2007: 83). Yet the abrupt switch of focus in the editing (from Jesus talking to the disciples to Mary teaching a child) does not elevate the position of Mary. She is another mouthpiece for the Gospel message, which indicates the importance of Jesus's words rather than her own personal status. As she speaks, Mary is making bread, but it is presented as a domestic task rather than a form of Eucharistic symbol.

Jean Delannoy gives Mary a continuously visible, if not always a speaking, role in *Mary of Nazareth*. She is a silent witness at the Sermon on the Mount, follows Jesus during the entry into Jerusalem on a donkey, waits in an adjoining room during the Last Supper, and goes to the Garden of Gethsemane on the night of her son's arrest. Connor's *Mary, mother of Jesus* also develops Mary's presence at key events, such as the entry into Jerusalem. Her individual perspective is underlined by point-of-view shots as she makes her way along behind Jesus, especially when she looks up to see Pilate watching ominously from a window. In the light of Vatican II, P. G. Hinnebusch claims that Mary is seen to embody 'person, freedom, responsibility, commitment, involvement, witness' (1969: 54). The titular protagonists of *Mary of Nazareth* and *Mary, mother of Jesus* are representations of this re-visioned Mary. However, it is when the Passion of Jesus begins that she achieves her full significance.

THE WITNESS

Mary's role on Calvary has been played by a succession of actresses across cinema history, but it was Mel Gibson's *The Passion of the Christ* that drew full attention to her presence. The director's personal vision illuminates the Marian dimension that exists, in a variety of guises, in most cinematic Passion narratives.

The controversies surrounding Gibson's film have been well documented, with the disputed anti-Semitism and undisputed violence forming the central tenets of the arguments. Yet *The Passion of the Christ* also had an ecumenically unifying aspect, which saw evangelicals lauding a film whose themes and structure 'point to a heightened Catholic sensibility' (Martin 2004: 97). The screenplay is inspired by the writings of the Catholic mystics Mary of Agreda (1602–1665) and Anne Catherine Emmerich (1774–1824) (see Miller 2005: 83–113); it features extrabiblical episodes that are familiar from the Catholic devotion called The Stations of the Cross; and it gives a central role to Mary. Some critics maintained that 'Gibson also cuts away from Jesus's suffering for scenes showing Mary's symbolic connection with Jesus as co-redeemer, following the Roman Catholic theological perspective that Mary participates in the salvation of humankind' (Staley and Walsh 2007: 153).

Indeed, in trying to explain this possible anomaly, in which Christians of all denominations responded positively to a film with a highly Catholic dimension, Darrell Bock explained that evangelicals 'gave Mel a pass on the Mary perspective' (in Caldwell 2004: 218). And in his introduction to *The Bible on the Big Screen*, Stephen Lang remarks on Mary's substantial role in the film but admits that 'as an evangelical myself, I did not find that offensive, since love for one's son is not something specifically Catholic, and one of the Gospels does say that Jesus's mother was present at the cross' (2007: 16).

The Passion of the Christ has been repeatedly criticised as inflammatory, with claims 'that its depiction of Jewish villainy – exaggerated well beyond what is in the Gospels and violating what historical knowledge we have of early-first-century Judea – will give aid and comfort to anti-Semites everywhere' (Fredriksen 2004: 46). However, it has also been noted that Mary is (unusually) played by a Jewish actress (Maia Morgenstern). Her opening words ('Why is this night different from every other night?') and Magdalene's reply ('Because once we were slaves and we are slaves no longer….on this night we were led from captivity to freedom') are taken from the question and answer format of the Jewish Passover. This addition to the script was made at Morgenstern's suggestion, with her personal understanding of the symbolism of the Seder (see Bartunek 2005: 54). 'Remember that Jesus was born of a Jewish mother of the seed of David and the people of Israel' is the second of the Ten Points of Seelisberg that was published by the International Council of Christians and Jews in 1947 (see Barcroft 2002: 283). Amidst the outcry over anti-Semitism in Gibson's film, a number of critics singled out the importance of Mary as a Jewish mother (see Levine 2004: 200; and Prothero 2004: 275–6) through whose eyes the audience often watches events.

Beginning with a quotation from Isaiah 53 ('He was wounded for our transgressions… by his wounds we are healed'), *The Passion of the Christ* is interested in the links between the Old and New Testaments, and how the Messianic prophecies are fulfilled in Jesus, whose sacrifice frees humankind from the bondage of sin (see Martin 2004: 105). The film's very first shot is of the moon – a moon that indicates the time of the Jewish Passover but is also a major Marian symbol of virginity and femininity (as Godard's eighteen moon shots in *Hail Mary* indicated) that links Mary to the mystery of life. The moon is an element in the traditional iconography of the Immaculate Conception, in which Mary crushes the serpent beneath her foot. Gibson presents the moonlit Garden of Gethsemane as 'the new Garden of Eden, the biblical place of testing and temptation, the place of spiritual battle described in Genesis' (Bartunek 2005: 17-18), in which Jesus is the New Adam. When Jesus is tormented by an androgynous Devil (Rosalinda Celentano), his ultimate resistance is signalled when he crushes the snake beneath his foot.

The Devil has been visualised in Passion narratives before. In *The Greatest Story Ever Told*, he appears in the crowd in front of Pilate as a heckler, calling out for Jesus to be crucified; and in *The Last Temptation of Christ*, it is a young girl who tempts Jesus to come down from the cross in the dream sequence. But *The Passion of the Christ* provides a direct visual confrontation between Mary and satanic forces on the road to Calvary. The personal encounter between Mary and the Devil across the Via Dolorosa evokes the iconography of the Immaculate Conception (see Duricy 2004). As Mary walks along the left side of the path, her eyes meet those of the Devil on the other side. Notably Mary does not drop her gaze but stares straight at the Devil unafraid, and she is the one who looks away first to return her attention to Jesus, signalling her victory in this personal battle of wills.

The relationship between Mary and Jesus is one of the most striking elements of Gibson's film, as the mother supports her son during his trial, torture and execution. When Jesus is struck violently by the soldiers who come to arrest him in Gethsemane, the scene cuts to Mary, sitting up suddenly in bed. Magdalene's puzzlement ('What, Mary? What is it?') indicates that Mary's intuitive reaction is born of the maternal instinct that only she shares with her son. During the first Marian flashback to Nazareth, Mary pours water out for Jesus (with all its solemn connotations of cleansing and baptism), and he raises his hands to splash her in a playful gesture. The drops of water on Mary's cheeks are immediately replaced by tear stains as the narrative returns to the present tense, and Mary becomes the sorrowful witness at the trial of her son.

The bond between Mary and Jesus is magnified in a later scene in the Palace of Caiaphas, when Mary suddenly walks ahead of the group, as if her senses are awakened. There are hellish flames burning in braziers around her as she follows an invisible trail around the room, passing behind the pillars and then kneeling on the floor and putting her head to the ground. The camera pans slowly down to the room below in which Jesus is a prisoner, his hands chained to the ceiling. He looks upwards, as if also aware of his mother's presence above him.

In *The Passion of the Christ*, Mary's words ('It has begun, Lord' and 'So be it') imply 'that she knew everything that was going to unfold, at least in broad strokes' (Bartunek 2005: 52). Mary's eyes meet those of Jesus, and he continues to look back towards her as he is dragged away by the guards. When Jesus is tried before Pilate, a dove – presumably representing the Holy Spirit – appears in the sky as if to signal divine blessing over the events. As the crowd shout for Jesus to be crucified, John looks at the ground, and Magdalene covers her ears and lowers her eyes. Only Mary stands upright, staring ahead.

A biblical line such as 'They scourged him' is turned into a blood bath in *The Passion of the Christ* (see Wallis 2004: 122), and the beating reminds the audience that Jesus is the Son of God: 'No real human being, no matter how strong, could possibly have survived this' (Thistlethwaite 2004: 135). But during the flogging, Jesus looks towards Mary in the crowd as if to gain strength from her, reminding the audience of his humanity: 'His mother's presence and love renews His determination, a moment of intimacy between Jesus and Mary that Satan attempts to mock' (Bartunek 2005: 96). The Devil glides through the crowd at Jesus's scourging, carrying a 'demonic' baby, and offering an unnatural Madonna and child image that acts as a counterpoint to Mary's comportment during the flagellation scene.

Mary's eyes are full of tears as she sees her son, covered in welts, his hands trembling. Kristeva notes that tears 'are the metaphors of non speech, of a "semiotics" that linguistic communication does not account for' (1986: 174). Indeed, in the missionary films *The Jesus Film* and *Dayasager*, Mary does not speak at the Crucifixion, but her tears are a 'non speech' that is clearly understood across linguistic divides.

At one point during the flagellation scene in *The Passion of the Christ*, Mary's head bends slightly away from the sight and her tears flow as she says: 'My son... when, where, how will you choose to be delivered of this?' Her words indicate that she believes that Jesus has the power to stop this agony, but she does not yet realise how much longer the suffering will continue. As the torture proceeds, Mary closes her eyes and turns away, giving the audience a moment of relief from the torture. The ongoing beating is perceptible in the background but the shallow focus allows Mary to distance herself from it, and the sound of the whipping is more muted as the non-diegetic musical score is foregrounded. Mary moves along the edge of the square, with her hands joined, as if she were a nun walking through the cloisters in prayerful contemplation. Then the audience's attention is returned fully to the laceration while Mary leans her head on a pillar and cries. But when Magdalene joins her and sinks at her feet, it is Mary who consoles the younger woman, putting her arm around her and demonstrating her own continuing fortitude.

As Staley and Walsh point out, Mary 'is arguably the most important character other than Jesus's in Gibson's film (2007: 155). The screenplay notes that it is Mary's dignity that catches the attention of Pilate's wife, Claudia (see Bartunek 2005: 84). Crying herself, Claudia comes forward carrying white cloths, which she hands to Mary without words (the scene being inspired by one of Emmerich's visions). The two women look at each other before Claudia hurries away, her head bowed. It is through Mary's point-of-view that the audience contemplates the whips and the blood. Then Mary kneels on the floor and attempts to wipe up the precious blood of her mutilated son.[8] Thistlethwaite maintains that '[c]enturies of traditional Mariology are revived in this picture. Mary, immaculately conceived, is the only human who really can look upon Jesus's brutalization and crucifixion without guilt' (2004: 133). But if Mary looks 'without guilt', she remains a sorrowful witness.

THE VIA DOLOROSA

The Bible does not record a meeting between Jesus and his mother on the road to Calvary. However, the encounter which forms the fourth stage in the Stations of the Cross is central to Gibson's recording of the Passion narrative, as in previous filmic interpretations. Notably, the silent *From the Manger to the Cross* was actually filmed on the traditional Via Dolorosa (The Way of the Cross) in Jerusalem, linking the cinematic text with the historical location and the ongoing Christian devotion. Mary rushes forwards to embrace Jesus in Olcott's film but is brutally pushed back by a soldier.

In New Testament films, the key supporters along the Via Dolorosa may vary in number, identity and significance but the most frequent protagonists are Mary, Magdalene and John. Pasolini's *The Gospel according to St Matthew* is particularly memorable because Mary struggles to fight her way through the soldiers. The camera (and, therefore, the audience) is caught up in the trauma, and the medium shots of the bustling crowd give a sense of drama and movement. There is no non-diegetic music at this moment – just the soundtrack of an angry mob.

However, in Julien Duvivier's *Golgotha* (1935) (which is also a film of crowds and mobile cameras), Mary (Juliette Verneuil) and her female companions initially watch at a distance by an archway and their stillness contrasts with the heaving crowd. In Rossellini's *The Messiah*, Mary stands amidst a little group that is separate from the people who demand the crucifixion of Jesus. Pope Benedict XVI points out that, in the Bible, the few stalwart followers of Jesus are 'the small band of people who remain true in a world full of cruelty, cynicism or else with fearful conformity' (2007: 87). By distinguishing the witnesses from the other onlookers, spatially within the frame or through editing, the filmic narratives often make this point. In *The Passion of the Christ* Mary, Magdalene and John form a separate group, with Mary generally at the heart of the trio. Her central positioning signifies her importance.

There are shots in *The Passion of the Christ* that are reminiscent of Duvivier's *Golgotha*. Duvivier presents Jesus's point-of-view of the hostile crowd (a shot that Gibson will emulate[9]), and shows Mary, Magdalene and John walking a different path away from the crowds (as in *The Passion of the Christ*). However, when Mary meets Jesus on his journey in *Golgotha*, Mary calls out 'My son!' but Jesus is too battered to respond and there is no connection (which contrasts with Gibson's representation of the same meeting) and Mary faints to her knees. As Jesus takes up the cross in *The Passion of the Christ*, he embraces it and says: 'I am your servant, Father. Your servant, and the son of your handmaid.' These words evoke Psalm 86, but the handmaid reference brings Mary into the equation and reminds the audience of Mary's decision at the Annunciation, whose repercussions are coming to a culmination on this day.

The suggestion that Mary was embracing a role as 'coredeemer' in *The Passion of the Christ* divided critics. Some commentators embraced or rejected this appellation, while others did not recognise it within the film's diegesis. Staley and Walsh identified Mary in the 'Roman Catholic role of coredeemer, suffering with her son and willing him forward to his ultimate goal of dying on the cross' (2007: 155). In contrast, Johnston countered:

'Although Gibson personally might believe that Mary is a coredemptrix, participating in the redemption of humankind, such theology is nowhere evident in the movie' (2004: 67–8). Stephen Prothero contends that Mary 'carries the weight not only of the anguish of all bereaved mothers everywhere, but also of the sacred secret that her son is (with her help) making all things new' (2004: 275–6). Robert Johnston argues that 'Gibson chooses to use Mary more devotionally, as an eyewitness to these terrible final events in her son's life. Mary becomes the viewer's eyes and heart' (2004: 68).

In fact, there is evidence for all these varied perspectives in *The Passion of the Christ*. These opposing views reveal the complexity of Mary's reactions at her son's death in all the on-screen interpretations, as well as serving as a reminder of Simeon's words that Jesus will be 'a sign of contradiction'. Mary's attitude along the way to Calvary is neither uniform across the filmic Passion narratives nor always consistent within each individual text. Usually, moments of courage are followed by agony and physical fragility. Mary may faint or fall (once or several times). Whether such incidents are natural moments of weakness or symbolically linking her visually to the suffering of her son (who falls three times under the cross according to Catholic tradition) is left to the interpretation of the spectator. For example, there is no Via Dolorosa in *The Messiah* but Mary stumbles twice as she runs towards Calvary, as if taking on the role of her son vicariously. The first stumble might have even been an unintentional slip on the part of the actress; but the second fall is clearly scripted, as her white veil falls off and she replaces it with a black shawl (the Western colour of mourning) from a merchant who is standing on the right of the frame.

The sense that Mary supports Jesus's mission is usually transmitted by nods and glances exchanged between mother and son, as seen in DeMille's *The King of Kings* and *The Passion of the Christ*. In Gibson's film, there is a reaction shot of Mary's face, as she covers her mouth with her left hand and gulps, as a soldier flourishes a whip and tears strips of wood out of the table before using the instrument of torture on her son's flesh. Jesus looks directly at his mother and she returns his gaze, with a faint nod of understanding that he must bear this torture.

In Ray's *King of Kings*, Mary's eyes meet those of Jesus and follow him on his way. She clutches her veil to her throat but does not cry out, and her personal response is not articulated. However, in Connor's *Mary, mother of Jesus*, which offers a focused Marian narrative, Mary's feelings are voiced throughout the Passion. When Magdalene runs to Mary's house to tell her of Jesus's arrest, the cockcrows in the background alert the audience not only to the early morning time frame but also to Peter's act of betrayal (see Jn 18:27). Mary falls to her knees and needs to support herself on the stone doorpost, breathing heavily and praying: 'You gave him to me to bring into this world. I tried to keep him safe. Please, God, don't take him now, like this.' Then she struggles to her feet and says, 'Thy will be done.' This is her own Gethsemane moment.

When Jesus appears before Pilate in *Mary, mother of Jesus*, Mary verbally expresses her comprehension of her son's sacrifice. While Magdalene screams for Jesus to be saved rather than Barabbas, Mary's eyes meet those of Jesus and, although pale and anguished, she says, 'It is us he is to save, not himself.' There is no question here of Mary taking on the role of a co-redeemer. Indeed, in a later scene, Mary's sense of assurance wavers when Jesus falls under the weight of the wooden beam across his shoulders, with a rope around his neck. During the carrying of the cross, Connor shoots Jesus in slow motion (a technique favoured by Gibson, who frequently used speeds of forty frames per second), which gives a sense of significance to the actors but also prolongs the agony. Mary walks along with the market stalls (the pots and pans of domestic life) acting as a barrier between herself and Jesus.[10] She screams an aggressive 'No!' and tries to rush forward but is prevented by a soldier, leaving Magdalene as her only support.

When the disciples Andrew and James run away in *Mary, mother of Jesus*, Mary openly calls them cowards. It is unusual to hear the disciples verbally chastised for their inaction by Mary, although their weakness is often indicated by editing. In DeMille's *The King of Kings*, there is a shot of the apostles, who are hiding in a building as the cross passes by outside, so that Mary as the 'first disciple' on the street is clearly distinguished from the frightened men cowering behind the shutters.

Maria, Daughter of Her Son shares some similarities with *The Passion of the Christ*, avoiding a straight linear structure. While Gibson uses flashbacks to open out the narrative, Costa (as previously noted) begins with the Crucifixion and then looks back over Mary's life. Mary is also present when Jesus is flogged (as in Gibson's film) and both films give prominent roles to a number of women, including Pilate's wife. However, in *Maria, Daughter of Her Son*, Mary appears to have no comprehension of the necessity of Jesus's death to fulfil his messianic purpose, and she pleads with Pilate's wife: 'I carried him in my womb, I nursed him, brought him up, loved him. I lived only for him and have none other than him. Please, save him.' However, Pilate's wife does not have the power to intervene despite her fears (she reveals that she had a dream of Mary weeping), and there is no gesture of compassion. Therefore, in Mary's reaction to her son's suffering, *Maria, Daughter of Her Son* is closer in approach to *Mary, mother of Jesus*. When Mary meets Jesus on the journey to

Calvary in *Maria, Daughter of Her Son*, it is Jesus who says, 'Mother, please don't cry.' But she continues to moan, 'No, my child, my baby.'

In *The Passion of the Christ*, Mary, Magdalene and John support each other at different times through the torture of Jesus: 'In this interplay, the trio becomes an icon of the Christian community' (Bartunek 2005: 98). When Jesus falls for the first time, Magdalene is in the lead, while Mary lingers behind, leaning into a wall. As she hesitates for the first time (a moment of weakness that may indicate her own Gethsemane moment), she finds it hard to breathe. She can hear Jesus being beaten and the thud of the cross as he falls to the ground. When John goes back to fetch her, he calls her 'mother' (indicating her status amongst the disciples even before Jesus's entrustment of Mary to John on the cross), and this appellation evokes the second Marian flashback. Mary remembers Jesus as a little boy, falling down outside the house. As he stumbles, Mary knocks over a pot in her eagerness to rush to his aid with her arms outstretched.

Shots from this childhood incident are now interspersed with the present events on the Via Dolorosa, as Mary runs towards her son with the same gesture. In the past and present, she kneels down beside him and says: 'I'm here,' in words that were dubbed in postproduction (see Bartunek 2005: 117) to underline the maternal link. In her memory, Mary can pick up her little boy and comfort him. But she cannot save her grown son, who touches her face and says: 'See, Mother, I make all things new' (see the Book of Revelation 21:5). While the on-screen Marys cry for the agony to stop in the films of Connor and Costa, Gibson's Mary helps Jesus to rise to his feet and assists his journey rather than trying to prevent it. Although there are clearly elements of co-operation here, Prothero identifies a more universal message for Christians as Mary gives her son strength: 'she reassures us that, like her, we can summon the resolve to accompany Jesus to the cross, to see his divinely ordained mission through to the bitter end' (2004: 275).

In fact, more obvious symbolism of the co-redemption occurs in Delannoy's *Mary of Nazareth* – the work of a Protestant rather than a devout Catholic. Mary is at the front of the crowd during the trial with John and Magdalene, and she cries out in pain and staggers almost to her knees when she sees her son with the crown of thorns. Her suffering is met with a burst of laughter from the crowd, so that she, too, receives their jeers. On the journey to Calvary, Mary falls when Jesus

FIG. 14 Symbolism of the co-redemptrix in *Mary of Nazareth*

stumbles and blood is visible on her forehead beneath her veil as if she were wearing an invisible crown of thorns. It is an obvious visual link to join her suffering directly to the Passion of Jesus. While there is no biblical evidence for this *stigmata*, Delannoy is drawing attention to the co-redemption issue. In *Mary of Nazareth* there is a vision of the 'uniquely active and effective participating role of Mary in the mystery of Redemption' (Seifert 1996: 167).

STABAT MATER

Standing by the cross of Jesus were his mother and his mother's sister, Mary the wife of Clopas, and Mary of Magdala. When Jesus saw his mother and the disciple there whom he loved, he said to his mother, 'Woman, behold, your son.' Then he said to the disciple, 'Behold, your mother.' And from that hour the disciple took her into his home. (Jn 19:25–27)

The films discussed here, including Pasolini's *Gospel according to St Matthew*, explicitly place Mary at the foot of the cross as in John's Gospel.[11] Only *The Jesus Film* maintains its focus on Luke's Gospel by presenting Mary as a woman (dressed in blue) as one of the crowd. There is one shot of her face, in which she is visibly crying, but she plays no prominent role amidst the bystanders.

Mary's location at the Crucifixion is interpreted poignantly in the thirteenth-century Latin hymn *Stabat Mater*, which features prominently in Arcand's *Jesus of Montreal*. The hymn conjures up an image whose various interpretations have theological repercussions. Does Mary stand stoically or fall prostrate? Is she silent or distraught? How close to the cross is she? These issues have been addressed in art across the centuries, as seen in the rapid montage of religious paintings of the Crucifixion in *Jesus Christ Superstar* (1973), although Mary plays no other role within the diegesis of Norman Jewison's film.

Theologians themselves have been divided in their reflections on Mary's actions on Calvary, with some of the Church Fathers giving rather misogynistic interpretations. Cyril of Alexandria, for example, proposed that Mary suffered anguish because 'a mere woman, ignorant of all mystery, was deceived into thoughts of this kind' (in Price 2007: 64). In contrast, François de Sales (d.1662) 'reminded his audience that Mary was not faint-hearted, but stood stalwartly at the Cross, exhibiting no signs of feminine hysteria and weakness' (Warner 1990: 218).

Emilio Cordero, George Stevens and Roberto Rossellini offer examples of de Sales's reflection. In *Mater Dei*, Mary does not cry. She has her hands crossed across her chest in a similar gesture to her sign of agreement in the film's earlier Annunciation scene. As she is also dressed in the same colour (green, the colour of hope), the two events are visibly linked: 'The *fiat* of Mary at the Annunciation finds its fulfilment in the *fiat* at the foot of the Cross. To be faithful is to remain faithful in private to what we proclaimed in public' (Delessale in Anon. 1997: 151).

In *The Greatest Story Ever Told*, Mary is watching motionless with her hands clasped as Jesus sets out with his cross. She is pictured in the centre of the screen between John and Magdalene (her frequent position in *The Passion of the Christ*) and she remains standing upright, dressed in iconic pale blue. Mary (and the audience) is distanced from the cross and she never enters the frame with Jesus. Although there are tears in her eyes in a two-shot that she shares with John, as she hears Jesus's words ('Mother, there is your son. There is your mother'), the scene has a still, tableau-like quality. As Jesus says, 'It is finished,' Mary's hands rise slightly upwards as if in offering. Then she joins her fingers in prayer. Although her eyes are moist, she makes no sound (in keeping with the fact that she utters very few words in the course of the film, and the majority of those in voice-over). After Jesus says, 'Father, into your hands I commit my spirit,' there is a freeze-frame that underlines the Holy Card approach.

As in Delannoy's *Mary of Nazareth*, in which Jesus appears nailed to a cross that is superimposed in the centre of the scene, the Passion is curtailed in Rossellini's *The Messiah*. The scourging happens off-camera and Jesus is already hanging on the cross when the audience sees him. Mary stands calmly at a substantial distance from the cross, holding the hand of Magdalene, who sits on the earth and sobs at her feet. Jesus speaks no words on the cross and there is no interaction between himself and the onlookers. The camera zooms in on his face, giving the audience a closer perspective than the witnesses on the ground. But when Jesus dies and his head falls forward, there is a reaction shot of Mary, who closes her eyes and lets her head drop down silently in tandem with her son. Unlike in the work of some of his Italian counterparts, there is no outpouring of grief on Mary's part in Rossellini's film. Baugh argues that Jesus is consequently re-dimensioned: 'Jesus arrives quickly on Calvary and almost as quickly dies. It seems oddly like the noble, stoical death of a hero, like that of Socrates, rather than what it was in reality and in the Gospel accounts: a horrible and shameful death as a criminal' (1997: 91).

Indeed, even the silent filmed tableaux of *The Life and Passion of Jesus Christ* offer Mary a more emotive role. When Jesus addresses Mary on the way to Calvary, she swoons and is held upright by John's left arm. Mary appears to faint again as she climbs up the slope but is able to stand upright as Jesus is nailed to the cross. This mixture of emotions – from weakness to strength (and vice versa) – provides a template for many future filmic interpretations. Although Elizabeth Johnson has complained that the dogma of the Immaculate Conception has sometimes allowed Mary to be presented as if she lived above the trials of human existence, she admits that the 'exception is the sorrow she felt at the cross, but even here, it is said, she willingly sacrificed her son for the redemption of the world' (2003: 108). It is the dichotomy between maternal suffering at the death of a child and understanding of the divine nature of Jesus's sacrifice that creates the dramatic tension.

In *The Life and Passion of Jesus Christ*, Mary is standing as Jesus is crucified but her body leans backwards as if she is physically recoiling. Her lips move visibly, presumably in prayer as her eyes are raised to heaven. She kneels at the foot of the cross and clings to the wood, sobbing, until Jesus dies, and she seems oblivious to the flashes of lightning. Then she rises up, reaches out her hand towards Jesus and takes comfort by holding onto John, who is also crying. Her raised hand is a sign of offering. In the language of *Marialis Cultus* (1974), Mary is the 'Virgin presenting offerings'. Nevertheless, the Catholic Church is insistent that her role is not priestly, as that might give 'ammunition to the lobby for the female priesthood' (Warner 1990: 221). Although Mary has a unique role, she is not seen to participate in a ministerial sense, 'which in the presence of the Supreme Priest in the act of His Sacrifice would have been utterly superfluous' (Bossard and Rum in Anon. 1997: 455).

Mary is watching as Jesus is nailed to the cross in *From the Manger to the Cross*. She is on her knees and clinging to John for support. But as the cross is lifted, she too raises her arms upwards (as a possible gesture of offering) but then she sways with her hands clasped to her chest in anguish. The progression of her gestures reflects the two aspects to her role: the mother who understands her son's mission; and the mother who suffers to watch her son tortured. Although she has been present throughout the execution scene, the intertitle does not directly mention her until the end, when the quotation from John 19:25 appears on the screen. The title card is followed by a shot of Mary as she beats her hands against the wood of the cross as a manifestation of her suffering.

However, as the film contains no Resurrection scene, it is important for the Christian audience that the last image is more uplifting. Mary has her arms raised up towards Jesus on the cross in the most obvious symbolisation of 'presenting offerings'. This image is followed by the title card with the verse from John 3:16: 'For God so loved the world, that he gave his only begotten Son, that whosoever believeth in him should not perish, but have everlasting life.' In comparison, as La Marre's *Color of the Cross* contains no Resurrection scene, the images of a distraught Mary (Debbi Morgan), screaming and crying, serve to undermine the message of Redemption.[12]

Baugh describes DeMille's *The King of Kings* as 'a Breughel painting: the death of the God-man was too awesome and mysterious an event to be seen in the all-revealing close-up shots that are a staple of more recent Jesus-films' (1997: 13). However, Mary adds a note of humanity. Despite the earlier faint smile and nod of acknowledgement when Jesus passed her on the way to Calvary, Mary now holds out her hand in a gesture of protest towards the cross and covers her ears as the nails are hammered. There is no sign here of a co-redemptive role. She glances briefly towards heaven and clasps her hands. However, when Jesus is on the cross, he again exchanges glances with Mary, who nods her head in apparent comprehension, while other women are prostrate with grief behind her. Later, Mary comes and stands at the foot of the cross, touching the wood and gazing up at her son as if in a gesture of acceptance. There is a low angle point-of-view shot from Mary's perspective as Jesus gazes down on her, creating a bond between mother and son.

During the storm and the darkness that covers the earth, Mary sits on the ground near the cross, protected by John. A beam of sunlight illuminates the body of Jesus, as well as John and Mary, who are at the foot of the cross, uniting the believers with Jesus. Mary raises up her hands towards Jesus, and a white bird (a symbol of the Holy Spirit) flies around them.

In Duvivier's *Golgotha*, Mary forces her way to the cross first, accompanied by John who holds her hand. Mary and Magdalene stand out from the crowd because of their similar darker cloaks, giving them a sense of sisterhood that is also found in *The Passion of the Christ*. When a soldier tries to stop Mary, she bravely resists him, saying: 'I am the mother of Jesus.' Therefore, her appearance also gives the onlookers pause for thought. When a man in the crowd mocks Jesus, saying, 'A few women and a peasant, that is all that he has,' another bystander looks towards Mary and adds, 'His mother.' These words visibly affect the High Priest Caiaphas, who is also present.

A similar incident occurs in *The Passion of the Christ*, after Mary comes to Jesus's side after he falls. The Roman soldier named Cassius queries the identity of Mary. On learning that she is 'the Galilean's mother', he hesitates, looking at Mary in her grief, before he is dragged away by his colleague. The incident was intended to show Mary as a *mediatrix*, drawing people to Christ (for Cassius will fall on his knees when Jesus dies as a sign of conversion to the faith). Pelikan argues that 'there has probably been no symbol or concept in Christendom that has carried out this "pontifical" vocation of mediation with more success and more amplitude than Mary' (1996: 78).

In Ray's *King of Kings*, Mary and John stand together but separate from the other followers on Calvary. The camera is positioned at the top of the cross, so that it rises as the cross is put into position and the audience has a view from above Jesus's head – the popular 'eye of God' shot. As the motion stops, Mary (supported by John's arm) comes into view at the foot of the cross. The red sleeves hanging beneath Mary's cloak look like streams of blood and her face is ghostly white as she kneels by the cross, but the blood that runs down Jesus's body and drips from his wounds does not touch her. Baugh notes that Jesus dies 'a thoroughly sanitised, domesticated version of that atrocious death' that is 'oddly disconnected with his life and mission' (1997: 23). There is a low-angle shot of Jesus as he says, 'Woman, behold your son,' followed by a shot of Mary looking upwards. However, the cutting of the second part of Jesus's utterance ('Son, behold your mother') changes the sense of the message, asking Mary to look upon her crucified son, rather than take John as her adopted son.[13] This is one of the theological inaccuracies for which the film was criticised.

Reviewers also commented negatively on the passivity of Jesus. 'Jeffrey Hunter [...] doesn't look as if he's suffering at all and you don't feel it' was the verdict of Scorsese (in Telford 1997: 134). Therefore, when Scorsese made his own Life of Christ film, it was unsurprising that he presented a Jesus who suffered greatly. At Calvary in *The Last Temptation of Christ*, Jesus looks around and asks, 'Mother, Magdalene, where are you?' The camera adopts his point of view, scanning the spectators to focus on a group of four women dressed similarly in dark colours. Three of the women kneel, with Mary in the centre, while Magdalene remains standing (for it is Magdalene who is the focus of attention in Scorsese's film rather than Mary). Jesus says, 'Mother, I'm sorry for being a bad son' (revealing that he still has no understanding of his purpose) but he is held back as he tries to move towards her. Mary sobs aloud in pain and bends her head as Jesus cries out in anguish as his hand is nailed to the cross.

In *Jesus of Nazareth*, Mary is not visible on the road to Calvary. In a scene before the Passover, she tells the rabbi that she will see Jesus 'when it is time' and this 'time' is revealed as the Crucifixion itself. Mary arrives some time after Jesus has been nailed to the cross and misses some of Jesus's important words. A soldier tries to prevent Mary from approaching the cross, but a centurion (whose servant had earlier been cured by Jesus) recognises her and takes her hand, leading her through. It is another visual example of the way in which Mary's presence brings other people nearer to Jesus.

When Magdalene is also prevented from going closer to the cross, she insists, 'Please, I'm one of the family.' When the centurion looks for confirmation, Mary nods her head and says. 'Yes, she is one of the family,' and Magdalene smiles in gratitude. Baugh suggests here that 'having Mary tell a lie, while certainly non biblical, is not a problem for Zeffirelli' (1997: 76). Yet, rather than a lie, Mary's welcoming of Magdalene is a reiteration of the 'mothers and brothers' pericope that Mary herself had uttered in her own version earlier in the narrative: 'Anyone who obeys our Father in Heaven is his brother, his sister, his mother.'

Mary is crying in *Jesus of Nazareth*, as are the other women, but she remains standing. After Jesus gives Mary into John's care, the disciple leads Mary away from the foot of the cross and she looks back at Jesus across John's shoulder. Gaventa points out that, in the Gospel of John, there is no reference to John and Mary after the 'Behold, your son' verse and that, from the narratorial perspective, 'Jesus has no mother' from this point onwards (1999: 94). However, although Zeffirelli might initially appear to be adhering to this viewpoint, as the focus is on Magdalene rather than Mary as Jesus dies, Mary returns memorably to the centre of the frame in the Deposition scene.

THE MATER DOLOROSA

Mary as the *Mater Dolorosa* (the Mother of Sorrows) is clearly visualised in Connor's Marian narrative *Mary, mother of Jesus*; the films of the Italian directors Pasolini, Costa and Zeffirelli; and Gibson's *The Passion of the Christ*. In *Mary, mother of Jesus*, John holds Mary's hand as they approach the cross, where a soldier is gleefully holding the robe that Mary had once made for Jesus. When Jesus refuses the offer of myrrh mixed with wine to ease the pain, the reaction shot of Mary indicates that she wants him to drink it, and she raises her hands to her own lips. Mary sobs, with her hands covering her mouth; and then she holds her hands in a gesture of prayer, with tears on her cheeks. As the soldiers nail Jesus's feet, Mary's own body writhes in agony and she falls to her knees. Her body visibly jerks in revolt as Jesus cries out in anguish, and she stretches out her left hand, as if trying to shield him from this pain.

Each act of torture perpetrated against Jesus is followed by a reaction shot of Mary, so they are in a dialogue of suffering. There is a high-angle shot from above the cross that unites Jesus and the witnesses, and the shadow of the cross forms a cord linking Mary and the followers to Jesus.[14] As Jesus cries, 'My God, why have you forsaken me?' Mary stands at the foot of the cross with her hands extended in prayer and recites the Our

FIG. 15 A dialogue of suffering in
Mary, mother of Jesus

Father to the line 'trespass against us'. Then she clasps her hands and pleads: 'Don't take him!' The rain comes down (the single 'God's tear' in *The Passion of the Christ* is multiplied into a torrent). As Jesus says, 'It is finished,' Mary's hands are lifted up in a gesture of offering (as in *The Greatest Story Ever Told*). But as Jesus dies, Mary screams 'No!' (the second time that she has cried this word aloud during the Passion) and rushes forward, extending her hand towards Jesus's feet. She is not co-operating in this act of torture.

In Pasolini's *The Gospel according to St Matthew*, the viewers are often placed in the position of a figure in the crowd – their vision temporarily obscured by distance or people's heads as they strive to make sense of what is happening. When colour film was first invented, it tended to connote fantasy rather than reality, and Pasolini's neo-realist approach offers a grittiness that is evidently missing from the Technicolor epics. However, the audience does not have the benefit of traditional Marian iconography, and the spectator may initially find it difficult to locate Mary amongst the group of people who approach the cross. The use of black and white means that Mary is not an iconic figure and, in this aspect, Pasolini was prefiguring a form of liberation Mariology, in which the domesticated handmaid of popular piety is reassessed as the human woman of Nazareth who survives personal trials.

However, Mary is soon recognisable in medium shot because she appeared earlier in the diegesis, and she is later distinguished by framing that isolates her from the group. Two women try to hold Mary upright and there is a close-up of her anguished face, although her cries are covered by the musical score. Although Mary does not share the frame with her son, there are a series of shots of Jesus on the cross followed by one of her suffering face, so that they are linked by the editing (as in *Mary, mother of Jesus*). At moments Mary shuts her eyes when she looks towards Jesus, and the mobile camera replicates her movements as she falls and trembles, reflecting her unsteadiness. Kneeling on the ground, she keens and holds onto the two women for support.

As a result of its reverse structure, Costa's *Maria, Daughter of Her Son* plunges the viewer into the heart of the Crucifixion without preamble in its opening scene. Mary, who is identified by her position next to John, cries out in anguish, 'My baby!' and holds her right hand against her chest. She beats her breast with each blow of the hammer putting the nails into Jesus's feet, and then runs forward crying, 'No! Stop! Please! Have mercy! My baby!' (There is no evidence that she truly understands her son's sacrifice.) She runs to the cross with her hands outstretched and touches Jesus's feet, which is as far as she can reach, before she is dragged away by a Roman soldier. Her cry ('Great gift of love!') will later be revealed as the expression that she used when she held the baby Jesus in her arms at the Nativity. Mary screams as a soldier stabs Jesus with a spear, and she faints to the ground as Jesus dies. She rests in John's arms – a form of *pietà* – as Jesus hangs on the cross. The scarlet bracelet (which the audience will later learn is a love token from her marriage to Joseph) is visible on her wrist as a symbolic wound.

In *The Passion of the Christ*, Mary, John and Magdalene fight their way to the front. Magdalene is on her knees but Mary is standing, looking straight at Jesus. As their eyes meet, she kneels on the ground and Jesus gets to his feet, perhaps given the strength by Mary's prayers. As the nails are driven into Jesus's hands, Mary physically recoils as if struck herself with each blow of the hammer (as Mary did in *Mary, mother of her son*). When the soldier stretches Jesus's arm to reach the nail hole, breaking the bone, there is a focus on Mary's tearstained face. A nail is hammered into Jesus's feet, and Mary closes her eyes and grabs hold of the gravel that makes up the ground.

However, as the cross is raised to its position, Mary stands up and lets go of the gravel, the idea for this gesture coming from Maia Morgenstern herself (see Bartunek 2005: 145). Mary's action here offers an interesting counterpoint to *The Last Temptation of Christ*, in which Scorsese markedly transforms the image of the Devilish spirit who tempts Jesus from the cross in Kazantzakis's text. In his novel, Kazantzakis describes the 'angel': 'His body was supple and firm, a blue-black disquieting fluff enwrapped his legs, from the shins to the rounded thighs; and his armpits smelt of beloved human sweat. [...] He folded his two wide green wings as though he did not want to frighten Jesus too much' (1975: 454). On screen, Scorsese's 'angel' has changed both sex and colour coordination. The young girl blends into the warm brown tones of the earth – an indication that her words speak of earthly interests and temporal passions rather than a heavenly message. In the novel, the angel tempts Jesus with the words: 'Once upon a time your heart did not want the earth; it went against her will. Now it wants her – and that is the whole secret' (1975: 457). Scorsese's use of colour underlines this earthly dimension. Consequently, when Mary lets go of the earth in *The Passion of the Christ*, it is a visual indication that she is free of the temptation to cling onto Jesus for earthly (albeit human) motives and accept that she must give him back to God for a divine purpose.

There is a flashback to the wine at the Last Supper in *The Passion of the Christ*. When Mary goes to the foot of the cross and kisses the feet of Jesus, the red blood then evokes the communion wine. It is also notable that the blood from Jesus's wounds is transferred onto her skin, linking her to his suffering and the iconography of the co-redemption. Again, this incident contrasts with the scene in Scorsese's *The Last Temptation of Christ*, for when the 'Devilish' young girl kisses the feet of Jesus, the blood does not mark her lips.

As Jesus says, 'It is accomplished' in *The Passion of the Christ*, Magdalene is still sobbing but Mary stands up straight and looks at her son. His heartbeat slows and stops. Mary says 'Amen', although the word does not appear in the subtitles (see Bartunek 2005: 145). Bartunek argues: 'This whole experience has been a living prayer for Mary, an offering of herself, her son, and her love' (2005: 145). There is silence. Then the teardrop falls from heaven that causes the earth to tremble. Jesus is stabbed with the lance, and water and blood flow down (a symbol of Baptism and of the Eucharist). The death of Christ symbolises the birth of the new Church, of a new Creation in the eyes of Christians. It is symbolic that the blood covers the now repentant soldier, who falls to his knees, and also bathes Mary and John, the first members of the new Church.

UNIVERSAL SIGNIFICANCE

When Jesus dies in *The Gospel according to St Matthew*, the screen goes dark and there are quotations from Matthew's Gospel in voice-over: 'You will listen, but for you there is no understanding. You will watch, but for you there is no perceiving. The heart of this people has become dull. Their ears are slow to listen, they keep their eyes shut. So they may never see with those eyes, or hear with those ears.' Critics have commented on Pasolini's view of himself as an 'angry, intellectual, cultural and moral prophet, rejected by his own people' (Baugh 1997: 100), identifying with the figure of Jesus in *The Gospel according to St Matthew*. This autobiographical dimension is evidently underlined by Pasolini's casting of Susanna Pasolini in the role of Mary. Yet, beyond this very specific case in which the director's mother plays the role, Mary at the foot of the cross has a more universal significance.

Marina Warner points out that Mary 'made the sacrifice on Golgotha seem real, for she focused human feeling in a comprehensible and accessible way' (1990: 211) and that she consequently became 'an approachable, kindly figure who could be depended on for pity and comfort' (1990: 216). When the mother of the unrepentant thief stumbles against Mary in

DeMille's *The King of Kings* (and says, via the intertitle, 'That one is my boy!'), Mary embraces the sorrowful mother. With her right hand on the woman's head, Mary stretches her left hand upwards to touch the wood of the cross, so that they are two mothers united in sorrow. 'In the *Order of Christian Funerals* the Church asks that the grief of parents over a dead child may be assuaged by the maternal presence of Mary who stood by her dying Son on Calvary' (Buono in Anon. 1997: 92). And within women's cultural reflections during time of war, the image of Mary on Calvary has been a source of inspiration to express their suffering at the mutilation and death of their sons on the battlefield (see, for example, O'Brien 2007b).

The continuing impact of the New Testament story is seen in Dornford-May's *Son of Man*, which updates the story to contemporary Africa and presents Jesus as a charismatic leader who speaks a pacifist message in an age of violence.[15] However, when Jesus is brutally killed, his death is not presented as a public execution but as a thuggish murder at night 'behind closed doors'. Consequently, there are no 'words from the cross' and the universal significance of his sacrifice is undermined. Jesus's body is put in the boot of a car and driven to a lonely spot to be buried.

It is at this point that Mary plays a significant role within the diegesis. Mary is not present at Jesus's death, but she becomes a 'mother of the disappeared' who refuses to be cowed. Joining the followers of Jesus, she goes to the authorities and bangs on the window, holding up a picture of her son in a quest for answers about his fate. When Mary learns the location of her son's grave, she visits the burial site and begins to dig with her bare hands to reach the body. The followers hang Jesus's corpse upon a cross (with red cloths to indicate the blood flow) in plain view of the authorities. Jesus's initial 'resurrection' is a symbol of defiance, as his supporters join together at the foot of the cross, dancing and singing 'The land is covered in darkness'. When the military try to disperse the people, Mary continues dancing with her back to the soldiers. As shots are fired, she has to fling herself to the ground. But then she stands up, faces the gunmen, and continues her defiant song and dance. Other people come to join her.

Writing in 2004 before the films *Color of the Cross* or *Son of Man* were released, Robert Franklin argued:

Since the slave period, blacks have understood and portrayed Jesus as a Suffering Saviour and a grassroots leader who was the victim of state-sponsored terror. Black theology has focused on the humanity and socially marginal status of Jesus. [...] When African Americans revisit the Passion scene, we know what the young Jewish mother Mary felt. We know the agony of those disciples who yearned to avenge their leader but were too powerless and afraid to try. (In Wallis 2004: 114).

These issues come particularly to the fore in the work of Dornford-May. However, rather than presenting a powerless victim, *Son of Man* offers a markedly feisty Mary who is prepared to stand up for the truth as a 'first disciple'.

THE PIETA

The New Testament does not recount that Mary took the body of her son into her arms at the Deposition and not all directors choose to give her this role. In *The Gospel according to St Matthew*, Mary stands to one side as the crown of thorns is tossed unceremoniously away onto the ground. (In comparison, in *The Passion of the Christ*, a shot of the crown of thorns and the nails becomes a notably iconic image.) More surprisingly, given the focus of his film, Jean Delannoy also avoids a scene that would have placed Mary in the centre of the frame in *Mary of Nazareth*.

But the image of the *Pietà* – made so famous by Michelangelo's beautiful marble sculpture – has entered the human cultural consciousness, and it has been embraced by directors of Passion narratives, with notable variations in style and impact. When Jesus's corpse is unearthed in *Son of Man*, there is a (literally) moving *Pietà* scene as Mary sits in the back of an open truck, with her son's body across her lap, travelling along the road.

In Ray's *King of Kings*, John helps lift down Jesus's body, which is then wrapped in a pure white cloth and laid on the ground in front of Mary. There is a high camera angle that reveals that the body does not look particularly bruised and the bindings are very white. Mary kneels silently by Jesus's head, and her facial expression indicates that she wants to be alone with the body of her son. The audience are not invited to join Mary in her suffering (which obviously marks a major contrast with Gibson's film, in which the audience is implicated). It is a private moment of contemplation, in which the cross continues to cast a shadow over the body of Jesus.

In *Jesus of Nazareth*, Jesus is taken down from the cross in the rain and his body is laid on the ground. Mary runs forward and cries and screams over the

FIG. 16 The suffering of a mother holding her dead child in *Jesus of Nazareth*

body in lamentation. She lifts Jesus up by the shoulders and holds him in her arms, then she lays him down and continues to keen over the body. Zeffirelli describes the intensity of the scene with Olivia Hussey:

> She was so totally immersed in her role, in her world of utter grief, that at the climax, sobbing in the rain pelting the lifeless body of her martyred son, she drew him to herself with amazing strength. Olivia actually lifted Robert Powell, a seventy-kilo man, as though she were really taking an infant into her motherly embrace. A moving scene, perhaps the most dramatic of them all. (1984: 73–4)

In his autobiography, Zeffirelli also makes a link to twentieth-century wartime memories 'of that terrible morning in 1944 when I had watched the mothers keening over their sons hanged by the Germans' (1986: 280).

Warner points out that there are Gothic and Renaissance treatments of the *Pietà* in which 'the slumped body of Christ is disproportionately small and the face of the Virgin anachronistically young in order to recall, with tragic irony, the mother who once held a baby in her arms' (1990: 209). In *The Messiah*, Rossellini has retained Mary's eternal youth, and this is nowhere more evident than in the *Pietà* scene. Reinhartz refers to Brunette's argument that the camera zoom draws attention to 'the prurient gaze of the nearby men' (2007: 83). But the men are standing behind Mary – so their vision is obscured. Only the audi-

FIG. 17 Michelangelo's *Pietà* brought to the screen in *The Messiah*

ence has a full view of Mary and her son, and the stillness and initial silence of the image creates one of cinema's most evocative incarnations of the artwork of Michelangelo in St Peter's Basilica in Rome.

In *Mary, mother of Jesus*, the body is taken down from the cross and laid on the ground in the rain. Mary removes the crown of thorns and the rope around Jesus's neck – the symbols of torture – and cradles her son's bloodstained head. Magdalene (at his feet) and John are also kneeling, crying. The three of them are alone with the body by the cross. When a similar grouping was observed in *The Passion of the Christ*, John Wallis complained that the sympathetic Jews Nicodemus and Joseph of Arimathea were replaced by Mary, Magdalene and John (2004: 120). But Joseph of Arimathea is one of the protagonists at the cross in Gibson's film,

FIG. 18 Breaking the fourth wall in
The Passion of the Christ

along with the repentant Roman soldier, as representatives of a wider humanity. Diane Apostolos-Cappadona remarks that Mary is moved 'from an elevated seat [as in *The Messiah*] to a position on the ground as a Madonna of Humility' (2004: 106).

In *The Passion of the Christ*, Mary breaks the fourth wall and looks directly at the audience. Her right hand is slightly open, as if she offers Jesus to the spectators. Apostolos-Cappadona compares Mary's role to the traditional interlocutor figure in painting, who 'serves as the connective between the action within the frame and the viewers outside its borders. Here is the anguished mother petitioning the world to witness the unnatural act that has been unleashed on her innocent son' (2004: 106).

In response to the perceived anti-Semitism in his film, Gibson claimed: 'This film collectively blames humanity [for] the death of Jesus. Now there are no exemptions there. All right? I'm first on the line for culpability' (in Meacham 2004: 13). The revelation that Gibson had filmed his own hand hammering in one of the crucifixion nails was a further illustration of this perspective. And there is no doubt that the final image of the film, in which Mary looks directly into the camera, is striving to implicate the whole audience in the sacrifice.

conclusion

In the Catacomb of Priscilla in Rome there is a fresco of a mother and child – the earliest documented portrait of the Virgin Mary. Tourists walk into the underground passageway and crane their necks to see the third-century artwork illuminated by torchlight, marvelling at the realisation that this is known as *the first* extant representation of the mother of Jesus. Cinematic portraits of Mary, projected onto screens in darkened rooms, form part of a very long heritage.

But in adding to the Marian artwork that already exists in paint, clay, marble and mosaic, filmmakers are facing a number of very specific challenges. Which director has the ability to handle the spiritual dimension via the cinematic medium? Who has the literary verve and theological understanding to write scenes that will transform the Scriptures into a screenplay? Is the aim to create an original *oeuvre*, to hearten the committed Christian, to develop an evangelistic tool or to create revenue for the film studio? Is there a need to be 'revolutionary' in style or content in order to appeal to audiences born two thousand years after the events portrayed?

In the history of religious films, it has been difficult to predict the 'winning combination' of profit and spiritual inspiration. A film about the Crucifixion with dialogue in Aramaic and Latin (originally intended to be released without subtitles) did not suggest big box-office, and Mel Gibson invested $25 million of his own money in *The Passion of the Christ* without any guarantee of financial return. Indeed, Robert Johnston argues that Gibson's film 'is not first of all about entertainment. Few who have gone to see it would even say it was enjoyable' (2004: 58). But although Gibson's film did not win universal approval, the fact that it earned over $300 million in the first year of its release (and over $600 million altogether) led to Hollywood's reawakened interest in religious topics.

Yet, although monetary gain might obviously play a part in filming a biblical screenplay, many directors of religious films profess loftier ambitions. Pasolini was inspired by the 'dialogue with artists' instigated by Pope John XXIII. Martin Scorsese wanted 'to make the life of Jesus immediate and accessible to people who haven't really thought about God in a long time' in *The Last Temptation of Christ* (in Marsh and Ortiz 1997: 137). And Jean Delannoy, who lived for a hundred years, wanted to end his career 'with something beautiful', and chose the life of Mary for his final film. Even Jean-Luc Godard (like Gibson) invested his own money in *Hail Mary*, and he explained his motivations:

> I think there's something so strong in the way the Bible was written, how it speaks of events that are happening today, how it contains statements about things which have happened in the past. I think, well – it's a great book! And somehow I think we need faith, or I need faith, or I'm lacking in faith. Therefore maybe I needed a story which is bigger than myself. (In Dieckmann 1993: 119)

The story of the mother of Jesus was 'bigger than himself' as Godard rightly indicated and demanded a particular sensitivity that he was unable to bring to his project. When Godard expressed his intention to take Shakespeare's *King Lear* and 'to do King Lear as King Leone, as a sort of patriarch-gangster... like a godfather' (in Brody 2008: 492), noone raised an eyebrow. But when Godard turned his attentions to the figure of the Virgin Mary, the most sacred female figure in Christian history, some members of the general public took to the barricades.

As is clear from the selection of films in this book, a filmmaker does not need a personal religious belief in order to make a non-parodic New Testament film. Pier Paolo Pasolini offers a very famous demonstration of this truth. Despite the fact that *The Gospel according to St Matthew* is directed by a Marxist atheist, the film was so appreciated by the Catholic Church that it appeared on the Vatican List of forty-five great films from the first century of the cinema. But Pasolini was 'an unbeliever ... who has a nostalgia for belief' (in Lang 2007: 180) and this nostalgia presumably served him well.

In an interview before making *Hail Mary*, Godard claimed that he would like to take Dolto's book *L'Évangile au risque de l'anaylse*, the characters of Joseph and Mary, three Bach cantatas and a book by Martin Heidegger, and ask IBM to 'make me a program that puts it all together' (in Laugier 1993: 29). But computer programs presumably do not (yet) understand the finer points of Marian doctrine, and when Godard undertook the task himself, it became clear that he did not either. Consequently, Godard earned the distinction of being the first director to receive a papal condemnation. In 1985, John Paul II sent a message of support to the film's opponents:

> The Sovereign Pontiff joins in the unanimous tribulation of the faithful of the Diocese of Rome concerning the programming of a film that insults and deforms the fundamental tenets of Christian faith, and desecrates the spiritual significance and historic value, and deeply injures the religious feeling of believers and the respect for the sacred and the Virgin Mary, venerated with so much love by Catholics and so dear to Christians. (In Locke 1993: 4)

While some commentators remarked on Godard's sincerity in tackling *Hail Mary* rather than it being a case of a director 'falling back on blasphemy to maintain a radical profile' (Mulvey 1993: 39), Godard faced a central problem that he had not encountered in his other experiments with collage. The Virgin Mary has a very specific significance in Christian Salvation History. She is not simply a blank canvas for the projections of the creative artist, or a name on which to hang an invented personality.

So, why do filmmakers continue to tackle religious subjects despite the inevitable pitfalls? In her fascinating book entitled *Glimpses of the Mother of Jesus*, Beverly Roberts Gaventa mentions that she 'would delight in hearing the content of Mary's pondering' over the birth of Jesus in the Gospel of Luke (1999: x). A scriptwriter would take this statement from Gaventa's work and use it to spark the imagination. If theologians cannot provide the answers, filmmakers are all too willing to take up the challenge. Some critics might query the way in which secular writers read between the lines of the New Testament and draw out Mary's biography with their imaginative scenes. But there is a very human desire to understand the motivations of the protagonists in the Christian narrative, given that it forms the lynchpin of the faith of billions of people. By presenting the story of Mary of Nazareth, the filmmaker is inviting the spectator to review the life of Jesus from a woman's perspective. It is, therefore, rather disappointing that only a few of the directors who have embraced this subject matter are female (Catherine Hardwicke and Katharina Otto in this particular study), although women have contributed to the scripts from the early days of cinema onwards, as testified by the fact that Gene Gauntier wrote the screenplay for *From the Manger to the Cross*, as well as playing the part of Mary. Godard's experience does not mean that there is only one way to approach the narrative of Mary (for example, in the pious, often static, symbol of *Mater Dei* or *The Greatest Story Ever Told*). The feisty black African Madonna in Dornford-May's *Son of Man* demonstrates the ongoing significance of Mary's role in the Passion narrative. It also proves that it is not necessary to cause outrage in order to make the Marian narrative stirring and relevant for a twenty-first century audience.

In the films selected for analysis in this book, the final image of Mary in the diegesis is often one of the most memorable, with *The Passion of the Christ* being a case in point. As Maia Morgenstern herself said: 'But in the end it was just a matter of a mother's love for her son. She couldn't do anything else. What else could she do? She had to suffer with Him' (in Bartunek 2005: 145). Mary's aged, smiling face at the Resurrection in Pasolini's *The Gospel according to St Matthew*, or the tearstained face of the 'ever young' Mary in Rossellini's *The Messiah*, as she realises that her son has risen from the dead, offer the positive hope after the despair of Calvary. In *Son of Man*, Dornford-May's Mary sings and dances after her son's death in order to continue the message that he preached.

THE FILMIC EFFECT

The contribution that film makes to the Marian iconographic heritage is significant and extensive. While this study has focused on the narrative of Mary of Nazareth, the Marian image has made multifarious appearances throughout film history, whether as a symbol of Catholic culture, divine providence, or a plot device (see Duricy 2000). While revered religious paintings remain in museums under video surveillance, the image of Mary is no longer out of reach, as the tourist souvenirs at the Marian shrines amply demonstrate. In capturing Mary's life in moving pictures, magnifying it on film screens, and copying it onto DVD for home consumption, the process of filmmaking also brings the story back down to earth while continuing the search for the transcendent (see Malone 2005: 14). Benedict XVI argues that Jesus leads the Christian to God's light through parables: 'In order to make [God's light] accessible to us, he shows how the divine light shines through in the things of this world and in the realities of our everyday life' (2007: 192). André Bazin, who was convinced 'that the movie camera, by the simple act of photographing the world, testifies to the miracle of God's creation' (Matthews 1999: 23), would have agreed.

Across the centuries, two Mariologies developed: one placed Mary in heaven, beside God's throne and 'sharing in its majesty and inaccessibility'; and the other looked to her as a gentle mother figure (see Bingemer 1991: 101). Vatican II attempted to rectify the model of Mary as inaccessible, with titles and privileges that distanced her from humanity (see Beaudin 2002: 5) and to promote 'a common ecumenical understanding of Mary as one of us with a unique vocation' (see McLoughlin and Pinnock 2007: xii). Psychoanalyst Julia Kristeva singled out the painting of the Nativity (1470–75) by Piero della Francesca as an image that represented the 'the new cult of humanistic sensitivity' that 'assimilated the Virgin to Christ with an earthly conception of a wholly human mother' (1986: 171). In particular, filmmakers are able to contribute to that 'cult of humanistic sensitivity' by presenting Mary as a human being walking on solid ground.

The focus on the human woman of Nazareth, rather than the Queen of Heaven, links with aspects of liberation Mariology. Within theological studies, there have been attempts to replace the history of Mary that has been 'maximalist, triumphalistic, and fictionally imaginative' and to make her 'intelligible and imagineable as a woman, a poor person, a person of strong faith, and a model who is memorable in cult for her saintly Jewish humanness' (Brennan 1995: 53). In many ways, film is the obvious medium to translate this aim. Mary has been called 'a masterpiece of God, because in her we detect a surplus of the divine – the overflowing presence of God's goodness in an earthen vessel' (Roten 1998: 111), and some of the world's most beautiful actresses (albeit by Western standards) have incarnated the role of Mary. But in filmmaking it is the 'earthen-ness' of the vessel that often comes to the fore, meaning that filmic narratives provide the opportunity to reflect on Mary 'as a Jewish woman of her era, someone whose experience relates her to men and women everywhere' (Cunneen 1996: xix). For Christians, she is a woman whose faith and courage are imitable, even if her very unique role in God's plan of Salvation is not.

However, Godard made an important observation on the Marian image: he admitted the difficulty of framing Mary in close-up in *Hail Mary* because the Marian dimension was lost as Myriem Roussel became indistinguishable from any other beautiful actress (see Païni and Scarpetta:

1984: 8). The 'celluloid Madonna' is a flesh and blood Madonna. But in any attempt to understand the mother of Jesus, a certain respectful context is always preferable.

And is it possible to understand the significance of a woman who 'has been more of an inspiration to more people than any other woman who ever lived' (Pelikan 1996: 2)? Filmmakers (and academics) continue to try and fail. At the end of Connor's *Mary, mother of Jesus*, the disciple John tells Mary that her work is finished, but Mary counters: 'Our work has just begun.' Then she herself utters a variation on the Great Commission: 'Go out into the world, knowing our own weakness, try to teach as he taught, live as he lived, love as he loved.' She looks directly at the camera and smiles. In both *The Passion of the Christ* and *Mary, mother of Jesus*, the actress playing Mary breaks the fourth wall in order to draw the audience in; and in Gibson's film the camera tracks back to reveal the body of Jesus in his mother's arms. Joseph Cheah argues that when Christians talk about Mary, the first question should not be 'Who is Mary?' but rather, 'Who is Jesus?' (1995: 73-4). Even if these films are only partly successful in their depiction of the mother of Jesus, they still continue to pose that very question and invite the audience to respond.

notes

INTRODUCTION

1   For more information on *The Jesus Film* project, see the official website: http://www.jesusfilm.org/index.html. Dayspring International was founded by John Gilman (see http://www.dayspringinternational.org/). *Dayasagar* (which is also known under the titles *Karunamayudu* and *Ocean of Mercy*) features Indian actors and has been translated into fourteen Indian languages. For more details see the work of Dwight Friesen (2008).

2   See http://campus.udayton.edu/mary//resources/researchdatabase.html. This research tool is complemented by Michael Duricy's postgraduate thesis, in which he collated information on over a thousand films: *Mary in Film: An Analysis of Cinematic Presentations of the Virgin Mary From 1897–1999, A Theological Appraisal of a Socio-Cultural Reality* (2000).

3   *Mater Dei* (Emilio Cordero, 1950); *The Nativity* (Bernard L. Kowalski, 1978); *Mary and Joseph, A Story of Faith* (Eric Till, 1979); *For Love, Only For Love* (Giovanni Veronesi, 1993); *Mary of Nazareth* (Jean Delannoy, 1994); *Mary, mother of Jesus* (Kevin Connor, 1999); *Maria, Daughter of Her Son* (Fabrizio Costa, 2000); *Joseph of Nazareth* (Raffaele Mertes, 2000); and *The Nativity Story* (Catherine Hardwicke, 2006).

4   *The Virgin's Bed* (Philippe Garrel, 1969); *The Milky Way* (Luis Buñuel, 1969); *Hail Mary* (Jean-Luc Godard, 1984); *The Last Temptation of Christ* (Martin Scorsese, 1988); *Jesus of Montreal* (Denys Arcand, 1989); *The Second Greatest Story Ever Told* (Ralph Howard and Katharina Otto, 1994); and *Son of Man* (Mark Dornford-May, 2006).

5   The Archbishop of Paris, Cardinal Lustiger, wrote to President Mitterrand warning him 'about the misuse of public funds for a project founded on subverting scripture' (in Baugh 1997: 51).

chapter 1: CONTEXTS

1   For an insight into the scale of the field of Mariology, visit 'The Mary Page' of the International Marian Research Institute: http://campus.uday-ton.edu/mary/index.html. The Institute at the University of Dayton holds over 100,000 books and pamphlets on Mariological topics in over fifty languages.
2   Martin Scorsese remembers this image from his childhood: 'My grandmother... had the portrait of the Sacred Heart. And also the niche with the statue of the Virgin Mary grinding the snake under her foot' (in Baugh 1997: 57).
3   Interviewed in the documentary *The Muslim Jesus*, broadcast on ITV1 on 19 August 2007.
4   For information, visit http://www.nazarethvillage.com.
5   1,114 members of the Council voted to incorporate the Marian teaching into the document, as opposed to 1,074 who wanted a separate publication (see Johnson 2003: 127).
6   Vatican II documents and Papal documents are available online at http://www.vatican.va/.

chapter 2: ANNOUNCEMENT AND COMMISSION

1   The film was initially screened in 1902 but additional scenes were added to the version released three years later.
2   In the town of Nazareth, the Orthodox community commemorates the Annunciation at the church situated by the original village well. The Catholic community has built the Basilica of the Annunciation at the site identified as Mary's house.
3   St Isaac the Syrian stated that it is when the priest has prepared himself and is praying that the Holy Spirit enters the bread and wine on the altar; and, therefore, that it would be fitting for Mary to be prepared and in the act of praying when the Holy Spirit came upon her (see Daniel-Ange 2005: 145).
4   The DVD release of the film contains an accompanying organ soundtrack by Timothy Howard that does not vary in intensity or drama at the appearance of the angelic messenger.

5   Zeffirelli's *Jesus of Nazareth* and Costa's *Maria, Daughter of Her Son* are the only other films analysed in this study to situate the Annunciation in a 'bedroom' setting.

6   Mary believes that she is seriously ill rather than pregnant, so when the doctor informs her that she has 'about seven months,' she thinks that he is referring to her life expectancy rather than the time remaining until the birth.

7   The Church Fathers St Augustine and St Gregory argued that Mary must have already taken a vow of virginity at this point, or she would have naturally assumed that the child would be born of her forthcoming marriage to Joseph. However, this view is countered by those theologians who insist that celibacy within marriage was unlikely within ancient Israel (see Hahn 2001: 107). Amongst the films discussed here, only Costa's *Maria, Daughter of Her Son* contains a hint of a pre-Annunciation vow of virginity.

8   The Annunciation would provide fascinating material for John Thompson's 'commutation test', which works by substituting actors in the same scene to see what effect the replacement has on the meaning of a performance (Thompson 1978).

9   In Roger Young's film *Jesus* there is also only a verbal account within a flashback.

10 I discussed Godard's film in comparison to Jean Delannoy's *Mary of Nazareth* in an article published in the journal *Literature and Theology*, and some of those ideas are re-worked in Chapters 2, 3 and 5 of this book (see O'Brien 2001).

11 It is notable that Gabriel wants to pay his taxi fare in American dollars, underlining the ubiquitous importance of the American currency, even for an angelic visitor to Europe.

12 I am grateful to David Sakula for this observation.

13 The screenplay is reprinted in French and English in Locke and Warren (1993).

14 The same vernacular is used in Roger Young's *Jesus*, when Mary recalls Joseph's reaction to the news of her miraculous pregnancy: 'I think he thought I was crazy.' The dialogue in Young's film might evoke a scene from *Casablanca* (Michael Curtiz, 1942) for Joseph says, 'Out of all the places in the world, all the women in the world, God found you in this little village?' Viewers who also watched *The Matrix* (Andy and Larry Wachowski, 1999) might have noted Mary's insistence on calling Jesus 'The One' (see Staley and Walsh 2007: 204), providing a Messianic link.

In order to avoid the dangers of invented Marian dialogue, Mary (Maria Pia Calzone) figures as a markedly silent witness in Giulio Base's *The Final Inquiry* (2007), which centres on the efforts of a Roman soldier to investigate the life and death of Jesus.

15   Writing of the silent era, Adele Reinhartz also notes that in *INRI* (Robert Wiene, 1923), Mary (played by Henny Porten) is transformed 'from a virginal maiden to a resourceful, adventurous, and assertive woman who will go to any lengths to be with her son in his moment of need' (2007: 13).

chapter 3: MARY AND JOSEPH

1   See, for example, *Mater Dei*, *King of Kings*, *The Greatest Story Ever Told*, *The Messiah*, *The Jesus Film* and *Son of Man*.

2   Godard reportedly originally considered the French film star Jean Marais (b.1913) and the philosopher Bernard-Henri Lévi for the role of Joseph (see Brody 2008: 458), which would have considerably changed the dynamic.

3   Staley and Walsh contrast this scene with Ray's fleeting view of the pregnant Mary in *King of Kings* (2007: 193).

4   Hardwicke later uses the same narrative device in *The Nativity Story*.

5   When *Mary of Nazareth* was screened on US television, sponsored by E.P.T, the early pregnancy test 'for those who just want to be sure. It is the name women trust', the commercial break came just after Joseph learns that Mary is expecting a baby (see Staley and Walsh 2007: 199), thereby offering a further indication of intersections between the sacred and the secular.

6   In Catholic theology, 'the Divine Motherhood explains the human and supernatural perfection of Mary. It is the only case in which a "Son" was able to "fashion" His Mother as He wanted her to be' (Delesalle in Anon. 1997: 334). This theological issue is raised in the title of Costa's *Maria, Daughter of Her Son*.

7   Serge Moati's film *Jésus* presents a titular protagonist who demonstrates the happiness evidenced by Roger Young's Jesus in *Jesus* (1999) combined with the torment of Jesus found in Scorsese's *Last Temptation of Christ* (1988). There are several extra-biblical scenes involving Mary (Ludmila Mikaël) as a mother who is both fearful and encouraging of her son's mission; and she is present at the Crucifixion.

chapter 4: VIRGIN AND MOTHER

1   *The Greatest Story Ever Told* cost $20 million in 1965 and earned $8 million (see Lang 2007: 178). *Son of Man* was nominated for the Grand Jury Prize in the World Cinema category at the Sundance Film Festival in 2006.

2   Some biblical historians also argue that the birth of Jesus took place between 6 – 4BC (see Makarian 1995: 14) due to a miscalculation of the dates.

3   The fact that Mary listened to the words of a fortune teller caused some consternation amongst devout Catholic internet reviewers, even though Mary did not instigate the conversation.

4   Gloria Dodd points out the inaccuracy of describing Mary as an 'unwed mother' because Mary and Joseph had already completed the first stage of the marriage process at the Annunciation. But she acknowledges that 'Mary is still a model for unwed mothers, even though she was married' (2005: 124).

5   Victor Fleming's *Gone with the Wind* caused consternation for Joseph Breen, one of the Production Code officials, in relation to the birth of Beau Wilkes: 'Always fearful that any hint of discomfort connected to the birth process might dissuade some women from embracing motherhood, Breen insisted that shots of Melanie Wilkes gripping a towel, wincing in pain, and perspiring had to be eliminated' (Walsh 1996: 149).

6   In *The Saint Mary*, water flows out of the ground in a scene that is reminiscent of the spring appearing in the grotto at Lourdes in the films *The Song of Bernadette* and *Bernadette*. When Jean Delannoy's film *Bernadette* was shown at a youth festival to an audience of 1,500 Muslim students at Rabat, they were able to relate to the fact that God had chosen such a humble person in Bernadette to be His messenger on earth (see Delannoy 1998: 234).

7   Theologian Virginia Kimball, who has herself given birth to nine children, draws attention to the work of Dr Dick-Read, who 'identified an important factor: that fear leads to pain. The birth process itself is a natural functioning of muscles, designed by God, and with each contraction the baby moves further down the birth canal toward birthing. If the mother cooperates with the bodily process of birth, she understands that it is not pain she is experiencing but rather labor, and hard work at that' (see Kimball 2007).

8   Debates over the month of Jesus's birth (with suggestions including December, March, April and September) have taken up the energies of biblical historians (see Brown 1993: 607ff).

9   Lew Grade, the producer of *Jesus of Nazareth*, reportedly 'was emphatic that the film should be acceptable to all denominations' (see Zeffirelli 1986: 274).

10   Mertes also uses the slow motion effect in *Joseph of Nazareth* as Joseph stares at the world around him in bewilderment while Mary goes into labour.

11   In Genesis, God says that he will 'intensify the pangs of childbirth' (Gn: 3:16), suggesting that labour pain might have existed even before the Fall.

12   There are obviously exceptions to the hair colour rule, such as the blond children in *The Village of the Damned* (Wolf Rilla, 1960); and the Devil portrayed as a girl with blonde hair in *Tobey Dammit*, Fellini's contribution to the anthology film *Spirits of the Dead* (1968). I am grateful to Ian Cooper for the latter observation.

13   Godard screened Rossellini's 'Finding in the Temple' scene in his exhibition *Voyage(s) en utopie* at the Pompidou Centre in Paris in 2006. The ease with which the scene was recognisable (without context or sound) demonstrated the visual power of the narrative.

chapter 5: MOTHER AND DISCIPLE

1   In many of the New Testament films, such as *Jesus of Nazareth*, Mary peers at Jesus through the *mechitzah*, a partition separating the men from the women in the synagogue, and sees her son criticised and rebuked for his pronouncements. However, archaeologists claim that the synagogue in first-century Galilee 'was not an all-male affair' and 'that there is virtually no archaeological or literary evidence from this period to suggest that Jewish men and women had segregated seating in synagogues' (Johnson 2003: 168). The Nazareth Village project confirms this view.

2   Notably, in Mertes's *Joseph of Nazareth*, Mary has 'a tall table' in her own home before the birth of Jesus, indicating either a lack of interest in the authenticity of the *mise-en-scène* or Mary's progressive attitude to new furniture. The intimate 'home life' is also depicted in Luis Buñuel's surreal *The Milky Way* (1969) when Mary (Edith Scob) advises Jesus not to shave off his beard because it suits him, a recommendation that he follows.

3   The role of Magdalene is treated only perfunctorily in this study in relation to Mary, but is evidently an area for possible further investigation.

4   The fact that the performers were working without a discernible script and were reportedly high on drugs may explain the film's overall lack of coherency (see Zouzou 2003: 165–70). The mother/whore issue was also reworked by Garrel's compatriot Jean Eustache in *La Maman et la putain* (1973, France).

5   La Marre also presents an extrabiblical relationship between Judas and Magdalene in *Color of the Cross*.

6   The distinction becomes more obvious when Magdalene removes her veil to wipe Jesus's blood off the stone flags after the scourging. The scene also indicates that she is presented as the woman saved from stoning by Jesus, because she has a flashback to that incident when she kneels down.

7   The event is presented in even more graphic terms in *Mary, mother of Jesus* when John's headless body is thrown down into a pit in front of Mary and Elizabeth.

8   At a Catholic Mass, the priest cleans the chalice carefully after Communion to ensure that no drop of the transubstantiated wine is left (see *General Instruction of the Roman Missal* 2005: 61).

9   Lance Tracy uses this device to extended effect in *The Cross* (2001), which is shot predominantly through the eyes of Jesus.

10 The *mise-en-scène* also evokes the contemporary Via Dolorosa in Jerusalem, which pilgrims walk along making the Stations of the Cross amidst the hubbub of market traders.

11 St Matthew places the female witnesses 'at a distance', without explicitly naming 'the mother of Jesus': 'There were many women there, looking on from a distance, who had followed Jesus from Galilee, ministering to him. Among them were Mary Magdalene and Mary the mother of James and Joseph, and the mother of the sons of Zebedee' (Mt 27:55-56). In *The Visual Bible: Matthew* (Regardt van den Bergh, 1993), which is presented as a word for word dramatization of the *New International Version* of the Bible, Mary (Joanna Weinberg) is also placed by the cross.

12 Although La Marre has made a sequel, *Color of the Cross 2* (2008), which includes the Resurrection, the audience of his first film (which was initially presented as a complete text) is left with a sense of emptiness.

13 Yet, in an earlier scene when John accompanied John the Baptist on his visit to Mary, a smile had passed between Mary and John that suggested a future bond.

14 I am grateful to Gail Horsfield-Porter (who pointed out the umbilical cord link) for this observation.

15   There are also signs of miracles in the cure of a paralytic girl and the rais-
     ing of a dead man, and these events are recorded by artists as murals in
     the town. In the final scene, a risen Jesus with holes in his sleeves (obvi-
     ously symbolic of the crucifixion nails) is seen walking up the hillside with a
     host of angels. Although his resurrection is not experienced by his followers
     within the film's narrative, Jesus turns to face the camera with a joyous cry
     and this moment is caught in a freeze frame. The spectators in the cinema
     become his witnesses.

filmography

A Child called Jesus/Un Bambino di nome Gesù (Franco Rossi, 1987, Italy/
   West Germany)
Annunciation to Marie, The/L'Annonce faite à Marie (Alain Cuny, 1991,
   France)
Au Hasard Balthazar (Robert Bresson, 1966, France/Sweden)
Bernadette (Jean Delannoy, 1988, Switzerland/France/Luxembourg)
Birdsong/El cant dels ocells (Albert Serra, 2008, Spain)
Breathless/A bout de souffle (Jean-Luc Godard, 1960, France)
Casablanca (Michael Curtiz, 1942, US)
Color of the Cross (Jean Claude La Marre, 2006, US)
Color of the Cross 2: The Resurrection (Jean Claude La Marre, 2008, US)
Cross, The (Lance Tracy, 2001, US)
Da Vinci Code, The (Ron Howard, 2006, US)
Dayasagar (A. Bhimsingh, 1978, India)
Final Inquiry, The/L'inchiesta (Giulio Base, 2007, Italy/Spain/US/Bulgaria)
For Love, Only For Love/Per amore, solo per amore (Giovanni Veronesi,
   1993, Italy)
From the Manger to the Cross (Sidney Olcott, 1912, US)
Gologotha (Julien Duvivier, 1933, France)
Gone with the Wind (Victor Fleming, 1939, US)
Gospa (Jakov Sedlar, 1995, Croatia/Canada/US)
Gospel according to St Matthew, The/Il Vangelo secondo Matteo (Pier Paolo
   Pasolini, 1964, Italy)
Gospel of John, The (Philip Saville, 2003, US)

Greatest Story Ever Told, The (George Stevens, 1965, US)

Hail Mary/Je vous salue, Marie (Jean-Luc Godard, 1984, France/Switzerland/ UK)

INRI (Robert Wiene, 1923, Germany)

Intolerance (D. W. Griffith, 1916, US)

Jesus (Roger Young, 1999, US)

Jésus (Serge Moati, 1999, France)

Jesus Christ Superstar (Norman Jewison, 1973, US)

Jesus Film, The (Peter Sykes and John Krisch, 1979, US)

Jesus of Montreal/Jésus de Montréal (Denys Arcand, 1989, Canada)

Jesus of Nazareth (Franco Zeffirelli, 1977, Italy/UK)

Joseph of Nazareth/Giuseppe di Nazareth (Raffaele Mertes, 2000, Italy)

King of Kings, The (Cecil B. DeMille, 1927, US)

King of Kings (Nicholas Ray, 1961, US)

Last Temptation of Christ, The (Martin Scorsese, 1988, US)

Life and Passion of Jesus Christ, The/La Vie et la Passion de Jésus-Christ (Ferdinand Zecca and Lucien Nonguet, 1905, France)

Maman et la putain, La (Jean Eustache, 1973, France)

Maria, Daughter of Her Son/Maria, figlia del suo figlio (Fabrizio Costa, 2000, Italy)

Mary and Joseph, A Story of Faith (Eric Till, 1979, Canada/West Germany/ Israel)

Mary, mother of Jesus (Kevin Connor, 1999, US)

Mary of Nazareth/Marie de Nazareth (Jean Delannoy, 1994, France/Belgium/ Morocco)

Mater Dei (Emilio Cordero, 1950, Italy)

Matrix, The (Andy and Larry Wachowski, 1999, US/Australia)

Messiah, The/Il Messia (Roberto Rossellini, 1975, Italy)

Milky Way, The/La Voie lactée (Luis Buñuel, 1969, France/West Germany/ Italy)

Miracle of Our Lady of Fatima, The (John Brahm, 1952, US)

Miracle Maker: The Story of Jesus, The (Derek Hayes, 1999, UK)

Miraculé, Le (Jean-Pierre Mocky, 1986, France)

Monty Python's Life of Brian (Terry Jones, 1979, UK)

Nativity, The (Bernard L. Kowalski, 1978, US)

Nativity Story, The (Catherine Hardwicke, 2006, US)

Omen, The (Richard Donner, 1976, US)

Passion (Jean-Luc Godard, 1982, France/Switzerland)

Passion, The (Michael Offer, 2008, UK)

Passion of the Christ, The (Mel Gibson, 2004, US)

Saint Mary, The (Shahriar Bohrani, 2001, Iran)

Second Greatest Story Ever Told, The (Ralph Howard and Katharina Otto, 1994, US)

Son of Man (Mark Dornford-May, 2006, South Africa)

Song of Bernadette, The (Henry King, 1943, US)

Spirits of the Dead (Frederico Fellini, Louis Malle and Roger Vadim, 1968, France/Italy)

Star Wars: Episode 1 – The Phantom Menace (George Lucas, 1999, US)

Village of the Damned, The (Wolf Rilla, 1960, UK)

Virgin's Bed, The/Lit de la Vierge, Le (Philippe Garrel, 1969, France)

Visual Bible: Matthew, The (Regardt van den Bergh, 1993, South Africa)

вibliography

Académie Mariale Pontificale Internationale (2005) *La Mère du Seigneur: Mémoire – Présence – Espérance*. Paris: Éditions Salvator.

Aichele, G. and Walsh, R. (eds) (2002) *Screening Scripture: Intertextual Connections between Scripture and Film*. Harrisburg, Pennsylvania: Trinity Press International.

Anglican-Roman Catholic International Commission (ARCIC) (2005) *Mary. Grace and Hope in Christ*. London: Morehouse Publishing.

Anker, R. M. (2004) *Catching Light: Looking for God in the Movies*. Grand Rapids, Michigan: Wm. B. Eerdmans Publishing Company.

Anon. (1997) *Dictionary of Mary*. New Jersey: Catholic Book Publishing Company.

Apostolos-Cappadona, D. (2004) 'On Seeing The Passion: Is There a Painting in This film? Or Is This Film a Painting', in S. B. Plate (ed.) *Re-viewing The Passion: Mel Gibson's Film and its Critics*. New York: Palgravc Macmillan, 97–108.

Ashe, G. (1976) *The Virgin*. London: Routledge and Kegan Paul.

Ashley, B. M. (1985) *Theologies of the Body: Humanist and Christian*. Braintree, Massachusetts: The Pope John Center.

Askren, C. L. R. (1989) 'Moon Games in Jean-Luc Godard's *Je vous salue, Marie*', in *Postscript*, V. 8, n.3 (Summer), 28–39.

Babington, B. and Evans, P. (1993) *Biblical Epics: Sacred Narrative in the Hollywood Cinema*. Manchester: Manchester University Press.

Balasuriya, T. (1997) *Mary and Human Liberation: The Story and the Text*. Harrisburg, Pennsylvania: Trinity Press International.

Ball, A. (2004) *The Other Faces of Mary: Stories, Devotions and Pictures of the Holy Virgin around the World*. New York: The Crossroad Publishing Company.

Barcroft, J. (2002) 'Jewish-Christian relations', in W. McLoughlin and J. Pinnock (eds) *Mary for Earth and Heaven: Essays on Mary and Ecumenism*. Leominster: Gracewing, 283–92.

Bartunek, J. (2002) *Inside the Passion: An Insider's Look at The Passion of the Christ*. West Chester, Pennsylvania: Ascension Press.

Baugh, L. (1997) *Imaging the Divine: Jesus and Christ-Figures in Film*. Lanham: Sheed & Ward.

Bearsley, P. (1983) 'Observations on Frederick M. Jelly, "Towards a Theology of the Body through Mariology"', in *Marian Studies*, Vol. XXXIV, 85–90.

Beattie, T. (2002) *God's Mother, Eve's Advocate*. London: Continuum.

—— (2007) 'Mary in Patristic Theology', in S. Boss (ed.) (2007) *Mary: The Complete Resource*. London: Continuum, 75–105.

Beaudin, B. (2002) *La conversion de Marie*. Montreal: Médiaspaul.

Beaumont, E. (1968) 'Claudel and Sophia', in R. Griffiths (ed.) *Claudel: A Reappraisal*. London: Rapp and Whiting, 93–111.

Bellour, R. and Bandy, M. L. (eds) (1992) *Jean-Luc Godard: Son + Image 1974–1991*: New York: The Museum of Modern Art.

Ben-Chorin, S. (2001) *Marie: Un Regard juif sur la mère de Jésus*. Paris: Desclée de Brouwer.

Benedict XVI (2007) *Jesus of Nazareth*. London: Bloomsbury.

—— (2008) *Angelus*, 20 July. On-line. Available http://www.vatican.va/holy_father/benedict_xvi/angelus/2008/documents/hf_ben-xvi_ang_20080720_sydney_en.html (21 July 2008).

Benko, S. (2004) *The Virgin Goddess. Studies in the Pagan and Christian Roots of Mariology*. Leiden, The Netherlands: Brill.

Bergala, A. (1999) *Nul mieux que Godard*. Paris: Éditions Cahiers du cinéma.

Bingemer, M. C. L. (1991) 'Woman: Time and Eternity: The Eternal Woman and the Feminine Face of God', in A. Carr and E. Schüssler Fiorenza (eds) *The Special Nature of Women?* London: SCM, 98–107.

Birchard, R. S. (2004) *Cecil B. DeMille's Hollywood*. Kentucky: University Press of Kentucky.

Boss, S. (2000) *Empress and Handmaid: On Nature and Gender in the Cult of the Virgin Mary*. London and New York: Cassell.

—— (2003) *Mary*. London: Continuum.

—— (ed.) (2007) *Mary: The Complete Resource*. London: Continuum.

Boulding, C. (2002) 'The treatment of the Holy Spirit and the Virgin Mary in the documents of Vatican II – analysis and reflection', in W. McLoughlin and J. Pinnock (eds) *Mary for Earth and Heaven: Essays on Mary and Ecumenism*. Leominster: Gracewing, 135–44.

Bouquet, S. (2003) *L'Évangile selon Saint Matthieu*. Paris: Cahiers du cinéma.

Bray, X. (2004) *El Greco*. London: National Gallery Company Ltd.

Brennan, W. (1995) 'Recent Developments in Marian Theology', in *New Theology Review*, Volume 8, Number 2 (May), 49–58.

Brody, R. (2008) *Everything is Cinema: The Working Life of Jean-Luc Godard*. London: Faber and Faber.

Brown, R. E. (1993) *The Birth of the Messiah: A Commentary on the Infancy Narratives in the Gospels of Matthew and Luke*. New York: Doubleday.

Brown, R. E., Donfried, K. P., Fitzmeyer, J. A. and Reumann, J. (eds) (1978) *Mary in the New Testament*. New York/Mahwah: Paulist Press.

Buby, B. A. (1994) *Mary of Galilee: Volume 1: Mary in the New Testament*. New York: Alba House.

—— (2000) *A Journey through Revelation*. New York: Alba House.

Butt, R. (2008) 'Judgment day for BBC's premiere of The Passion', *The Guardian*, 1 March. On-line. Available http://www.guardian.co.uk/media/2008/mar/01/bbc.religion (5 June 2008).

Caldwell, D. (2004) 'Selling Passion', in *Perspectives on the Passion of the Christ*. New York: Miramax Books/Hyperion, 211–24.

Campbell, R. H. and Pitts, M. R. (1981) *The Bible on Film: A Checklist, 1897–1980*. Metuchen, New Jersey: Scarecrow.

Carlson Brown, J. and Parker, R. (1989) 'For God So Loved the World?', in J. Carlson Brown and C. R. Bohn (eds) *Christianity, Patriarchy and Abuse: A Feminist Critique*. New York: The Pilgrim Press, 1–30.

Carmody, D. Larnder (1992) *Mythological Woman: Contemporary Reflections on Ancient Religious Stories*. New York: Crossroad.

Carr, A. and Schüssler Fiorenza, E. (eds) (1991) *The Special Nature of Women?* London: SCM.

Carroll, E. R. (1994) 'The Virgin Mary and Feminist Writers', in *Carmelus*, Vol. 41, 49–62.

—— (2002) 'What are they saying about Mary today? A review of current literature', in W. McLoughlin and J. Pinnock (eds) *Mary for Earth and Heaven: Essays on Mary and Ecumenism*. Leominster: Gracewing, 30–41.

Catechism of the Catholic Church (1994) Dublin: Veritas Publications.

Cheah, J. (1995) 'Asian Women's Mariology in Christological Context', in *Marian Studies*, Vol. XLVI , 71–88.

Clarke, R. (2002) 'The Bearer of God and the politics of Ireland', in W.

McLoughlin and J. Pinnock (eds) *Mary for Earth and Heaven: Essays on Mary and Ecumenism.* Leominster: Gracewing, 293–299.

Claudel, P. (1965) *Théâtre II.* Paris : Éditions Gallimard.

Clément, C. and Kristeva, J. (1998) *Le Féminin et le sacré.* Paris: Stock.

Clinton, P. (1999) 'Visually dazzling *Phantom Menace* lacks heart, soul'. Online. Available http://edition.cnn.com/SHOWBIZ/Movies/9905/13/review.phantom.menace/ (12 May 2008).

Cognet, L. (1967) 'Les Difficultés actuelles de la dévotion mariale', in *Recherches sur l'intercession de Marie, II, Controverses et théologie,* Bulletin de la Société Française d'Études Mariales, 37–43.

Craciun, I. (2002) 'Theotokos in a Trinitarian perspective', in W. McLoughlin and J. Pinnock (eds) *Mary for Earth and Heaven: Essays on Mary and Ecumenism.* Leominster: Gracewing, 42–52.

Cunneen, S. (1996) *In Search of Mary.* New York: Ballantine Books.

Daly, M. (1984) *Pure Lust: Elemental Feminist Philosophy.* London: The Women's Press.

—— (1986) *Beyond God the Father: Towards a Philosophy of Women's Liberation.* London: The Women's Press.

Daniel-Ange (2005) *Touche pas à ma mère.* Paris: Éditions du Jubilé.

Deacy, C. (2001) *Screen Christologies: Redemption and the Medium of Film.* Cardiff: University of Wales Press.

Deacy, C. and Williams Ortiz, G. (2008) *Theology and Film: Challenging the Sacred/Secular Divide.* Oxford: Blackwell.

de Beauvoir, S. (1949) *Le deuxième sexe I.* Paris: Gallimard.

Delannoy, J. (1998) *Aux yeux du souvenir: Bloc-notes 1944/1996.* Paris: Les Belles Lettres.

de Margerie, B. (1987) 'Mary in Latin American Liberation Theologies', in *Marian Studies,* Vol. XXXVIII, 47–62.

Dieckmann, K. (1993) 'Godard in His "Fifth Period": An Interview', in M. Locke and C. Warren (eds) *Jean-Luc Godard's Hail Mary: Women and the Sacred in Film.* Carbondale and Edwardsville: Southern Illinois University Press, 119–23.

Dodd, G. (2005) 'The Nuptial Meaning of the Body in the Marriage of Mary and Joseph', in D. H. Calloway (ed.) *The Virgin Mary and the Theology of the Body.* Stockbridge, Massachusetts: Marian Press, 107–24.

Dolto, F. (1977) *L'Évangile au risque de la psychanalyse I.* Paris: Seuil.

Donnelly, D. K. (1994) 'Mary: A Sign of Contradiction to Women?', in F. A. Eigo (ed.) *All Generations Shall Call Me Blessed.* Villanova, Pennsylvania: The Villanova University Press, 107–42.

Duricy, M. (2000) *An Analysis of cinematic presentations of the Virgin from 1897–1999: A theological appraisal of a cultural reality*, unpublished thesis in partial requirement of the Licentiate of Sacred Theology, Dayton, Ohio: University of Dayton.

—— (2003) 'The Life of the Virgin Mary in Film', in *Ephemerides Mariologicae* Vol. LIII – Fasc. III–IV, 479–88.

—— (2004) 'IMRI's Media Specialist comments on Gibson's *Passion*'. On-line. Available http://campus.udayton.edu/mary//news04/20040305.html (12 April 2008).

Ebertshäuser C., Haag, H., Kirchberger, J. H. and Sölle, D. (1998) *Mary: Art, Culture, and Religion through the Ages*. New York: The Crossroad Publishing Company.

Elliott, J. K. (1993) *The Apocryphal New Testament: A Collection of Apocryphal Christian Literature in an English Translation*. Oxford: Oxford University Press.

Emmerich, C. (2003) *The Dolorous Passion of Our Lord Jesus Christ*. El Sobrante, California: North Bay Books.

Endean, P. (2007) 'How to Think about Mary's Privileges: A Post-Conciliar Exposition', in S. Boss (ed.) *Mary: The Complete Resource*. London: Continuum, 284–291.

Evdokimov, P. (1994) *Woman and the Salvation of the World*, trans. by Anthony P. Gythiel. Crestwood, New York: St Vladimir's Seminary Press.

Fitzgerald, M. L. (2007) 'Mary as a sign for the world according to Islam', in W. McLoughlin and J. Pinnock (eds) *Mary for Time and Eternity*. Leominster: Gracewing, 298–304.

Franciscan Friars of the Immaculate (1998) *Marian Shrines of France*. New Bedford, Massachusetts: Academy of the Immaculate.

Fraser, P. (1998) *Images of the Passion: The Sacramental Mode in Film*. Westport, Connecticut: Praeger Publishers.

Fredriksen, P. (2004) 'Gospel Truths: Hollywood, History, and Christianity', in *Perspectives on the Passion of the Christ*. New York: Miramax Books/Hyperion, 31–47.

Friesen, D. H. (2008) 'Karunamayudu: Seeing Christ anew in Indian Cinema', in D. Shepherd (ed.) *Images of the Word: Hollywood's Bible and Beyond*. Atlanta: Society of Biblical Literature, 165–88.

Gambero, L. (1999) *Mary and the Fathers of the Church: The Blessed Virgin Mary in Patristic Thought*. San Francisco: Ignatius Press.

Garrel, P. and Lescure, T. (1992) *Une caméra à la place du cœur*. Aix en Province: Admiranda/Institut de l'image.

Gaventa, B. Roberts (1999) *Mary: Glimpses of the Mother of Jesus*. Edinburgh: T & T Clark Ltd.

—— (2005) '"All Generations Will Call Me Blessed": Mary in Biblical and Ecumenical Perspective', in A.-J. Levine with M. Mayo Robbins (eds) *A Feminist Companion to Mariology*. London: T & T Clark International, 121–29.

Geiger, A. (2006) '*The Nativity Story* Not on Par with *The Passion of the Christ*'. On-line. Available http://www.airmaria,com/vlog.stnd.stnd0001Revw.asp (25 March 2008).

General Instruction of the Roman Missal (2005) London: CTS.

Girard, R. (1987) *Things hidden since the Foundation of the World*. London: The Athlone Press.

Go, P. (1976) 'Sexuality in the Proclamation of Pius XII', in F. Böckle and J.-M. Pohier (eds) *Sexuality in Contemporary Catholicism*. New York: Crossroad, 4–21.

Godard, J.-L. (1985) *Jean-Luc Godard par Jean-Luc Godard I*. Paris: Éditions de l'Étoile – Cahiers du cinéma.

Goldberg, D. J. and Rayner, J. D. (1989) *The Jewish People*. London: Penguin.

Grace, P. (2009) *The Religious Film*. Oxford: Wiley-Blackwell.

Greeley, A. M. (1990) *The Catholic Myth: the behavior and beliefs of American Catholics*. New York: Scribner.

Greeley, A. M. and Greeley Durkin, M. (1984) *How to save the Catholic Church?* London: Viking.

Greene, N. (1990) *Pier Paolo Pasolini: Cinema as Heresy*. Princeton: Princeton University Press.

Greydanus, S. D. (2006) '*The Nativity Story* and Catholic Teaching'. On-line. Available http://www.decentfilms.com/sections/articles/nativitycritics.html (23 June 2008).

Groupe des Dombes (1998) *Marie dans le dessein de Dieu et la communion des saints II: Controverse et conversion*. Paris: Bayard.

Hahn, S. (2001) *Hail Holy Queen: The Mother of God in the Word of God*. New York: Doubleday.

Hamington, M. (1995) *Hail Mary? The Struggle for Ultimate Womanhood in Catholicism*. New York: Routledge.

Harris, R. (1999) *Lourdes: Body and Spirit in the Secular Age*. London: Penguin.

Haskins, S. (1993) *Mary Magdalene: Myth and Metaphor*. New York: Riverhead Books.

Hazleton, L. (2004) *Mary: A Flesh and Blood Biography of the Virgin Mother*. New York: Bloomsbury.

Heft, J. L. (1980) 'Mary in the Doctrine of Urs von Balthasar', in *Marian Stud-*

ies Vol. XXXI, 1980, 40–65.

Hinnebusch, P. G. (1969) 'Our Lady and Salvation in the Twentieth Century', in *Marian Studies*, Vol. XX, 49–64.

Hurley, M. (2002) 'Ecumenism and mariology today', in W. McLoughlin and J. Pinnock (eds) *Mary for Earth and Heaven: Essays on Mary and Ecumenism*. Leominster: Gracewing, 185–208.

Jelly, F. M. (1983) 'Towards a Theology of the Body through Mariology', in *Marian Studies*, Vol. XXXIV, 66–84.

John Paul II (1999) 'Letter of his Holiness Pope John Paul II to Artists'. On-line. Available http://www.vatican.va/holy_father/john_paul_ii/letters/documents/hf_jp-ii_let_23041999_artists_en.html (12 February 2008).

—— (2000) 'Act of Entrustment'. On-line. Available http://www.vatican.va/holy_father/hf_jp-ii_hom_20001008_act-entrustment-mary_en.htm (19 February 2008).

Johnson, E. A. (1985) 'The Marian Tradition and the Reality of Women', in *Horizons*, Vol. 12/1, Spring, 116–35.

—— (2003) *Truly our Sister: A Theology of Mary in the Communion of Saints*. New York: Continuum.

Johnston, R. K. (2004) 'The Passion as Dynamic Icon: A Theological Reflection', in S. B. Plate (ed.) (2004) *Re-viewing The Passion: Mel Gibson's Film and its Critics*. New York: Palgrave Macmillan, 55–70.

Jomier, J. (2002) *The Bible and the Qur'an*. San Francisco: Ignatius Press.

Kazantzakis, N. (1961) *The Last Temptation*. London: Faber and Faber.

Kimball, V. M. (2007) 'Mary's Labor: An Orthodox Perspective'. On-line. Available http://www.catholicweb.com/media_index.cfm?fuseaction=view_article&partnerid=48&article_id=3116 (2 April 2008).

Kinnard, R. and Davis, T. (1992) *Divine Images: A History of Jesus on the Screen*. New York: Citadel.

Korn, E. and Pawlikowski, J. (2004) 'Commitment to Community: Interfaith Relations and Faithful Witness', in *Perspectives on the Passion of the Christ*. New York: Miramax Books/Hyperion, 181–96.

Kristeva, J. (1986) 'Stabat Mater', in T. Moi (ed.) *The Kristeva Reader*. Oxford: Blackwell, 160–186.

Land (1965) 'Film Reviews: *The Greatest Story Ever Told*', in *Variety*, 17 February.

Lang, J. S. (2007) *The Bible on the Big Screen: A Guide from silent films to today's movies*. Grand Rapids, Michigan: Baker Books.

Langkau, T. (2007) *Filmstar Jesus Christus*. Berlin: Lit Verlag.

Larrañga, I. (1991) *The Silence of Mary*. Boston: Pauline Books and Media.

Laugier, S. (1993) 'The Holy Family', in M. Locke and C. Warren (eds) *Jean-Luc Godard's Hail Mary: Women and the Sacred in Film*. Carbondale and Edwardsville: Southern Illinois University Press, 27–38.

LaVerdiere, E. (2004) *The Annunciation to Mary: A Story of Faith*. Chicago: Liturgy Training Publications.

LaVerdiere, E. with Bernier, P. (2007) *The Firstborn of God. The Birth of Mary's Son Jesus*. Chicago: Liturgy Training Publications.

Laurentin, R. (1984) *Marie mère du Seigneur: Les plus beaux textes de deux millénaires*. Paris: Desclée.

—— (1989) 'La figure de Marie dans la perspective du féminisme américain', in *La Figure de Marie: Lumière sur la femme, Études mariales*. Paris: O.E.I.L., 83–111.

Leahy, B. (2002) 'Mary, mother of the Church', in W. McLoughlin and J. Pinnock (eds) *Mary for Earth and Heaven: Essays on Mary and Ecumenism*. Leominster: Gracewing, 300–13.

Levine, A.-J. (2004) 'First take the log out of your own eye: Different viewpoints, different movies', in *Perspectives on the Passion of the Christ*. New York: Miramax Books/Hyperion, 197–210.

Locke, M. (1993) 'A History of the Public Controversy', in M. Locke and C. Warren (eds) *Jean-Luc Godard's Hail Mary: Women and the Sacred in Film*. Carbondale and Edwardsville: Southern Illinois University Press, 1–9.

Locke, M. and Warren, C. (eds) (1993) *Jean-Luc Godard's Hail Mary: Women and the Sacred in Film*. Carbondale and Edwardsville: Southern Illinois University Press.

Loughlin, G. (2004) *Alien Sex: The Body and Desire in Cinema and Theology*. Oxford: Blackwell Publishing Ltd.

Lytal, C. (2006) 'Q & A: Nativity's Catherine Hardwicke'. On-line. Available http://www.premiere.com/directors/3300/q-a-catherine-hardwicke.html (22 May 2008).

Maeckelberghe, E. (1991) *Desperately Seeking Mary: a feminist appropriation of a traditional religious symbol*. Kampen, The Netherlands: Kok Pharos Publishing House.

Makarian, C. (1995) *Marie*. Paris: Lattès/Desclée de Brouwer.

Malone, P. (1992) 'Mary on the Screen', in *Compass Theology Review* 26, No.4, 25–31.

—— (2005) *Can Movies be a Moral Compass?* London: St Pauls.

Marsh C. and Ortiz, G. (eds) (1997) *Explorations in Theology and Film*. Oxford: Blackwell Publishing Ltd.

Martin, J. (2004) 'The Last Station: A Catholic Reflection on *The Passion*', in *Perspectives on the Passion of the Christ*. New York: Miramax Books/Hyperion, 95–110.

Massingberd Ford, J. (1972) 'Our Lady and the Ministry of Women in the Church', in *Marian Studies*, Vol. XXIII, 79–112.

Matter, E. A. (1983) 'The Virgin Mary: A Goddess?', in C. Olsen (ed.) *The Book of the Goddess Past and Present*. New York: Crossroad, 80–96.

Matthews, P. (1999) 'Divining the real', in *Sight and Sound*, August, 22–25.

Maunder, C. (2007) 'Mary in the New Testament and Apocrypha', in S. Boss (ed.) *Mary: The Complete Resource*. London: Continuum, 11–46.

McHugh, J. (2002) 'The Wedding at Cana (John 2.1-11)', in W. McLoughlin and J. Pinnock (eds) *Mary for Earth and Heaven: Essays on Mary and Ecumenism*. Leominster: Gracewing, 3–9.

McKnight, S. (2007) *The Real Mary: Why Evangelical Christians Can Embrace the Mother of Jesus*. Brewster, Massachusetts: Paraclete Press.

McLoughlin, W. and Pinnock, J. (eds) (2002) *Mary for Earth and Heaven: Essays on Mary and Ecumenism*. Leominster: Gracewing.

—— (2007) *Mary for Time and Eternity*. Leominster: Gracewing.

Meacham, J. (2004) 'Who really killed Jesus?', in *Perspectives on the Passion of the Christ*. New York: Miramax Books/Hyperion, 1–15

Merton, T. (1972) *New Seeds of Contemplation*. New York: New Directions.

Miller, D. (2007) 'Mary: Grace and Hope in Christ: The ARCIC Statement', in W. McLoughlin and J. Pinnock (eds) *Mary for Time and Eternity*. Leominster: Gracewing, 15–21.

Miller, M. Migliorino (2005) *The Theology of the Passion of the Christ*. New York: St Pauls/Alba House.

Moore, K. Z. (1994) 'Reincarnating the Radical: Godard's *Je vous salue Marie*', in *Cinema Journal* 34, No 1, Fall, 18–30.

Morrey, D. (2005) *Jean-Luc Godard*. Manchester: Manchester University Press.

Morris, M. (1998) 'Some Protestant and Catholic Images of Mary in nineteenth-century and twentieth-century Art', in *Marian Studies*, Vol. XLIX, 41–67.

Mulvey, L. (1975) 'Visual Pleasure and Narrative Cinema', *Screen*, 16, 3, 6–18.

—— (1993) 'Marie/Eve: Continuity and Discontinuity in J-L Godard's *Iconography of Women*', in M. Locke and C. Warren (eds) *Jean-Luc Godard's Hail Mary: Women and the Sacred in Film*. Carbondale and Edwardsville: Southern Illinois University Press, 39–53.

O'Brien, C. (2001) 'When radical meets conservative: Godard, Delannoy and the Virgin Mary', in *Literature and Theology*, Vol. 5.2, 174–86.

—— (2007a) 'Mary in Film', in S. Boss (ed.) *Mary: The Complete Resource*.

London: Continuum, 532–36.

—— (2007b) 'Sacrificial rituals and wounded hearts: the uses of Christian symbolism in French and German women's responses to the First World War', in A. S. Fell and I. Sharp (eds), *The Women's Movement in Wartime: International Perspectives, 1914–19*. Basingstoke: Palgrave Macmillan, 244–59.

O'Donnell, C. (2007a) 'Issues of method at ESBVM congresses', in W. McLoughlin and J. Pinnock (eds) *Mary for Time and Eternity*. Leominster: Gracewing, 27–48.

—— (2007b) 'Models in Mariology', in W. McLoughlin and J. Pinnock (eds) *Mary for Time and Eternity*. Leominster: Gracewing, 65–89.

Ostling, R.N. (1991) 'Handmaid or Feminist?', in *Time* (December 30), 58–62.

Oursler, F. (1951) *The Greatest Story Ever Told*. New York: Permabooks.

Owen, R. (2006) 'Pregnant Mary embarrasses Vatican', Timesonline, 24 November. On-line. Available http://entertainment.timesonline.co.uk/tol/arts_and_entertainment/article647967.ece (12 July 2008).

Païni, D. and Scarpetta, G. (1984) 'Interview with Godard', in *Artpress: Spécial Godard*, Hors série No.4, December–January/February, 4–18.

Paris, J. (1997) *L'Annonciation*. Paris: Éditions du Regard.

Paul VI (1974) *Marialis Cultus*. On-line. Available http://www.vatican.va/holy_father/paul_vi/apost_exhortations/documents/hf_p-vi_exh_19740202_marialis-cultus_en.html (16 July 2008).

Pelikan, J. (1996) *Mary Through the Centuries: Her Place in the History of Culture*. New Haven and London: Yale University Press.

Perry, M. and Schweitzer, F. M. (2004) 'The Medieval Passion Play Revisited', in S. B. Plate (ed.) *Re-viewing The Passion: Mel Gibson's Film and its Critics*. New York: Palgrave Macmillan, 3–19.

Perry, T. (2006) *Mary for Evangelicals: Toward an Understanding of the Mother of the Lord*. Downers Grove, Illinois: InterVarsity Press.

Plate, S. B. (ed.) (2004) *Re-viewing The Passion: Mel Gibson's Film and its Critics*. New York: Palgrave Macmillan.

Popelard, M.-D. (2002) *Moi Gabriel, vous Marie. L'Annonciation: une relation visible*. Rosny-sous-Bois: Éditions Bréal.

Prédal, R. (1988) *Jean-Pierre Mocky*. Pairs: Lhermier, Editions des quatre-vents.

Price, R. (2007) 'Theotokos: The Title and its Significance in Doctrine and Devotion', in S. Boss (ed.) *Mary: The Complete Resource*. London: Continuum, 56–73.

Prothero, S. (2004) 'Jesus Nation, Catholic Christ', in *Perspectives on the Pas-*

sion of the Christ. New York: Miramax Books/Hyperion, 267–81.

Quéré, F. (1982) *Les femmes de L'Évangile*. Paris: Éditions du Seuil.

Rahner, H. (1961) *Our Lady and the Church*. London: Darton, Longman and Todd.

Ranke-Heinemann, U. (1990) *Eunuchs for the Kingdom of Heaven: The Catholic Church and Sexuality*. London: Penguin.

Reinhartz, A. (2007) *Jesus of Hollywood*. New York: Oxford University Press.

Rossier, F. (2004) 'Kecharitomene (Lk 1:28) in the Light of Genesis 18:16–33: A Matter of Quantity', in *Marian Studies*, Vol. LV, 159–83.

Roten, J. G. (1991) 'Un Féminisme marial? Marie et la femme dans l'enseignement de Paul VI', in *Études Mariales: Le Mystère de Marie et la femme d'aujourd'hui*. Paris: Médiaspaul, 23–72.

—— (1998) 'Mary and the Way of Beauty', in *Marian Studies*, Vol. XLIX, 109–27.

—— (1999) 'Marian Studies-Doctrine', in *Marian Studies*, Vol. L, 163–70.

—— (2001) 'Marie dans le Cinéma', *Études Mariales: Bulletin de la Société Française d'Études Mariales*, 58, 102–128.

—— (2007) 'The Never Ending Challenge of Religious Films'. On-line. Available http://campus.udayton.edu/mary/religiousfilms.html (27 March 2008).

Roubach, S. (2007) 'Stabat Mater Dolorosa: The Virgin Mary in Film', *Open Theology*, No.2, December. On-line. Available http://www.opentheology. org/index.php?option=com_content&task=view&id=71&Itemid=42 (5 March 2010).

Ruether, R. Radford (1993) *Sexism and God-Talk*. Boston, Massachusetts: Beacon Press.

Saward, J. (2002) *Cradle of Redeeming Love. The Theology of the Christmas Mystery*. San Francisco: Ignatius Press.

Schaberg, J. (1987) *The Illegitimacy of Jesus: A Feminist Interpretation of the Infancy Narratives*. San Francisco: Harper and Row.

—— (2005) 'Feminist Interpretations of the Infancy Narrative of Matthew', in A.-J. Levine with M. Mayo Robbins (eds) *A Feminist Companion to Mariology*. London: T & T Clark International, 15–36.

Schrader, P. (1972) *Transcendental Style in Film: Ozu, Bresson, Dreyer*. California: University of California Press.

Shinners, J. R. Jr. (1989) 'Mary and the People: The Cult of Mary and Popular Belief', in D. Donnelly (ed.) *Mary, Woman of Nazareth: Biblical and Theological Perspectives*. New York: Paulist Press, 161–86.

Schüssler Fiorenza, E. (1995) *Jesus: Miriam's Child, Sophia's Prophet: Critical*

Issues in Feminist Christology. London: SCM.

Sean, C. (1969) 'Mary, Model of Modern Woman', in *Marian Studies*, Vol. XX, 29–40.

Seifert, J. (1996) 'Mary as Coredemptrix and Mediatrix of all Graces – Philosophical and Personalist Foundations of a Marian Doctirne', in M. I. Miravalle (ed.) *Mary: Coredemptrix, Mediatrix, Advocate. Theological Foundations II, Papal, Pneumatological, Ecumenical*. Santa Barbara, California: Queenship Publishing Company, 149–74.

Silverman, K. and Farocki, H. (1998) *Speaking about Godard*. New York and London: New York University Press.

Smith, W. B. (1980) 'The Theology of the Virginity In Partu and its Consequences for the Church's Teaching on Chastity', in *Marian Studies*, Vol. XXXI, 99–110.

Spretnak, C. (2004) *Missing Mary: the Queen of Heaven and her re-emergence in the modern church*. New York: Palgrave Macmillan.

Stack, O. (ed.) (1969) *Pasolini on Pasolini: Interviews with Oswald Stack*. The Cinema One Series, 11. Thames and Hudson.

Staley, J. L. and Walsh, R. (2007) *Jesus, the Gospels, and Cinematic Imagination: A Handbook to Jesus on DVD*. Louisville and London: Westminster John Knox Press.

Stern, R. C., Jefford, C. N. and DeBona, G. (1999) *Savior on the Silver Screen*. New York: Paulist Press.

Sterritt, D. (1993) *The Films of Alfred Hitchcock*. Cambridge: Cambridge University Press.

—— (1999) *The Films of Jean-Luc Godard: Seeing the Invisible*. Cambridge: Cambridge University Press.

Stone, B. P. (2000) *Faith and Film: Theological Themes at the Cinema*. St. Louis, Missouri: Chalice Press.

Stourton, E. (1998) *Absolute Truth: the Catholic Church in the World Today*. London: Viking.

Tatum, W. Barnes (1997) *Jesus at the Movies: A Guide to the First Hundred Years*. Santa Rosa, California: Polebridge Press.

Telford, W. R. (1997) 'Jesus Christ Movie Star: The Depiction of Jesus in the Cinema', in C. Marsh and G. Ortiz (eds) *Explorations in Theology and Film*. Oxford: Blackwell Publishing Ltd, 115–139.

The Koran (2003) translated with notes by N. J. Darwood. London: Penguin.

Thistlethwaite, S. (2004) 'Mel makes a War Move', in *Perspectives on the Passion of the Christ*. New York: Miramax Books/Hyperion, 127–45.

Thompson, J. O. (1978) 'Screen Acting and the Commutation Test', *Screen*,

19/2, 55–69.

Tilby, A. (2001) *Son of God*. London: Hodder and Stoughton.

Turner, V. and Turner, E. (1978) *Image and Pilgrimage in Christian Culture: Anthropological Perspectives*. New York: Columbia University Press.

Wallis, J. (2004) 'The Passion and the Message', in *Perspectives on the Passion of the Christ*. New York: Miramax Books/Hyperion, 111–125.

Walsh, F. (1996) *Sin and Censorship: The Catholic Church and the Motion Picture Industry*. New Haven and London: Yale University Press.

Ware, K. (2002) '"The Earthly Heaven": The Mother of God in the Teaching of St John of Damascus', in W. McLoughlin and J. Pinnock (eds) *Mary for Earth and Heaven: Essays on Mary and Ecumenism*. Leominster: Gracewing, 355–68.

Warner, M. (1990) *Alone of all Her Sex: The Myth and Cult of the Virgin Mary*. London: Picador.

Warren, C. (1993) 'Whim, God and the Screen', in M. Locke and C. Warren (eds) *Jean-Luc Godard's Hail Mary: Women and the Sacred in Film*. Carbondale and Edwardsville: Southern Illinois University Press, 10–26.

Winter, T. (1999) 'Pulchra ut luna: Some Reflections on the Marian Theme in Muslim-Catholic Dialogue', in *Journal of Ecumenical Studies*. Extract online. Available http://www.questia.com/googleScholar.qst;jsessionid=LlLL8YP0y3vPhC1ygz1716LmJJbRX0RVGqnGWLDrZy82Qq1h5s90!1427019383?docId=5001896751 (27 January 2008).

—— (2007) 'Mary in Islam', in S. Boss (ed.) *Mary: The Complete Resource*. London: Continuum, 479–502.

Woodward, K. L. (1997) 'Hail, Mary', in *Newsweek*, 25 August, 39–45.

Yarnold, E. (2002) 'Co-redemptrix', in W. McLoughlin and J. Pinnock (eds) *Mary for Earth and Heaven: Essays on Mary and Ecumenism*. Leominster: Gracewing, 232–46.

Zeffirelli, F. (1984) *Franco Zeffirelli's Jesus: A Spiritual Diary*. San Francisco: Harper & Row.

—— (1986) *The Autobiography of Franco Zeffirelli*. London: Weidenfeld & Nicolson.

Zouzou (2003) *Jusqu'à l'aube*. Paris: Éditions Flammarion.

Zwick, R. (1997) 'Maria im Film', in W. Beinert and H. Petri (eds) *Handbuch der Marienkunde*. Regensburg: Verlag Friedrich Pustet, 270–317.

index

films